Praise for Hockey For Dummies, 2nd Edition

"My dog, Blue, and I ran out to get *Hockey For Dummies,* 2nd Edition. We give it two paws up!"

> — Don Cherry, Former NHL Coach and Coaches' Corner Commentator for *Hockey Night in Canada*

"I've seen lots of books on the game, but nothing gives die-hard fans and new-comers to the sport the inside edge like *Hockey For Dummies,* 2nd Edition. JD's insight and sense of humor continue to come through as he discusses new players, new teams, and other recent developments in the game."

> — Scotty Bowman, NHL's Winningest Coach and Coach of the Detroit Red Wings, 1997 and 1998 Stanley Cup Champions

"Listen to the Beezer: *Hockey For Dummies* is a must read for all hockey fans!"

> — John Vanbiesbrouck, Goaltender, New York Islanders

"Nothing gets by John Davidson. If the first edition didn't already make you a fan, then *Hockey For Dummies,* 2nd Edition, will."

> — Mark Messier, Center, New York Rangers

Hockey For Dummies,® 2nd Edition

SEP -- 2010

gift

19

The rink

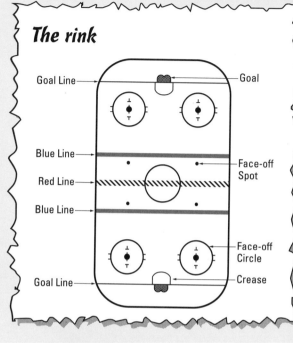

- Goal Line
- Goal
- Blue Line
- Red Line
- Blue Line
- Face-off Spot
- Face-off Circle
- Goal Line
- Crease

Tips on shooting and passing the puck

- ✔ The younger the player, the shorter the pass.
- ✔ Cradle the puck with your stick when you receive it.
- ✔ Don't pass to the player; pass to where he or she is going. And try to put the puck on the blade of the recipient's stick.
- ✔ Don't pass over two lines; that's against the rules, and the official will blow the whistle. Then he'll call a face-off, most likely in your defensive zone.
- ✔ Whenever possible, keep your passes on the ice. But if you must elevate the puck to get it to your teammate, try to make it land flat on the ice so it is easier to receive.

Penalties

Tripping: When a stick or any portion of a player's body is used to cause an opposing player to fall.

Hooking: When a player impedes the progress of an opponent by "hooking" him with his stick.

Interference: When a player interferes with or impedes the progress of an opponent who does not have the puck. Also assessed to a player who deliberately knocks the stick out of an opponent's hand, or who prevents a player who has dropped his stick (or any other piece of equipment) from picking it back up.

Elbowing: When a player uses his elbow to foul an opponent.

Slashing: When a player hits an opponent with his stick, or "slashes" him, either to impede his progress or cause injury.

Cross checking: When a player makes a check with both hands on the stick.

Butt ending: When a player jabs an opponent with the top end of his stick.

Spearing: When a player stabs at an opponent with the blade of his stick, whether he makes contact or not.

Fighting: Called "fisticuffs" in the National Hockey League rule book, it is assessed when players drop their gloves and throw punches at each other.

Checking from behind: Whistled when a player hits an opponent who is not aware of the impending contact and therefore cannot defend himself from behind.

Kneeing: When a player fouls an opponent by kneeing (of course!).

Roughing: Called when a player strikes another opponent in a minor altercation that the referee determines is not worthy of a major penalty.

Hockey For Dummies, 2nd Edition

Cheat Sheet

Positions

Goalie: Perhaps the toughest position in all of sports (remember, this book is being written by a former netminder), the goalie is the one player who can control a team's confidence. His job is to keep the puck out of the net, and if he's good, he can take his team a long way. Good goalies win championships.

Defensemen: A team at full strength has two — one on the left side and another on the right. Nowadays, there are three primary kinds of defensemen. One is creative and offensive-minded; he likes to handle the puck and lead the team up ice, but is not too physical. Another is defensive-minded, a stay-at-home bruiser who plays a physical game and doesn't often venture out of his zone with the puck. And there are those rare athletes who are a combination of the two.

Right wing: He works the right side of the ice for the most part. Needs to be a physical player who is good along the boards and in the corner. He is responsible for the opposition's left defenseman in the defensive zone.

Left wing: Traditionally a left-handed shot, but the NHL is seeing more right-handers playing this position now, a practice picked up from the Europeans. A right-hander has a better angle to shoot from when he's coming in on his wing. Like the right wing, he needs to be able to dig out the puck from the corners and battle in front of the net.

Center: He quarterbacks his club at both ends of the ice. Must be good at face-offs and passing, doesn't hurt if he possesses a good shot as well. Coaches want a lot of creativity in this position — and a lot of hockey smarts.

Hockey do's and don'ts

- Learn to skate properly, even if you're playing goalie. You can't do anything in hockey if you can't skate.

- Make sure your equipment — whether it's your skates, your stick, or your sweater (that's what the pros call a hockey jersey) — fits well.

- On the bench, be alert. Watch what the opposing team is doing, and be prepared to play both ways, offensively and defensively.

- Don't be a puck hog; pass to your teammates.

- Don't stay out on your shift for too long. If you're working hard, an average shift on the ice should last no longer than a minute. Come off when it's your turn.

- Be ready when it's your turn to go onto the ice.

- Wear a helmet. But remember: Just because you have head protection, don't think you are invincible.

- Be careful with your stick. Just because everybody wears headgear, don't think they're invincible either.

- Don't check people from behind.

- Keep your head up when you're going into the boards. If it's tucked in, the chances of a serious head injury rise if someone hits you from behind.

- Don't yap at the ref or the other team. It's okay to be emotional and pull for the people on your team. But don't give the ref a hard time, or the opposing players.

- Get yourself in good physical shape.

- Work on your shooting and passing.

Wiley, the Wiley Publishing logo, For Dummies, the Dummies Man logo, the For Dummies Bestselling Book Series logo and all related trade dress are trademarks or registered trademarks of Wiley Publishing, Inc. All other trademarks are property of their respective owners.

For Dummies: Bestselling Book Series for Beginners

Hockey

FOR

DUMMIES®

2ND EDITION

Hockey
FOR
DUMMIES®
2ND EDITION

by John Davidson
with John Steinbreder

Foreword by Wayne Gretzky
Preface by Mike Myers

Wiley Publishing, Inc.

Hockey For Dummies®, 2nd Edition

Published by
Wiley Publishing, Inc.
909 Third Avenue
New York, NY 10022
www.wiley.com

Copyright © 2000 by Wiley Publishing, Inc., Indianapolis, Indiana

Published simultaneously in Canada

No part of this publication may be reproduced, stored in a retrieval system, or transmitted in any form or by any means, electronic, mechanical, photocopying, recording, scanning, or otherwise, except as permitted under Sections 107 or 108 of the 1976 United States Copyright Act, without either the prior written permission of the Publisher, or authorization through payment of the appropriate per-copy fee to the Copyright Clearance Center, 222 Rosewood Drive, Danvers, MA 01923, 978-750-8400, fax 978-750-4744. Requests to the Publisher for permission should be addressed to the Legal Department, Wiley Publishing, Inc., 10475 Crosspoint Blvd., Indianapolis, IN 46256, 317-572-3447, fax 317-572-4447, or e-mail permcoordinator@wiley.com

Trademarks: Wiley, the Wiley Publishing logo, For Dummies, the Dummies Man logo, A Reference for the Rest of Us!, The Dummies Way, Dummies Daily, The Fun and Easy way, Dummies.com and related trade dress are trademarks or registered trademarks of Wiley Publishing, Inc., in the United States and other countries, and may not be used without written permission. All other trademarks are the property of their respective owners. Wiley Publishing, Inc., is not associated with any product or vendor mentioned in this book.

For general information on our other products and services or to obtain technical support, please contact our Customer Care Department within the U.S. at 800-762-2974, outside the U.S. at 317-572-3993, or fax 317-572-4002.

Wiley also publishes its books in a variety of electronic formats. Some content that appears in print may not be available in electronic books.

Library of Congress Cataloging-in-Publication Data:

Library of Congress Control Number: 00-104226

ISBN: 0-7645-5228-7

Manufactured in the United States of America

10 9 8 7 6 5

About the Authors

John Davidson has been a hockey analyst for the Madison Square Garden Network since 1984 and also serves as an analyst for ABC Sports in the United States and CBC in Canada. A longtime goaltender who broke in with the St. Louis Blues in 1973 and retired as a New York Ranger ten years later, JD is also a regular panelist for *Hockey Night in Canada.* In addition, he has his own weekly radio show, *Inside the NHL,* and an Internet show on the NHL's Web site, nhl.com. He has won four New York Sports Emmys and one Ace Award and has covered three Winter Olympics (with a fourth to come in 2002 at Salt Lake City). He lives in Bedford, New York, with his wife Diana, their daughters Lindsay and Ashley, and three very vocal dogs.

John Steinbreder is a senior writer for *Golfweek* magazine. The author of five books, he also writes a regular column for *Chief Executive* magazine and is a contributing editor at *Met Golfer* and *Sporting Classics.* Previously, John worked as a reporter for *Fortune* magazine, a writer/reporter for *Sports Illustrated,* and a special contributor for ESPN. He has also written articles for several major newspapers and magazines, including *Time, The New York Times Magazine, The Wall Street Journal, Forbes FYI,* and *Sky.* He lives in Easton, Connecticut, with his daughter Exa and still gets to play the occasional game of pond hockey.

(Photo by Alison Dunn)

Dedication

To our parents, Eunice and Jack Davidson and Sandy and Cynthia Steinbreder, for giving us the chance to pursue our dreams. And to our families, Diana, Lindsay, and Ashley Davidson and Exa Steinbreder, for the love and support they have given us along the way.

Authors' Acknowledgments

Writing, like hockey, is a team effort, and we could not have done this book without an enormous amount of help from our friends and colleagues. First off, thanks to Mark McCormack, Sandy Montag, and Mark Reiter of the International Management Group for bringing us into this project and doing their best to keep us both solvent. We are also appreciative of the good work Stacy Collins of Hungry Minds did in getting this book off the ground and all her support along the way. And we are grateful for the fine editing skills of Alissa Cayton and Gregg Summers and the technical assistance we received from John Halligan and Arthur Pincus.

The folks at the National Hockey League lent an invaluable hand, and we would like to thank everyone who is a part of that organization, especially Gary Bettman and Bernadette Mansur. Doug Palazzari, Chuck Menke, and Heather Ahearn of USA Hockey also contributed a great deal to our efforts, and so did Bob Nicholson and Johnny Misley of the Canadian Hockey Association. Thanks also to the people at the International Ice Hockey Federation, the American Hockey League, and the International Hockey League for their input.

We turned to a number of other sources as we put this opus together and are grateful for their time and support. Scotty Bowman and Colin Campbell graciously shared their insights on the game, and so did Emile Francis, Don Cherry, Dick Irvin, Mark Messier, Brian Leetch, Wayne Gretzky, Mike Gartner, Gary Roberts, Mike Vernon, Sergie Nemchinov, Al MacInnis, Ron Hextall, Eric Lindros, Brett Hull, Cammi Granato, Sami Jo Small, and Hayley Wickenheiser. Thanks also to Mike Folga, Jim Ramsay, Michael Cosby, Bob Schank, and Howie Wenger for providing us with a wealth of information on conditioning and equipment; Stan Fischler for the terrific books he has written on the game; Scott Cooper, the world's number 1 Ranger fan; and hockey fans everywhere who bring such passion and enthusiasm to the sport. Finally, we would like to express our appreciation to Mike Myers and Wayne Gretzky for penning the Preface and Foreword.

On a personal level, JD would like to thank the MSG Network for putting such a high quality product on the air, his play-by-play partner Sam Rosen, John Whalen and Michael McCarthy of MSG, John Shannon of *Hockey Night in Canada,* and, of course, his wife Diana, his daughters Lindsay and Ashley, and his brothers — Wilson, Marshall, and Murray — and their families.

As for John Steinbreder, he would like to thank Dave Seanor, Jim Nugent, Rance Crain, Ken Hanson, Jeff Babineau, Dale Gardner, Alayna Gaines, Brad Klein, and everyone else at The *Golfweek* Group for making his job there the best he has ever had. He is also grateful for the fabulous work Duncan Christy, Christopher Buckley, Patrick Cooke, Robin McMillan, Chuck Wechsler, and J.P. Donlan continue to throw his way. In addition, he is appreciative of the support of his mother Cynthia; the friendship of his neighbors Arvid and Pam; the sage counsel he so often receives from Pat Tone and Mike Dailey; the FC work he has done with John Kennedy; the Sunday morning chats with Kendall; the duck hunts with Tyler, Billy, and DG; the times he gets to talk hockey with Nat, Pete, and JB; and the days and nights he gets to spend with his daughter Exa, a sweet girl who never gets angry when her father switches the television channel from *Rugrats* to a New York Rangers hockey game.

Publisher's Acknowledgments

We're proud of this book; please send us your comments through our online registration form located at www.dummies.com/register.

Some of the people who helped bring this book to market include the following:

Acquisitions, Editorial, and Media Development

Project Editors: Alissa Cayton, Gregg Summers

  (Previous Edition: Bill Helling)

Acquisitions Editor: Stacy S. Collins

Copy Editor: Gregg Summers

Acquisitions Coordinator: Lisa Roule

Technical Editors: Arthur Pincus, President of Arthur Pincus Media; John Halligan, Historian for the National Hockey League

Editorial Manager: Jennifer Ehrlich

Editorial Assistant: Jennifer Young

Cover Credit: International Stock© Bob Firth Photography

Production

Project Coordinator: Emily Wichlinski

Layout and Graphics: Karl Brandt, John Greenough, Jason Guy, Clint Lahnen, Barry Offringa, Tracy K. Oliver, Kristin Pickett, Jacque Schneider, Jeremey Unger, Erin Zeltner

Proofreaders: Laura Albert, Vickie Broyles, Joel Showalter

Indexer: John Sleeva

Publishing and Editorial for Consumer Dummies

Diane Graves Steele, Vice President and Publisher, Consumer Dummies
Joyce Pepple, Acquisitions Director, Consumer Dummies
Kristin A. Cocks, Product Development Director, Consumer Dummies
Michael Spring, Vice President and Publisher, Travel
Brice Gosnell, Publishing Director, Travel
Suzanne Jannetta, Editorial Director, Travel

Publishing for Technology Dummies

Andy Cummings, Acquisitions Director

Composition Services

Gerry Fahey, Vice President, Production Services
Debbie Stailey, Director of Composition Services

Contents at a Glance

Cartoons at a Glance

By Rich Tennant

page 153

page 7

page 67

page 179

page 217

page 273

Fax: 978-546-7747
E-mail: richtennant@the5thwave.com
World Wide Web: www.the5thwave.com

Table of Contents

· ·

Foreword

My first experience with a pair of skates and a hockey stick happened before I turned 3. My coach, also known as "Dad," instructed me from the comfort of our kitchen, while I played on the home-made rink that had once been our backyard. Dad wasn't trying to build a hockey star from our kitchen; he was only trying to stay warm. Even back then, hockey was my life. I lived, breathed, slept, dreamed, and played hockey. Reading John Davidson's *Hockey For Dummies*, 2nd Edition, takes me back to those days growing up in Ontario. It reminds me of all the important lessons I learned, and all the great moments I've experienced as a player.

For those of you who are new to the game I love, *Hockey For Dummies* is the most comprehensive, easily understood source of hockey history and instruction I've ever come across. Not only was "JD" a superb player in the NHL, he is also an extremely skilled commentator sharing his knowledge of the game with fans all over North America. From hat tricks to power plays, *Hockey For Dummies* provides the reader with the wisdom of an expert.

John has also included advice from some of his pals in the NHL (check out my section on passing!). This is the sort of "inside information" you ordinarily get at an expensive hockey camp. But it's all collected here — and I think even my father could pick up one or two new secrets. From cover to cover, you'll get all the basics. If you're a fan or a serious player, I'd bet you can dip into any page and learn. Whoever you are, *Hockey For Dummies* has something for every hockey lover.

— **Wayne Gretzky**
NHL's All-Time Leading Scorer

Preface

Congratulations! You have chosen to learn about the best sport invented by man. The perfect combination of soccer, basketball, and football. The best water sport ever . . . on frozen water, that is.

To those of you who are just getting acquainted with the world of hockey, it might seem as foreign to you as the movie *Rollerball* and equally as physical. It is a fast-paced, contact game that's played on a hard surface with a hard puck with hard sticks surrounded by hard boards played by hard men — and women.

It's true that hockey has sometimes been referred to as the "fourth sport" in the United States, but now the NHL has teams in warm-weather climates like Georgia, Florida, and Arizona — and with the explosive popularity and growth of in-line skating, hockey is now accessible to everyone!

There's nothing like watching Paul Coffey streak down the ice at Mach 2. And there's nothing like the sound of an Al MacInnis slap shot. The perfection of Jaromir Jagr's wrist shot. The balletic grace of a Darius Kasparaitis body check. Or, last but not least, the perfection of a Wayne Gretzky flip pass as it "feathers" though sixteen legs — landing flat onto the stick of a man just as he's crossing the blue line.

Maybe many of you cannot yet grasp what I have described. So read on, my children, and discover a kind of love that I and others have known all along . . . it's a special love. Why, it's the love of hockey.

Game on!

— Mike Myers
Canadian Actor, Comedian, and Hockey Fan

Introduction

Welcome to *Hockey For Dummies,* 2nd Edition, the book that tells you everything you've always wanted to know — and then some — about the most exciting sport in the world. It's skaters streaking down the ice at breakneck speeds. It's slap shots screaming past goalies. It's deft stick handling, crisp passing, crunching body checks, fantastic playmaking, and even a bit of fighting (in the pros). As a sport, hockey has everything — which is why we're writing about it.

About This Book

We want this book to appeal to every level of player and fan, from the 8-year-old boy competing on Saturday mornings in his local youth hockey league to the 65-year-old grandmother who hasn't missed a New York Rangers game at Madison Square Garden in 20 years. We hope the native Floridian who knows next to nothing about the sport will find it easier to watch and understand after perusing this volume; and we'd like it to be as compelling a read for the longtime fan or player who thinks he, or she, knows it all. We even want to give the National Hockey League pros that JD (John Davidson) hangs around with something different to talk about in the locker room. Perhaps it will be the names they find on his Top Ten Lists. Maybe it will be his strategies for penalty kills and power plays. Whatever the attraction, we hope that they, and all our other readers, find *Hockey For Dummies,* 2nd Edition, interesting, useful, and fun.

This book recounts the workings of the NHL, explains the type of equipment players use, describes the rules of the game and the philosophies of the different coaches, and gives tips on watching hockey on television and improving your slap shot and board work. It is both history journal and instructional guide. And it might even make you laugh a little, too.

Some of you, we believe, will be hard-core hockey fans who grew up playing on the frozen ponds in your neighborhoods and following your favorite NHL teams. Even if you know and love the game already, you'll find plenty of new information in this book. An equal number of you may be fairly new to the game. You may live in warm-weather places — such as Atlanta, Miami, and Phoenix — that only recently have gotten interested in hockey. Many of you may not know the difference between a cross check and a slap shot. You may not understand how many points a team gets for a regular-season win or what makes the playoff system work. You may even think that skates are those strange-looking stingrays that swim in the ocean and that John Davidson, whose name appears on the cover of this book, is actually the one-time singer and game show host, not the former standout goalie who is now the game's best-known television analyst. We forgive you for any of these transgressions if you promise to buy this book. And then we'll help you become as knowledgeable and passionate about the sport as your Snow Belt brethren. We might also talk you — and your children — into playing the game yourself. In fact, we can even show you different ways to enjoy the sport, even if it's the middle of summer and there's no ice around. We like hockey so much we'll do anything to play it. Well, almost anything.

Why You Need This Book

Beginners need this book because nothing else will give them as complete an introduction to the game and an understanding as to how it works. Do you know what the left wing does? The right defenseman? Not to worry, we explain both of them. Do you know how to buy hockey equipment for yourself or your children (or for that matter, your grandchildren)? Do you know how many teams now play in the NHL? Do you know how players in that league train or what they practice before a game? Do you have any idea what they say to each other on the ice? Newcomers to the game may ask these and many, many more questions. And we happily answer them.

At the same time, however, we also try to pique the interest of those who know the sport better. And that's the real beauty of this volume. It addresses the needs of the neophyte without talking down to the casual player, or the rabid NHL season ticket holder, or the high school scoring star, or those bangers who earn their keep in the top pro league. It has plenty of good information for everybody.

There are several reasons why JD is the perfect person to write this book — and the one who gets top billing on the cover. A goalie who was born in Ottawa, Ontario, and raised in Calgary, Alberta, he played ten seasons in the NHL, some as a member of the St. Louis Blues but mostly with the New York Rangers. The highlight of his playing career was leading the Rangers to the Stanley Cup Finals in 1979, which they lost in a hard-fought series to the Montreal Canadiens. Back and knee injuries forced JD to retire in 1983, but he didn't just shrink away from the game. He spent a year as an analyst for New York Rangers broadcasts on the Madison Square Garden Network and then moved to a similar position with the wildly popular *Hockey Night in Canada,* which is as big up north as *Monday Night Football* is in the States. JD stayed there for two years before coming back to MSG, where he still works. He also serves as a game analyst for ABC. Over the years he has done games for the three other major broadcast networks and covered three Winter Olympics (and will soon cover another Winter Olympics in 2002). In addition, he has won four New York Sports Emmys and one Cable Ace Award. He knows the sport and is as able as anyone to simplify the game and convey its intricacies to fans of all levels and backgrounds. That's what makes him so good on TV, and a natural to do this book.

How to Use This Book

You shouldn't read this book as you read a novel, from cover to cover. Pick the different chapters that interest you most and go from there. Beginners may want to start with the glossary so they have a better sense of Hockey Speak before they start turning the other pages. Parents and kids who play in one of the many recreational leagues, or just on the local rink or pond, may want to turn to Chapters 2, 3, 14, 15, 16, and 17 first, while those more into spectating should enjoy what we have in Chapters 4, 5, 11, 12, and 13. And JD's Top Ten Lists should be of interest to anybody who has followed the game. You may want to read only bits and pieces of the book at a time or sit down for an extended session. However you do it, we want to make sure you are discovering more about the game and having fun in the process.

How This Book Is Organized

We have taken great care in organizing this book. We begin with an explanation of how hockey began and what it's all about, and then describe the equipment needed to play the game and the rules. Later on, we get into the NHL, discuss things like training and coaching, talk about the best ways to watch the game from the stands or in your living room, and outline what you need to know to play hockey yourself. We finish up with JD's Top Ten Lists and the appendixes, which tell you how to talk a good game and where to find a place to play. This book is simple yet comprehensive.

Part I: Getting Started — Before They Drop the Puck

First, we describe how the sport began and where it was originally played. In addition, we explain the various positions on the ice and what each person is responsible for doing so you and your friends don't scurry around like a bunch of maniacs. We also tell you what a hockey rink is and what it looks like. We talk about the equipment hockey players use and the rules they must follow on the ice. We know, it sometimes looks like complete anarchy out there. But it's not. There's rhyme and reason to it all.

Part II: How the Big Boys (And Girls) Do It

Here, we look at the NHL, the premier hockey league in the world, and go over everything from when it was started (1917) to what the Stanley Cup is (hockey's version of the World Series) to how fast the players are (in a word, very). Then we get into the minors, the colleges, and the women's leagues (real women do play hockey). We include a section on training at the professional level and another on coaching that gets into everything from shooting drills to matching lines. We next cover the power play, which is perhaps the most critical test of any hockey team — on offense or on defense. We also tell you how to defend against the power play. Finally, we examine the world of intimidation and hitting in hockey.

Part III: It's Easier from the Stands (A Lot Easier)

Some people prefer to play hockey, while others like to watch. This part clues you in on the best ways to follow the game on television. We also have tips on how to get the most out of a game from the stands and go over the various TV shows, newspapers, magazines, and online services you can turn to if you want to stay informed.

Part IV: So You're Ready for Your Shift

This part is mostly for players, and we have a number of the NHL's current and former stars giving tips: Wayne Gretzky on passing; Mark Messier on winning face-offs; and so on. Also, we tell you where to go and what to look for in youth and adult hockey leagues throughout the United States and Canada as well as some hockey schools and camps. In addition, we have information on what to do if you haven't any ice (such as street hockey and in-line skating, for example).

Part V: The Part of Tens

This part has the best things hockey has to offer, as compiled by JD himself, and other lists ranging from the top teams of all time to the most ferocious hitters.

Part VI: Appendixes

Hockey has a language all its own, and in Appendix A we give you the terms you'll need in order to talk hockey with the best of them. Appendix B lists various hockey organizations where you can get information on everything from Pee-Wees to the pros. In Appendix C, you can find an illustrated list of the hockey referee signals and when they are used. Finally, Appendix D gives you lists of information, from Hall of Fame members to NHL milestones.

Icons Used in This Book

We lead you through all this information with some icons developed especially for this book. They point you toward valuable advice and alert you to important hazards.

"Chateau Bow-Wow" is a standard expression in hockey describing the place players go when they mess up. Read this section, or you'll end up in JD's doghouse.

This icon lets players know when they are getting good advice — and some of this advice comes directly from NHL players.

This information bears repeating. Bears repeating.

Be careful with this stuff; you could hurt yourself.

This icon points out passages that make it easier for fans to watch their favorite sport, either on TV or from the stands.

Hockey coaches really are teachers on skates, so pay attention to these parts. You might learn something important.

Information for the big kids.

Information for the little ones.

Talk like this, and the guys in the cheap seats will understand you.

Words of wisdom from the hockey maven. Read this carefully, or he'll slash you.

Part I

Getting Started — Before They Drop the Puck

©RICHTENNANT

MYTHOLOGICAL HOCKEY

Jeez- I <u>hate</u> facing off with the Cyclops. That one stupid eye just throws my concentration.

In this part . . .

In this part, we get you started with an introduction to hockey and what it's all about, from the origins of the sport and the way players have dressed and protected themselves over the years to the rules of the game. We also tell you what the different players do — and we explain how you can outfit yourself and your kids in everything from shoulder pads and skates to sticks and gloves. We alert you to the things you can — and cannot — do when you are on the ice.

Chapter 1

What Is Hockey?

· ·

· ·

*P*eople have been playing hockey for longer than any of us has been alive, but we can't tell you exactly when it was invented, or by whom, because no one really knows for sure. We do have some sketchy details on how it got started, however, and we can describe the ways the game has grown and changed over the years. Once a relatively obscure source of recreation for people who lived in the north country, hockey is now played all over the world and has become one of the most popular winter sports. Frankly, we don't know what we'd do without it, and millions of other people feel the same way.

The Origins of the Game

Most historians place the roots of hockey in the chilly climes of northern Europe, specifically Great Britain and France, where field hockey was a popular summer sport more than 500 years ago. When the ponds and lakes froze in winter, it was not unusual for the athletes who fancied that sport to play a version of it on ice. An ice game known as *kolven* was popular in Holland in the seventeenth century, and later on the game really took hold in England. In his book *Fischler's Illustrated History of Hockey,* veteran hockey journalist and broadcaster Stan Fischler writes about a rudimentary version of the sport becoming popular in the English marshland community of Bury Fen in the 1820s. The game, he explains, was called *bandy,* and the local players used to scramble around the town's frozen meadowlands, swatting a wooden or cork ball, known as a *kit* or *cat,* with wooden sticks made from the branches of local willow trees. Articles in London newspapers around that time mention increasing interest in the sport, which many observers believe got its name from the French word *hoquet,* which means "shepherd's crook" or "bent stick." A number of writers thought this game should be forbidden because it was so disruptive to people out for a leisurely winter skate.

Hockey comes to North America

Not surprisingly, Canada was the site of the earliest North American hockey games. British soldiers stationed in Halifax, Nova Scotia, reportedly had organized contests on frozen ponds in and around that city in the 1870s, and about that same time students from McGill University in Montreal began facing off against each other on a downtown ice rink. The continent's first hockey league was said to have been launched in Kingston, Ontario, in 1885, and it included four teams.

Hockey became so popular in Canada that clubs from Toronto, Ottawa, and Montreal were soon playing games against each other on a regular basis. The English governor-general of Canada, Lord Stanley of Preston, was so impressed that in 1892 he bought a silver bowl with an interior gold finish and decreed that it be given each year to the best amateur team in Canada. That trophy, of course, has come to be known as the Stanley Cup and is awarded today to the team that wins the National Hockey League playoffs.

When Canadians first played hockey, the teams had nine men per side. But by the time the Stanley Cup was introduced, it was a seven-man game. The change came about accidentally in the late 1880s after a club playing in the Montreal Winter Carnival showed up two men short, and its opponent agreed to drop the same number of players from its team to even the match. In time, players began to prefer the smaller squad, and it wasn't long before that number became the standard for the sport. Each team featured one goaltender, three forwards, two defensemen, and a rover, who had the option of moving up ice on the attack or falling back to defend his goal.

The rise of professional hockey

Hockey was a strictly amateur affair until 1904, when the first professional league was created — oddly enough in the United States. Known as the International Pro Hockey League, it was based in the iron-mining region of Michigan's Upper Peninsula. That folded in 1907, but then an even bigger league emerged three years later, the National Hockey Association (NHA). And shortly after that came the Pacific Coast Hockey Association (PCHA). In 1914, a transcontinental championship series started between the two, with the winner getting the coveted cup of Lord Stanley. World War I threw the entire hockey establishment into disarray, and the men running the NHA decided to suspend operations.

But near the end of the war, the hockey powers-that-be decided to start a whole new organization that would be known as the National Hockey League (NHL). At its inception, the NHL boasted five franchises — the Montreal Canadiens, the Montreal Wanderers, the Ottawa Senators, the Quebec Bulldogs, and the Toronto Arenas. The league's first game was held

December 19, 1917. The clubs played a 22-game schedule and, picking up on a rule change instituted by the old NHA, dropped the rover and employed only six players on a side. Toronto finished that first season on top, and in March 1918 met the Pacific Coast Hockey Association champion Vancouver Millionaires for the Stanley Cup. Toronto won, three games to two. Eventually the PCHA folded, and at the start of the 1926 season, the NHL — which at that point had ten teams — divided into two divisions and took control of the Stanley Cup.

A Typical Hockey Rink

In the old days, hockey rinks were set up on ponds, lakes, and rivers, with the piled-up snow that had been shoveled off serving as the boundaries. But things are very different today. Sure, pond hockey still exists, but the professional game and the vast majority of amateur contests are now played indoors on regulation rinks.

As shown in Figure 1-1, the official size of an NHL rink is 200 feet long and 85 feet wide (61m and 25.9m). Surrounding the playing surface are the *boards*, walls usually made of fiberglass that must measure between 40 and 48 inches tall, with the ideal height being 42 inches (107.7cm).

Thirteen feet (4m) from each end of the rink is the goal, the posts of which are 4 feet high and 6 feet wide (1.2m and 1.8m). Each goal has a net, in front of which is a semicircular *crease* that has a radius of 8 feet (2.4m).

Additionally, two blue lines divide the area between the two goals into three parts; each line is 60 feet (18.3m) from its respective goal. The area between the blue line and the goal line is either the offensive zone or the defensive zone, depending on which team is attacking and which is defending the goal.

A red line then bisects the playing surface between the two blue lines, and that line (and the entire area between the blue lines) is called *center ice*. The rink also contains five face-off circles, two in each defensive zone and one at center ice where the puck is dropped between the opposing centermen at the start of each period. There are four other face-off spots, just outside the blue lines, where the puck may also be dropped after the referee calls an infraction in that area or stops play for some other reason.

Synthetic glass encircles the entire rink, except for the area just in front of the two player benches. Glass behind the benches protects those fans from the puck — and protects the players from the fans.

Hockey rinks for international competition, including the Winter Olympics, are 200 feet by 100 feet (61m by 30.5m). That makes them some 15 feet (4.6m) wider than those used in the NHL, a design characteristic that leads to more open play and gives the game greater flow but also takes away much of the

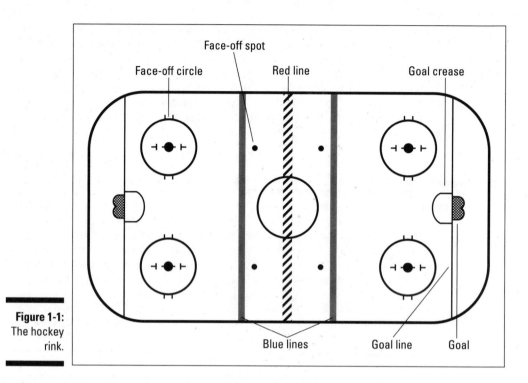

Figure 1-1:
The hockey
rink.

physical play that North American fans seem to appreciate. The majority of hockey rinks in the United States are built to NHL specs, but more and more international-sized arenas are being constructed.

How Hockey Is Played: The Positions

Hockey is played on ice with a frozen rubber puck and sticks made of wood and space-age materials like graphite, fiberglass, aluminum, and even titanium. Each team consists of six players, all of whom wear skates and various types of padding and protection, depending on their position. Obviously, goaltenders wear the most, and speedy playmakers or scorers the least. The goal of the game is to score goals by putting the puck in the opposing team's net and to keep it out of your own.

In most cases, a hockey team consists of a goalie (the *netminder*), two defensemen, and three forwards (one of which is called a center, and the two wings, left and right). (See Figure 1-2 for an approximate placement of these positions.) We say "in most cases" because different game situations may induce a coach to change things a bit. When looking for more offense, for example, a coach may send four forwards onto the ice instead of three.

As we discuss in greater depth in Chapter 3, hockey referees penalize players for infractions by taking them off the ice and making their team play for a period of time, generally two minutes, with one less skater than the other squad (which puts the numerically superior team into a situation called a *power play*; see Chapter 8 for all the details). So the team that has been penalized has only five, not six players on the ice. Sometimes, late in the game a club that is behind takes out its goaltender and replaces him with another player to create more offense.

As a rule, all hockey teams carry two goalies. Youth hockey clubs generally have enough players to put out three lines (each line consists of a centerman and two other forwards) and three sets of defensemen (each set is made up of one left defenseman and one right). NHL teams are allowed to suit up as many as 18 players, excluding goaltenders, for a game; that gives them enough for four lines. Traditionally, professional coaches in the United States and Canada have been flexible with the units they put onto the ice, letting different lines play with different sets of defensemen. But more and more, teams follow the European model and skate three units of five, meaning that they keep the sets of forwards and defensemen together all the time. The other players who dress for the game in that system are extras who usually play only when one of the regulars is injured or has an equipment problem, or in penalty-killing or power-play situations.

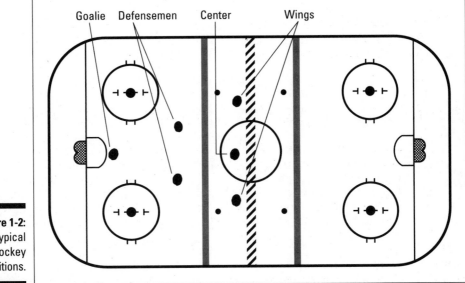

Figure 1-2:
Typical
hockey
positions.

Centers

The *center* is the team's quarterback, the one who directs the play in both the offensive and defensive zones, and centers come in all shapes and sizes. You have people like Eric Lindros and Mark Messier, who combine speed, power, and scoring ability, as well as uncanny leadership. Another type is the play-making center, like Mike Modano or Adam Oates, who can score but also excels at making the good pass and setting up teammates. And then there are two-way marvels, such as Peter Forsberg, who are scoring threats and tenacious defensive specialists as well. Different as they all may be in many ways, good NHL centermen usually have several things in common:

- ✔ They must be good on face-offs.
- ✔ They must be able to pass and shoot well.
- ✔ They must be able to lead the team on both ends of the ice.

The first-line center is generally a team's highest scorer, because he's either a great playmaker (passer) or finisher (goal scorer), or both. Most second-line centers have similar abilities, though they may not be on as high a level as the man anchoring line number 1. Third-line centers are supposed to be good on face-offs and strong on checking; their primary job in most cases is to keep the other team's top line from scoring.

Wings

Traditionally, *wings* (or *wingers*) went up and down the ice on their respective sides, the right wingers on the right and the left wingers on the left. And what determined which side the players played? Their shot. A right-handed shot was positioned on the right wing, and a left-handed winger played the left wing. The most notable exception to this rule was Maurice (Rocket) Richard, one of the greatest players ever, who shot left-handed but played right wing.

But thanks again to the European influence, you now frequently see left-handed shots playing on the right side, for example, because they have a better chance of *one-timing* shots (shooting right off the pass without breaking stride), which can be a very effective way of scoring a goal. Instead of stopping the puck and practically teeing it up (like Gary McCord, of *Golf For Dummies* fame), you strike the puck as it's moving. The benefit is that it cuts the release time in half and gives the shooter a better chance of scoring.

Several different types of wingers play in the NHL these days.

- ✔ One is a checker like Jere Lehtinen. His primary job is to stay on the other team's good players and make sure they don't score. He doesn't put many points on the board, but he provides an invaluable service to his team by keeping the other guys' big gun at bay.

✔ Next is the gritty, tough forward who makes plays along the boards and in the corners, plays the opponent's body well yet also knows how to score in the trenches, and ideally has a bit of a mean streak in him. Scott Mellanby is a good example of this kind of player, and so are Pat Verbeek and Keith Tkachuk.

✔ You also have the pure scoring wings, such as Brett Hull, who has a big shot, as well as the speed scorers, like Tony Amonte and Paul Kariya — flashy skaters who seem to fly down the ice.

✔ In addition, the league has a few wingers, such as Pavol Demitra, who can play it both ways, either as a scorer or a checker.

✔ And finally, the NHL has enforcers such as Tie Domi and Bob Probert, tough guys who hit and intimidate and are not afraid to drop their gloves and use their fists.

As is the case with centermen, coaches generally put their most talented offensive wingers on the first two lines and keep their defensive specialists for the third line. Many times, the fourth-line wingers are asked to pick up the pace of the game by hitting hard, creating turnovers, and being aggressive. Those who play on the fourth unit don't get nearly as much ice time as the others, so they usually try to do as much as they can during their shifts. They can really ignite a team if they get some good licks in and get the crowd going as well.

Goalies

Years ago, the big kid who couldn't skate traditionally stayed in goal, but not anymore. Goalkeepers today must be excellent skaters and first-rate stickhandlers or they won't last very long. Agility is key and so is athleticism, because the men in the net must be able to scramble around with all that equipment on. They must also have great hockey smarts and must not only read plays as they form but also react quickly to them. In addition, goalies must talk incessantly to their teammates, telling their defensemen who are working behind the net where to go with the puck and barking warnings to their forwards about which of the opponents are bearing down on them. Listen closely the next time you are at a game or watching one on TV, and you can hear the netminder shouting to his fellow players when the puck is deep in their end. (Dominik Hasek, who won the Most Valuable Player award in the NHL for the 1996–97 and 1997–98 seasons, talks more than any other goalie!)

Great goalies have great instincts, and they must also have a tremendous ability to concentrate and keep focused on what's going on. Remember, play does not stop very often in hockey. It's not like baseball, which seems to have more downtime than action, or football, in which players have time to rest and regroup before each play. Hockey is often continuous action, and a goaltender must be able to focus for the entire game. Concentration, in many ways, is the difference between a major-league and a minor-league goalie. And only a minor lapse can be the difference between a win and a loss.

A goalie gaffe

Consider a 1974 game that our very own JD played with the St. Louis Blues. "One of the opposing forwards, a player named Jerry Korab, wristed the puck down the ice from his own defensive zone, and I went over to stop it," the fearless coauthor and onetime goaltender says. "But I looked up for just one second to see where I was going to put the puck, and while I was doing that, it hit off the heel of my stick, went through my legs, and then trickled off the goalpost and into the net, before 16,000 people." The reason he messed up? Concentration, pure and simple. He lost his concentration for a moment, and it cost him and his Blues. Fortunately, JD quickly adds, his teammates picked him up, and St. Louis came back to tie the game 6–6.

Defensemen

These players have two jobs, really. *Defensemen* mainly defend their end of the ice and keep the other team from scoring. It's a position for which you must be physically dominating. You have to be able to clear men out from the front of the goal, to block shots, and to grapple with the opponent's forwards in the corner and along the boards. But after taking care of the defense, defensemen then have to switch to offense. The first pass is key to any successful rush up the ice, and the vast majority of the time, the defensemen have to make that pass. Defensemen often set the tone and get things going on the offensive end.

Occasionally a defenseman can also lead a team's offense, such as the great Bobby Orr, who won the James Norris Trophy for being the league's best defenseman eight consecutive times and captured two scoring titles. And there are some defensemen — such as Brian Leetch, Chris Chelios, Ray Bourque, and Chris Pronger — who can play the position extremely well both ways. But most defensemen are valued mainly for their ability to keep the other team from scoring and are not asked to do much else.

Chapter 2

Pads and Pucks: Gearing Up

· ·

· ·

*L*ike knights going off to battle, hockey players must cloak themselves in armor before heading out to the ice. Players today wear much more equipment than they did in the game's early years, and many players look like modern-day gladiators when they step onto a rink. That's good, too, because with the speed of the shots and the power of the checks, they need all the protection they can get.

The Modern Hockey Player's Gear

Hockey gear varies a great deal, depending upon the age, sex, and ability of the player and where he or she is competing. A member of the Vancouver Canucks, for example, is going to have much different gear than a weekend skater involved in a pickup pond game. In this section, we focus on a National Hockey League skater and all that he dons when it comes time to play. He has the most up-to-date equipment — and he wears a lot of it when he goes onto the ice (as shown in Figure 2-1).

Skates

Nothing is more important to an NHL player than his skates, and the ones on the market today are marvels of technology. The basic design has not changed that much in the past 30 years, but instead of using only leather for the boots, manufacturers now employ a combination of materials. The inside of many skates, for example, is made of *Clarino,* a synthetic leather that is easier to break in and more water-resistant.

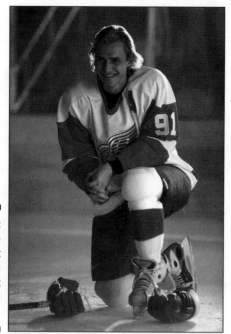

Figure 2-1:
Up-to-date
equipment
— and
plenty of it
(Sergei
Fedorov).

The heel and lace eyelets are still made completely of leather, but the rest of a skate's exterior also includes nylon; Kevlar, which is also used in bullet-proof vests; and graphite to keep it light, stiff (for better support and protection), and durable. As for the old metal runners, they have been replaced by a plastic holder in which a metal blade is inserted (see Figure 2-2).

Skate blades have different shapes, and the kind a player chooses depends on the type of performance he wants. The bottom of Brian Leetch's blades, for example, have what is known as a *deep hollow* — the thin area between each blade's two sharp edges has been hollowed out and curves a bit to the inside. Longtime NHL equipment manager Mike Folga sharpened Leetch's blades that way because the smooth-skating defenseman wants to be able to cut on the ice the way Warrick Dunn does on a football field; the deeper the hollow, the easier it is to make those types of moves. Another pair of talented defensemen, Ray Bourque and Paul Coffey, have somewhat flatter blades because they are more straight-ahead skaters. Same with center Mark Messier.

While goalies' skates have a somewhat different shape and design, they are made of the same materials. In addition, they have a plastic shell on the outside to provide better protection from pucks banging off the goalie's feet, and their blades are a bit wider.

Figure 2-2:
A typical
hockey
skate.

Sticks

Sticks are certainly the next most important piece of equipment. Some are made of traditional wood, and others feature aluminum, graphite, Kevlar, or titanium shafts into which wooden blades are cemented with hot glue. Perhaps half the players in the NHL use stick shafts made of those new materials, in part because they are more durable and cost-effective. The blades go for only $8 or $9 apiece, less than half the price of a complete wooden stick, and the savings can add up after a while. Additionally, some players like the feel of the aluminum or graphite shafts and believe they can get off a better shot with them. Goalies' sticks, which have a wide "paddle" partway down the shaft so that it is easier to block shots, are still made entirely of wood (wrapped with fiberglass).

Sticks come in different degrees of *flex:* medium, stiff, and extra stiff. The stronger player who hits more slap shots will probably want a stiffer stick because a *slap shot* is made with a full windup — and is the most powerful shot. A forward who shoots closer to the net and likes to *snap* his shots (with a shortened backswing and a quick follow-through) will probably opt for a stick that's more flexible. And all sticks have blades that are curved, even ones used by goalies, because that gives a shot — or pass — more lift and power.

The NHL has very specific regulations on sticks that may be used in league play. According to its rule book, sticks should be no longer than 63 inches (162cm) from the heel to the end of the shaft, and the blade may not be more than 12½ inches (32cm) long. In addition, a blade may be no more than 3 inches and no less than 2 inches wide (7.7 and 5.1cm), and the curve may not exceed ½ inch (1.3cm). For goalies, the widened part of the stick, or "paddle," can be a maximum of 26 inches (67cm) long, and the blade must not exceed 3½ inches (9.0cm) in width or 15 inches (39cm) in length. Figure 2-3 shows some sample sticks.

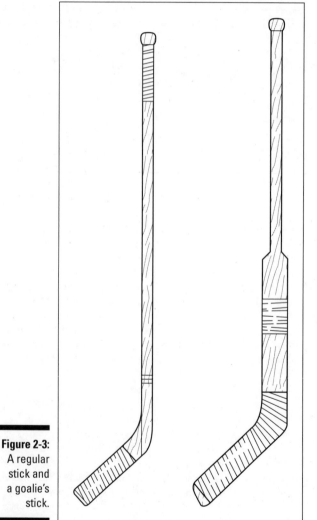

Figure 2-3:
A regular
stick and
a goalie's
stick.

Protection

The rest of a hockey player's equipment is designed primarily to protect him from sticks, pucks, elbows, goalposts, and opposing players, while enabling him to maneuver with as much speed and agility as possible. Helmets are a critical piece of gear for players on any level, and some pros like to attach a clear shield in front to protect their eyes. (All amateur players must wear a full face guard on their helmets in organized competition.) Figure 2-4 shows some typical protection.

Shoulder pads vary in size depending on the position a person plays and his preferences. Defensemen usually have heavier pads because they do more checking than other players and take a lot of punishment on the ice; some defensemen look like they should be playing linebacker for the Dallas Cowboys. Also, their shoulder pads often extend all the way to their waists because they often must drop to their knees to block shots and need padding across their chests. Some even have a pad that goes down their spines to protect them from slashes across the back. Forwards, on the other hand, might opt for lighter shoulder pads, depending on their role. Some forwards have the shoulder pads extended down their backs for further protection.

A checking wing will want more protection than a *sniper* (a pure goal scorer) who doesn't hit other players or the boards all that much. Wayne Gretzky's shoulder pads not only looked old but offered very little in the way of protection. But as a scorer and playmaker who didn't mix it up physically very much, he really didn't need much else.

A pro may also wear padded pants, a protective cup, shin guards, elbow pads, and gloves. Though protective equipment doesn't look that different from the gear players were wearing 20 years ago, the materials have changed a lot thanks to the development of new plastics, foams, and other materials that make it all lighter, stronger, and more durable. Even the *sweaters*, or jerseys, are better. Once made of wool because games were initially played outside, they had all the comfort of a rubber suit on a hot July day. But now they are made with very lightweight and breathable materials.

Goalie protection

Not surprisingly, goalies have a somewhat different ensemble. They wear masks in addition to their helmets, and many put on extra neck protection as well. Chest protectors are essential, and all goalies put padding down both their arms to their wrists. Goalies' gloves are quite different from those that their teammates wear. See Figure 2-5 for the goaltender's regalia.

Figure 2-4:
After skates and a stick, a hockey player's equipment is for protection (Eric Lindros).

Figure 2-5:
A modern goalie is well protected (Curtis Joseph).

The puck

Rule 25 of the NHL rule book provides a description of that little object known as the "puck" — a word whose origin may be seventeenth-century French from a verb that means "to poke." The handbook says:

"The puck shall be made of vulcanized rubber, or other approved material, one inch (1") thick and three inches (3") in diameter and shall weigh between five and one-half ounces (5½ oz.) and six ounces (6 oz.).

"The home team shall be responsible for providing an adequate supply of official pucks which shall be kept in a frozen condition. This supply of pucks shall be kept at the penalty bench under the control of one of the regular off-ice officials or a special attendant."

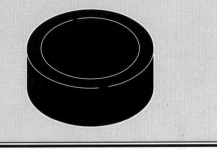

A glove known as a *blocker* goes on the hand that holds the stick, and a glove known as the *catcher,* which looks like an oversized first baseman's mitt, goes on the other hand. Goalies also wear large, pillow-like pads on the fronts of their legs that wrap around the tops of their skates and go up past their knees. Years ago, the outside of the pads was made entirely of leather and the inside was stuffed with deer hair. Those materials are also used to make the more modern version, but manufacturers also include a number of synthetic materials to make the pads lighter and more water-resistant.

What They Wore — and Didn't Wear — in Years Past

Hockey players of the past wore remarkably little equipment, and the gear they did have was very rudimentary. In the beginning, skates consisted of blades that were attached to shoes, and sticks were made from tree branches. The first goalie shin and knee pads had originally been designed for cricket. The quality of the gear progressed over the years, with true hockey skates being made and players wearing protective gloves. Shin guards eventually came into being, but many times they didn't do much to soften the blow of a puck or stick, and players were known to stuff newspaper or magazines behind them for extra protection. (Compare the players in Figure 2-6 to those you see today.)

Figure 2-6:
Hockey
circa
1943 —
before
helmets,
masks, and
curved
blades.

For many years the blades on sticks were completely straight, but New York Rangers star Andy Bathgate began experimenting with a curve in the late 1950s. During a European tour of Ranger and Chicago Blackhawk players, Bathgate showed his innovation to Bobby Hull and Stan Mikita, and they began playing with curved blades themselves. And it wasn't long before most NHL players had done the same thing.

Amazingly, goalies played without masks until 1959, when Jacques Plante wore face protection in a game in the old Madison Square Garden after he had taken a puck in the cheekbone from Bathgate. Plante's coach, Toe Blake, pressured him to shed the mask later on, and he did for a while. But he started wearing a mask again the following spring, and other goaltenders eventually followed suit. But it wasn't until 1973 that masks became universal for goalies; that year, journeyman goalie Andy Brown was the last netminder to appear in an NHL game without a mask.

It's also surprising that players didn't begin wearing helmets with any sort of regularity until the early 1970s; before that, the only people who wore them did so mostly because they were recovering from a head injury, or, in the case of one former Chicago Blackhawk forward, because they were embarrassed about being bald. (No, it wasn't Bobby Hull.) The league passed a rule before the 1979–80 season decreeing that anyone who came into the NHL from that point on had to wear a helmet. By the early 1990s there were only a few players left who went bareheaded, and the last one to do so was Craig MacTavish, who retired after the 1996–97 season.

Deciding What Equipment Is Best for You — and Your Kids

The best way to buy the right equipment is to find a store or outlet that specializes in hockey equipment and has knowledgeable salespeople who can not only help pick out the best gear for you and your kids but also make sure it all fits properly.

Getting the right skates

Let's start with skates. Most adults should get ones that are a size to a size and a half smaller than their usual shoe size. Children should drop half a size. It's important that the skates fit comfortably and snugly at the time of purchase; it's not like buying a sweater two sizes too big and waiting for a kid to grow into it. The best way to check is to push your toe, or your child's, to the front of the skate and then put a finger down behind the heel. If you can fit more than one in there, the skate is too big. The whole key to good skating ability is support, and you can't get support if the skate doesn't fit.

Getting the right helmet

When choosing a helmet, make sure you have the right width and that it does not wobble. Children should have protection for their ears. Players at all levels should wear a full face guard, either a clear shield or wire cage, and a chin cup.

Padding up: From the shoulders to the hands

Shoulder pads should be comfortable and not too bulky. You want the cup to fit right on the shoulder and the pad to almost rest against your neck; anything that's looser in that area may jam into you when someone checks you or you fall to the ice. And that will hurt. Defensemen should get shoulder pads with full frontal protection so they can block shots without worry; forwards can get away with a lot less.

Whether you get heavy-duty, football-like equipment or go for lighter-weight wear depends on your abilities and your level of play. Many adult and youth leagues don't allow checking, for example, so there's no reason to get big, expensive pads.

As for elbow pads, you want ones that fit properly on the point of the elbow and won't slip up and down. And you want to make sure that they're not so tight that they constrict the flow of blood. These days, elbow pads come in various lengths; some people prefer to wear a long glove and short elbow pads, while others — Brett Hull of the Dallas Stars is one who comes to mind — like a shorter glove and longer pads. You should have the forearm covered against slashes and stick checks so it is as well protected as the elbow.

Gloves used to be all leather, but now they're made mostly of Kevlar or nylon or some combination of the two. You want something with a strong thumb, which is an area where many injuries occur. For a good fit, you should have a little room at the end of your fingers.

From the waist down

Hockey pants used to be held up exclusively by suspenders, but now they come with belts, so it's not so hard tucking that sweater in the right side à la Wayne Gretzky. The key is getting pants with good thigh, hip, and tailbone protection.

Shin guards should fit in the center of the kneecap and go down to the top of the skate. They run from 7 inches in length to 17 inches. If you are a defenseman, you want to get ones with lots of padding because you will be blocking more shots than a forward, who should get lighter and smaller guards. Defensemen often have padding that wraps right around the back of their legs.

Choosing a stick

Choosing a stick is mostly a question of which size and type of shaft you prefer. The aluminum shafts are somewhat more expensive, but they do last longer and might not be a bad way to go for the more serious player. Kids, beginners, and very part-time players can get by just fine with wooden sticks.

The bottom line

So what will all this equipment cost? Plenty, if you go down and pick it all out at once. Outfitting one child will run anywhere between $300 and $400, while equipment for adults could go from $400 all the way up to $1,000 for top-of-the-line stuff. You should purchase equipment that best suits your level of play and commitment, and the same goes for the kids. Just don't take shortcuts on the critical gear, like helmets and skates. It pays to be safe and comfortable.

Taping a stick

What's the best way to tape a stick, and how do the pros do it? We turned to "The Great One," Wayne Gretzky, for his thoughts on the subject.

"A lot of people tape the blades and knobs of their sticks certain ways because of superstition," he says. "Some guys go from heel to toe on their blades, and others toe to heel. Paul Coffey, the great defenseman who was a teammate of mine in Edmonton years ago, would always use white tape. I, on the other hand, used black, and I would dust it with baby powder. I would put some powder in a thin sock, tie it up, and then hit the sock against the blade I just taped. And the powder would go through the sock and onto the tape. It helped take some of the stickiness out of the new tape on the stick and made the puck come off it a bit smoother.

"It is easier to control a puck, to handle the give and take of a pass, when you are using a taped stick," Gretzy continues. "But Paul and I would purposely not practice with tape on our stick blades because it forced us to concentrate harder. The puck was harder to handle that way, and somehow that made it easier for us when we played a game with our normal sticks.

"Most guys tape their entire blade, though there are some people like Bobby Orr, the longtime Boston Bruins defenseman, who put only a strip or two on. But, as I said before, that has more to do with superstition than anything else.

"As for the top [handle] of the stick, which people tape so it is easier to grip and also easier to pick up when it falls to the ice, the amount of tape used is related to the kind of grip the player wants and his size. A guy with big hands is apt to use more tape, while a guy with smaller hands will use less."

Some extra advice for parents outfitting children: Check out area stores for trade-in and swap programs. Many youth hockey leagues and sporting goods stores that supply them allow parents to trade in skates and pads for gear that fits as their children grow up, at minimal cost. Do it if you can.

Where to Buy What You — and Your Kids — Want

Finding first-rate hockey gear is not always the easiest task. The big sporting goods chains carry some equipment. Unless their primary orientation is hockey, however, they probably won't have the quality and selection you need if you want to buy skates, helmets, and sticks. Check your local Yellow Pages for the names of outlets that might specialize in hockey gear, and peruse *The Hockey News,* which often carries advertisements for that sort of store. You may also want to check out the pro shop at the local ice rink; they usually are well stocked with up-to-date equipment and have knowledgeable salespeople.

Sometimes you can find an independent retailer who has everything you need to play the game and offers not only a fair price but also expert help in sizing and selection. Our favorite in that category is Gerry Cosby's, which has a big store at Madison Square Garden in New York City and outlets in Princeton, New Jersey; Westbury, New York; and Sheffield, Massachusetts. Cosby's caters to athletes of all ages and abilities, from Pee-Wees to the pros. Many of the teams in the NHL buy some, if not all, of their equipment from Cosby's, and when Wayne Gretzky played for the New York Rangers, he outfitted his young sons in hockey gear at that store. Check it out if you're ever in the Big Apple.

If you can't make it to New York and don't have a good hockey store nearby, then look in *The Hockey News,* where you will find several national mail-order houses that specialize in hockey gear. But we still think it's best to go directly to a store to be properly fitted.

Fans who are more interested in making a fashion statement than a hat trick can buy NHL-licensed merchandise bearing the logo of their favorite team at a wide range of stores, from Kmart and Target to Saks Fifth Avenue and Bloomingdale's. The products available span the spectrum, from hockey sweaters and team hats to wallpaper and bedsheets. Most franchises have team stores of some sort in the city in which they are based and also out at their arena, and the big sporting goods chains such as Modell's and Foot Locker have some gear for sale. In addition, the NHL puts out a catalog for all its licensed merchandise goods, as well as other items such as autographed collectibles and electronic games.

Chapter 3

Rules of the Game

· ·

· ·

*W*alk into a hockey game that's tied with only a minute to go in the third period, and you're likely to find something resembling one of the street scenes from *A Tale of Two Cities*. (If you haven't read the book, picture torch- and pitchfork-carrying mobs, terrified aristocrats, and a lone, abandoned child, all milling around a very busy guillotine. Put this scene on an ice rink, make a few casting changes, and you have the tail end of a close game.) In other words, near chaos — and it appears as if all sense of order has gone. But appearances are deceiving. Hockey, like the other major sports, is governed by a strict set of rules, and games are much more controlled than they often seem. This chapter describes the National Hockey League's most important regulations and the roles of the people who must enforce them on the ice.

Scoring

The object of hockey is to score goals, and the team that scores the most wins the game. To score a goal, an attacking player must put the puck between the goalposts and over the red goal line. But how you get the puck over the goal line determines whether you get the point or not:

✔ You can use your stick to get the puck over the goal line.

✔ You can have the puck deflect into the net off any part of your body or skate.

The greatest assist and scoring feats

Most goals in a game: 7

Joe Malone

Quebec Bulldogs (1920)

Most goals in a season: 92

Wayne Gretzky

Edmonton Oilers (1981–82)

Most goals in a career: 894

Wayne Gretzky

Edmonton Oilers, Los Angeles Kings, St. Louis Blues, New York Rangers

Most points in a career: 2,857

Wayne Gretzky

Edmonton Oilers, Los Angeles Kings, St. Louis Blues, New York Rangers

Most assists in a season: 163

Wayne Gretzky

Edmonton Oilers (1985–86)

Most assists in a career: 1,963

Wayne Gretzky

Edmonton Oilers, Los Angeles Kings, St. Louis Blues, New York Rangers

Most points (goals and assists) in one game: 10 (6 goals, 4 assists)

Darryl Sittler

Toronto Maple Leafs (1976)

Most points (goals and assists) in one period: 6 (3 goals, 3 assists)

Bryan Trottier

New York Islanders (1978)

Because this last feat was accomplished against JD's Rangers, JD adds: "I must have been injured that night." (Be sure to check out Appendix D for many more hockey statistics and figures.)

A referee will allow a puck that has been deflected into the goal by a defender's body, skate, or stick to stand as a score as well. However, a member of the attacking team may not deliberately bat the puck into the net with any part of his body or kick it in with his foot. And anything that deflects in off the referee or linesmen doesn't count as a goal, either.

An offensive player who puts the puck into the net gets credit for scoring a goal. The player (or players) who made the pass(es) that immediately led to the goal receives an *assist*. No more than two players can receive an assist for each goal. Each player gets one point for a goal or assist, and the NHL player who amasses the most points during the season wins the scoring title and the coveted Art Ross Trophy.

Periods

NHL games are divided into three 20-minute periods. If the contest is tied at the end of regulation during the regular season, the teams play an additional period of sudden-death overtime that lasts no more than five minutes, with each side having only four skaters and a goaltender. The club that scores first wins. If no one scores, the game ends in a tie. During the playoffs, however, the overtime lasts until a goal is scored, with the teams breaking after every 20 minutes as they do during regular play.

Sometimes, the games go on like an all-night party, such as the time in 1936 when it took the Detroit Red Wings nearly six full overtime periods to score on the Montreal Maroons and win a playoff game 1–0. The winning shot went in at 2:25 a.m., after more than 175 minutes of playing time. That's almost three full games.

Rosters: Who Gets to Play

Teams may dress no more than 18 players, excluding goalies, for each game. A list of all eligible players must be given to the referee or official scorer beforehand, and after that no roster changes can be made. Teams may use any number of goalies that they wish.

Generally, a club has two goalies ready to go each game, one of whom starts while the other sits on the bench. If both should get hurt, the rules allow a team to put any other player in goal, provided he is on the roster.

NHL franchises often have several players that regularly practice with the team but do not dress for games. They make up a sort of unofficial *taxi squad* and play only sporadically during the regular season and hardly at all in the playoffs.

The shoot-out

Some minor and international leagues handle overtime a bit differently. They have their teams play a five-minute, sudden-death period, and if no one scores, the game is then decided by a *shoot-out*. Each team picks five players, and each one of them takes a *penalty shot* on the other's goalie, skating in by themselves with the puck from the red line (center ice) and trying to score. Whichever team scores more in its five chances is declared the winner; and if the squads remain tied after the first shoot-out, they start another. This method is very popular in some hockey circles because of the added excitement it generates. A shoot-out determined the 1994 Olympic gold medal champion at Lillehammer, when Sweden bested the Canadian national team.

General substitutions

Skaters can enter the game from the bench while play is in progress, provided that the people coming off the ice are within five feet of their bench and out of the play before the switch is made. That's known as *changing on the fly*. If a player doesn't get within five feet of the bench before his replacement hits the ice, his team is whistled for having too many men on the ice and loses a man to the penalty box for two minutes.

When play has stopped, the visiting team has the option of replacing its players on the ice. The referee allows a reasonable amount of time (5–10 seconds), and then he puts up his hands to indicate that the visitors cannot make any more changes. At that point, the home team may make its desired substitutions. This setup gives the home team the advantage in determining matchups, letting it put out the players it wants to face those on the opposing squad. To counter this, the visiting team often substitutes as soon as play begins again and gets the people it wants onto the ice by quickly changing on the fly. (See Chapter 8 to read about the interesting game of matchups and changes.)

Goalie substitutions

As for goaltenders, they may be substituted at any time (usually during a stoppage in play — but not always). The new player coming in after a stoppage is allowed warm-ups only if his team's two goaltenders have already been knocked out of the game and he is goalie number 3. In that case, the netminder is allowed two minutes to get ready, unless he is being inserted for a penalty shot. Then he must go to work stone cold.

Infractions

The dictionary tells us that an infraction is a "breach, violation, or infringement" of the rules; hardly a minute goes by in a game without one occurring. At last count, the NHL had 93 "official rules," all of which are laid out in a book that is 159 pages long. We don't have the time or space to go over each one of the rules, but we can describe briefly some of the most common breaches. (You can find the signals for these infractions in Appendix C.)

Icing

Icing is called when a player behind the red line in his end of the rink shoots a puck past the goal line in his offensive zone when both teams are playing at even strength. The officials stop play when an opponent other than the goalie touches the puck. (See Figure 3-1 for an illustration of icing from the defensive zone, from behind the goal line, and from the neutral zone.) Icing is considered an infraction because teams can do it to take away legitimate scoring chances from skaters on the offensive.

A club that has fewer players on the ice than its opponent (because of a penalty) may "ice" the puck as often as it likes in order to kill the penalty.

Offside

A player may not skate into his offensive zone ahead of the puck (see Figure 3-2). If that happens, a whistle is blown and a face-off is held just outside the zone where the breach — *offside* — occurred. What matters in determining offside is the position of the skates: Both skates must be all the way over the blue line before the puck for a player to be offside. The location of the stick does not matter.

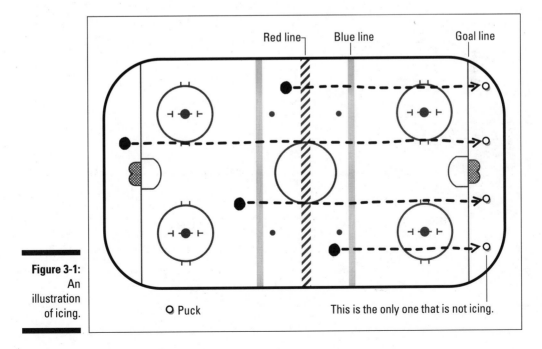

Figure 3-1:
An illustration of icing.

Red line · Blue line · Goal line

O Puck

This is the only one that is not icing.

Officials will also call offside if a player makes what is called a *two-line pass*. A defenseman with the puck in front of his own net, for example, cannot snap it to a teammate beyond the red line at center ice because it would have to go over two lines, first the blue and then the red, to get there. For that play to work, the player at center ice would have to skate inside the red line, closer to his own net, to receive the pass (see Figure 3-3).

Offside is called to keep players from hanging around the red line at center ice, or all the way down in their offensive zone, and waiting for a pass that will give them a *breakaway* (skating toward the goal with no defenders around except for the goalie) and an easy chance at a goal.

Keep in mind that if you — the receiver of the puck — precede the puck into your offensive zone, you are offside.

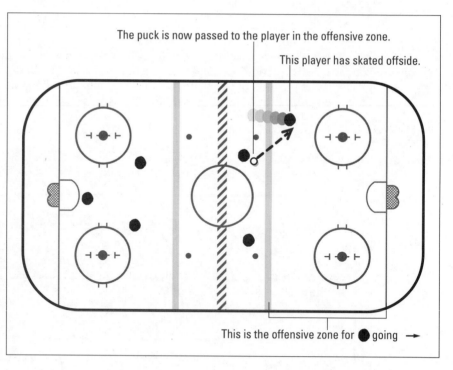

The puck is now passed to the player in the offensive zone.

This player has skated offside.

Figure 3-2:
Skating into the offensive zone ahead of the puck is offside.

This is the offensive zone for ● going →

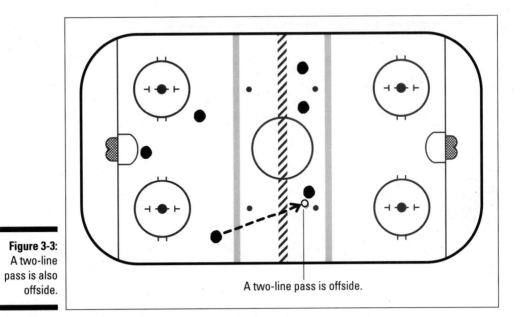

Figure 3-3:
A two-line
pass is also
offside.

A two-line pass is offside.

Types of Penalties

Unlike infractions, which result in a face-off, penalties usually call for some-one to spend some time in the penalty box. There are three types of penalties in hockey: *minor, major,* and *misconduct*. The severity of the action deter-mines the kind of penalty handed down. A player who accidentally trips an opponent, for example, faces a less stringent punishment (probably two min-utes in the penalty box) than one who punches another player in the mouth or hits him across the face with a stick (at least five minutes in the box, and maybe more). There is bad, and then there is really bad. And the badder a player is on the ice, the longer he will spend watching the game from the sidelines. (Refer to Appendix C for an illustration of the signals for these penalties.)

Minors

Most of the penalties called during an NHL game are minors, in which players are sent to the box for two minutes for things like roughing, slashing, trip-ping, holding, or hooking an opponent (see "How You Get a Penalty" later in this chapter). No substitute is allowed during that time. If a player mis-behaves a bit more, he might receive a double minor and have to serve two, two-minute penalties consecutively.

Majors

If the violation is even more egregious, such as for fighting, a ref hands out a major penalty, which lasts for five minutes. No substitute is permitted, and the team on which the foul was called is forced to compete with one less man. A player who is assessed a major for injuring an opponent in the face or head with his stick is automatically fined $100. And a skater who gets three majors in the same game is thrown out.

Misconducts

There are also three kinds of misconduct penalties.

- A *basic misconduct,* such as yelling at the referee, forces a skater to sit in the penalty box for ten minutes. Bad as that infraction might be, however, it does not lead to the loss of a man, and therefore no one goes onto the power play (see Chapter 9 for details on the power play).

- Get a *game misconduct,* however, and a player is tossed from the ice right away. Violators are also fined and face the possibility of suspension if their infraction, be it a vicious slash or brutal cross-check, is particularly egregious. (Many game misconducts are enhancements to other penalties.) Any skater who is whistled for a total of three game misconducts during the regular season is automatically suspended for one contest — unless the misconducts involve abuse of officials or stick-related fouls, in which case it takes only two in the same season to lead to suspension. Two game misconducts in the playoffs of any given year will result in the same action.

- Finally, referees may also call what is known as a *gross misconduct,* which also results in suspension from that game, a fine, and the possibility of even more serious league action.

Note: If a player receives a game or gross misconduct penalty, his team does not have to play the rest of the game a man down — the team is only short a player during the penalty time for the player who was tossed from the game. After the penalty time is up, a substitute can take the place of the evicted player.

Sometimes the infraction is so great that a penalty shot is called, and the player who was fouled gets to skate in on the goalie by himself and try to score. Officials call penalty shots for a variety of reasons, such as a player deliberately dislodging the goalpost during a breakaway for the other team, falling on the puck in his *crease* (the area in front of the goal), picking up the puck with his hand in the crease area, and taking a player down from behind on a breakaway. Penalty shots don't happen very often, but when they do, they create some of the most exciting moments in hockey, especially in a big game.

How You Get a Penalty

It's not really that hard to get a penalty. If a player slashes his opponent across the wrist with his stick, he's gone, most likely for two minutes but maybe even longer. Same thing if he knocks down a man from behind. Or holds him up in front of the net. Or mouths off to the referee. If a player breaks one of the league's rules, he'll probably receive a penalty (unless the referee doesn't see him or is inclined to let things go).

Just so you know what your favorite winger or centerman is not supposed to do when he skates onto the ice, we have compiled descriptions of the most frequently called penalties.

Roughing

Roughing is called after a player strikes an opponent in a minor altercation that the referee determines is not worthy of a major (see Figure 3-4). For example, if two players push and shove a lot and appear ready to fight but don't actually drop their gloves and start punching each other, then it's considered roughing. They may also be whistled for particularly rough behavior after play has stopped; a good face plant (such as grinding one's palm into an opponent's face) often leads to a roughing penalty, and so might an open-handed slap or an obvious elbow.

Hooking

If a player impedes the progress of another by "hooking" him with his stick and keeping him from making a play, then he is guilty of *hooking*. Generally that happens when a skater has scooted by the man guarding him, and the defenseman has no other recourse but to hold the player up by "hooking" him. Not only does that break up a play illegally, but it can also injure a player, especially if the stick comes up high and hits the opposing player in his face (see Figure 3-5). Hooking is also known as *waterskiing* — which gives you a good idea of what is involved.

Charging

An official may call a minor or major penalty on a player who skates or jumps into, or *charges,* an opponent in any way (as shown in Figure 3-6). Whether it's a major or minor penalty depends upon the seriousness of the infraction; the more dangerous the hit, the more likely it will be a major.

Figure 3-4:
Does this
look like
roughing
to you?

© NHL Images/Al Messerschmidt

Figure 3-5:
A fish-eye
view of
hooking.

© NHL Images/Allsport/Robert Laberge

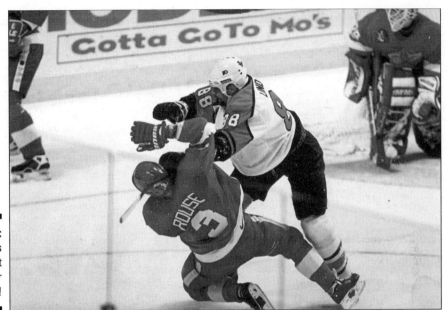

© NHL Images/Allsport/Rick Stewart

Figure 3-6:
Someone is
going to get
called for
charging!

Hockey and fighting

Fighting has long been an accepted part of professional hockey in the United States and Canada and is considered a natural by-product of a fast and furious game. Years ago, it was not unusual to see entire benches empty during a fight and have every player wrestling their opponents to the ice and throwing punches. But the NHL and other leagues began instituting much stricter rules about fighting, and anyone who leaves the bench to enter or start a brawl these days, or jumps into an altercation as the third man, is treated harshly with penalties and fines.

But unlike college and international hockey organizations, which prohibit fighting, the NHL and other professional leagues in North America still allow it to go on, though not without penalty. That bothers some fans, who would

like to see fighting completely banned. But the majority seem to enjoy the occasional scrap between players. And there are those who argue quite sensibly that fighting neutralizes the possibility of smaller players being intimidated by bigger ones, especially if both franchises have a fighter or two on their rosters; no one is going to be able to mess around with one of the smaller skaters if he knows he will then have to answer to one of the fighters. So it actually serves to better keep the peace. Also, the absence of fighting would likely lead to an increase in the number and severity of stick fouls (slashing, high-sticking, and so on), which can be even more dangerous, because players wouldn't have the same outlet for their frustration and rage.

Interference

A common penalty that occurs when a player interferes with or impedes the progress of an opponent who does not have the puck. It happens a lot in front of the net, where players fight for position, and also behind a play as a skater may try to hold up another as he tries to catch up with the puck. In addition, interference is called when a player deliberately knocks the stick out of an opponent's hand or prevents a player who has dropped his stick, or any other piece of equipment, from picking it back up.

Slashing

Players receive this penalty when they smack an opponent with their sticks, or "slash" an opponent, either to hold him up or cause injury. Generally, the slash has to be a fairly strong one for a referee to call this infraction; the rule book states that "non-aggressive stick contact to the pants or the front of the shin pads should not be penalized as slashing."

High sticking

Any contact made with a stick above an opponent's shoulders is not allowed, and the officials will assess a minor penalty (see Figure 3-7). This rule is supposed to protect players from being hit by a stick in the face, eyes, or head. Also, players cannot bat the puck above the normal height of the shoulders; officials stop play if that happens. In addition, any apparent goal scored as the result of a player striking the puck with his stick above the goal's crossbar is not allowed.

Checking from behind

The officials whistle this infraction when a player hits an opponent who is not aware of the impending contact and therefore cannot defend himself from behind. It is a very dangerous infraction that can seriously injure the person who is hit.

Fighting

It's actually called "fisticuffs" in the NHL rule book and is assessed when players drop their gloves and start to act like prizefighters. Players get rid of their gloves because they can hit harder and inflict more pain with their bare knuckles (see Figure 3-8). Chapter 10 has more information on fighting.

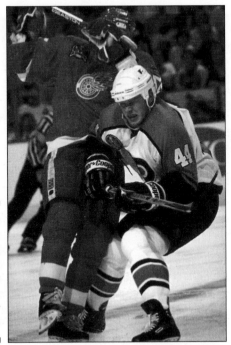

Figure 3-7: High sticking (with an elbow thrown in for roughing)!

Figure 3-8: Fisticuffs in the NHL.

Referees and Linesmen: Their Roles and Responsibilities

Each NHL game is now officiated by two *referees,* who wear orange armbands, and two *linesmen.* The referees are the ones who supervise the entire game, and in the case of disputes, their decisions are final. They report any serious infractions to league headquarters and are also in charge of arbitrating any controversial goals or calls. A referee also drops the puck at center ice at the start of each game.

The linesmen have only slightly lesser roles; they may call some penalties and are expected to help out each other, and the referees, should an extra set of eyes and ears be needed. And they are responsible for breaking up fights and handling all face-offs after the opening.

Hockey linesmen and referees have a tough job. They must skate up and down the ice to keep up with the play — and it is estimated that they skate up to seven miles per game! They must dodge pucks that fly by at speeds as high as 100 miles per hour. They must avoid getting hit by sticks, skates, and flying bodies as players fight for position and the puck. ***Note:*** If an official gets hit by the puck, play continues. But if a puck bounces off an official into the goal, that goal is not allowed.

And the officials must deal with a fair amount of verbal abuse as players and coaches argue calls and whine about the penalties that are and are not assessed. (Physical contact between refs and players — à la Roberto Alomar [baseball] or Dennis Rodman [basketball] — is rare, however, and on the few occasions that physical contact does happen, the leagues act swiftly and sternly.) The work of officials involves a tremendous amount of subjectivity; it's not always easy to discern what is and isn't a penalty — or a goal — when things happen as quickly as they do in hockey.

When it comes to calling a penalty, the officials are on their own. But as far as goals are concerned, they have some help. A *goal judge* at the end of each rink decides whether the puck has passed between the goalposts and entirely over the goal line. In addition, a *video goal judge* at each game checks the replays to determine what is and isn't a goal.

What the video goal judge reviews

The video goal judge is responsible for reviewing these situations:

✔ The puck crossing the goal line

✔ The puck in the net before a goalpost is dislodged

✔ The puck in the net before or after time expires at the end of a period

✔ The puck directed into the net by a hand or foot

✔ The puck deflected into the net off an official

✔ The puck directed into the net after being struck with a high-stick, above the height of the crossbar, by an attacking player

✔ The correct time on the official game clock (the game time is visible on the videotape)

Chapter 4

The National Hockey League

● ●

In This Chapter

▶ Discovering the origins of the NHL

▶ Following the standings

▶ Thinking about the Cup

▶ Wondering at the players' size, speed, and strength

● ●

*T*here are hundreds of active hockey associations around the globe, but none has the power, prestige, and players of the National Hockey League. And for that reason, we devote an entire chapter to the international organization that is home to the best teams in the world.

In the Beginning

The NHL was founded in Montreal in November 1917, and the league's first games were played the following month. Initially, the league had five franchises: the Montreal Canadiens, the Ottawa Senators, the Montreal Wanderers, the Quebec Bulldogs, and the Toronto Arenas. But Quebec decided not to operate that first season, so its players were allocated to the other teams. The clubs played a 22-game schedule, and Toronto was the only one that had a rink with man-made ice.

Things did not go smoothly in the beginning. Shortly after the season started, the Wanderers began having serious financial problems and got so low on players that the other teams offered to donate some of their own so that the club could continue competing. And then the Montreal Arena, which was home to both the Wanderers and the Canadiens, burned to the ground. That was enough for the owners of the Wanderers, and they withdrew the team from the league, leaving the NHL with only three teams. (The Canadiens moved their home games to the 3,250-seat Jubilee Rink.) Toronto won the championship that first tumultuous season, beating Montreal in a two-game playoff, and then went on to capture the Stanley Cup (more about that later) by topping the Vancouver Millionaires of the rival Pacific Coast Hockey Association (PCHA) in a best-of-five series.

Do we mean to say that the NHL was not the only professional hockey league operating at the time? Yes, indeed. In fact, the PCHA had been around for many years, and athletes had been getting paid to play hockey for even longer. Historians believe that several of the men who put together the earliest amateur hockey clubs quietly lined the pockets of their top players and shelled out whatever money they had to in order to get the very best talent. Many believe that the first unabashedly professional hockey team was the Portage Lakers of Houghton, Michigan, which was organized in 1902. And by the end of that decade, two leagues known as the National Hockey Association (NHA) and the Canadian Hockey Association (CHA) employed a number of professional players. In 1911, a pair of those stars, brothers Lester and Frank Patrick, decided to form a third league, the PCHA. (Unfortunately, we are unable to confirm long-standing rumors that the first player they ever signed was a strapping goalie named John Davidson.)

The seeds for the NHL were planted in the fall of 1917 when the NHA disbanded — partially due to the loss of players, many of whom had gone overseas to fight in World War I, and also because of the disdain team owners felt toward one of their own, Eddie Livingstone, who held the Toronto franchise. They disliked the man so much that they hatched a plan to start a new league without him, and after meeting in Montreal's Windsor Hotel, they agreed to reorganize as the National Hockey League. The new league played its first games on December 19, and Livingstone was nowhere to be seen.

The NHL limped through its first several years of operation. Only 700 fans showed up for the Wanderers' opening match with Toronto, for example, even though admission was free for soldiers in uniform. The 1919 Stanley Cup Finals were halted after five games because of a Spanish influenza epidemic, which sickened many of the players and claimed the life of the Montreal Canadiens' Joe Hall. And the existence of other leagues, such as the PCHA and the Western Canadian Hockey League, which started in 1921, kept the NHL from dominating the hockey scene. But one by one, the other associations folded, and 1926 marked the last year a team from outside the NHL played for the Stanley Cup. From that point on, the NHL had the professional game pretty much to itself.

A penny for his thoughts

The NHL had its share of colorful players in the early years, and one of the most outrageous was Ken Randall of the Toronto Arenas, who was suspended for a time during the inaugural season of 1917–18 because he owed $35 in back fines for arguing with referees. No problem, Randall said. He brought a bag of pennies to the rink before the start of one game and put it down on the ice as a form of partial payment. One of the opposing players jokingly hit the bag with his stick as he skated by, however, and the pennies spilled all over the rink, delaying the opening face-off until the players could pick up all the coins.

Where the NHL Is Today

The NHL has never been more popular or in better financial shape, and at the start of the 2000–01 season, the league boasted 30 franchises. Each team plays 82 regular-season games, beginning in October, and then a four-round playoff competition for the Stanley Cup begins in mid-April, with the finals ending in early June.

The NHL employs more than 750 players, and its games are televised all over the world. The Stanley Cup Championship, for example, is broadcast to more than 150 countries, from Albania to Zimbabwe, and watched in more than 300 million homes. (See "Battling for the Stanley Cup," later in this chapter.) Owners of NHL teams include corporate heavyweights like the Disney Co., and the teams now play in sleek new arenas that are modern entertainment centers with laser lights and rock music as well as food courts and luxury seating. (Refer to Appendix B for NHL league and franchise contact information.)

How the NHL Has Changed over the Years

The NHL has definitely changed over the years. Let us count the ways.

- The players have gotten bigger, stronger, and better, and so has the equipment.

- The games are faster, and the shots harder.

- The goalies all wear face masks and the forwards and defensemen helmets.

- Sticks are now made of materials like graphite and aluminum, and most of the players' protective padding consists of space-age plastics and fabrics.

- The league has more games, harder hitting, and more playoff action.

- Teams are based all over North America, from Vancouver, British Columbia, to Sunrise, Florida, and crowds of 19,000 are not unusual for a regular-season contest.

- And we mustn't forget the money. If a player made $2,000 a year in the early days of the NHL, he was pulling down big bucks. But the fellows today do a whole lot better: The average annual salary today exceeds $1 million.

Who's the Boss?

At the start of the 2000–01 season, the commissioner of the league was Gary Bettman, and he took office in February 1993. A native of New York City, Bettman worked for the National Basketball Association for 12 years, serving last as senior vice president and general counsel before coming to his senses and joining *The Coolest Game on Earth*™.

Bettman is the top dog, but there are a number of other men and women who help him run the league. Jon Litner, executive vice president and chief operating officer, is number 2. Another executive VP, and director of hockey operations, is Colin Campbell. Among his many duties is meting out punishments to players who behave badly. Bill Daly is an executive VP and the league's chief legal officer. Bernadette Mansur is in charge of corporate communications. Frank Brown is the VP of media relations, and Tom Richardson runs the Internet end of things.

Bettman is based in New York, and the league has other principal offices in Montreal and Toronto.

The NHL Teams

As we mentioned earlier, the NHL included 30 teams at the start of the 2000–01 season:

 Mighty Ducks of Anaheim

 Atlanta Thrashers

 Boston Bruins

 Buffalo Sabres

 Calgary Flames

 Carolina Hurricanes

 Chicago Blackhawks

 Colorado Avalanche

 Columbus Blue Jackets

 Dallas Stars

Detroit Red Wings

Edmonton Oilers

Florida Panthers	Philadelphia Flyers
Los Angeles Kings	Phoenix Coyotes
Minnesota Wild	Pittsburgh Penguins
Montreal Canadiens	St. Louis Blues
Nashville Predators	San Jose Sharks
New Jersey Devils	Tampa Bay Lightning
New York Islanders	Toronto Maple Leafs
New York Rangers	Vancouver Canucks
Ottawa Senators	Washington Capitals

The Columbus and Minnesota franchises are expansion teams new to the NHL in 2000–01.

The Conferences and Their Divisions

The NHL is divided into two conferences, Eastern and Western, and each of those has three divisions: the Northeast, Atlantic, and Southeast are part of the Eastern Conference, while the Central, Pacific, and Northwest are in the Western. Table 4-1 shows these conferences and their teams for the 2000–01 season.

Table 4-1	The NHL Conferences in 2000–01	
Eastern Conference		
Atlantic	*Southeast*	*Northeast*
New Jersey	Atlanta	Boston
NY Islanders	Carolina	Buffalo
NY Rangers	Florida	Montreal
Philadelphia	Tampa Bay	Ottawa
Pittsburgh	Washington	Toronto
Western Conference		
Northwest	*Pacific*	*Central*
Calgary	Anaheim	Chicago
Colorado	Dallas	Columbus
Edmonton	Los Angeles	Detroit
Minnesota	Phoenix	Nashville
Vancouver	San Jose	St. Louis

How the Standings Are Determined

Each team gets two points for a win during the regular season. In the event of a tie at the end of regulation play, each team earns one point. And if one of the teams scores a goal in the overtime period, it will earn an additional point. The teams in each conference with the most points at the end of the season finish highest in the standings. Table 4-2 shows how the standings added up at the end of the 1999–2000 season (W=wins; L=losses; T=ties; RT=regulation tie, which is the term for an overtime loss; PTS=points; GF=goals for; GA=goals against).

Table 4-2	The NHL 1999–2000 Final Standings						
Eastern Conference (Atlantic Division)							
	W	*L*	*T*	*RT*	*PTS*	*GF*	*GA*
Philadelphia	45	25	12	3	105	237	179
New Jersey	45	29	8	5	103	251	203

	W	L	T	RT	PTS	GF	GA
Pittsburgh	37	37	8	6	88	241	236
NY Rangers	29	41	12	3	73	218	246
NY Islanders	24	49	9	1	58	194	275

Eastern Conference (Northeast Division)

	W	L	T	RT	PTS	GF	GA
Toronto	45	30	7	3	100	246	222
Ottawa	41	30	11	2	95	244	210
Buffalo	35	36	11	4	85	213	204
Montreal	35	38	9	4	83	196	194
Boston	24	39	19	6	73	210	248

Eastern Conference (Southeast Division)

	W	L	T	RT	PTS	GF	GA
Washington	44	26	12	2	102	227	194
Florida	43	33	6	6	98	244	209
Carolina	37	35	10	0	84	217	216
Tampa Bay	19	54	9	7	54	204	310
Atlanta	14	61	7	4	39	170	313

Western Conference (Central Division)

	W	L	T	RT	PTS	GF	GA
St. Louis	51	20	11	1	114	248	165
Detroit	48	24	10	2	108	278	210
Chicago	33	39	10	2	78	242	245
Nashville	28	47	7	7	70	199	240

Western Conference (Northwest Division)

	W	L	T	RT	PTS	GF	GA
Colorado	42	29	11	1	96	233	201
Edmonton	32	34	16	8	88	226	212
Vancouver	30	37	15	8	83	227	237
Calgary	31	41	10	5	77	211	256

(continued)

Table 4-2 *(continued)*

Western Conference (Pacific Division)

	W	L	T	RT	PTS	GF	GA
Dallas	43	29	10	6	102	211	184
Los Angeles	39	31	12	4	94	245	228
Phoenix	39	35	8	4	90	232	228
San Jose	35	37	10	7	87	225	214
Anaheim	34	36	12	3	83	217	227

The Playoff Format

Basically, there are four rounds of best-of-seven-games series, beginning with the Conference Quarterfinals and then continuing with the Conference Semifinals, the Conference Finals, and then the Stanley Cup Championship. The top eight teams from each conference competed in the first round of the 1999–2000 playoffs, and the winners of those faced off in Round Two (the semifinals). Two teams from each conference battled for the Conference Finals titles in the third round, with the winners of each conference going against each other for the Stanley Cup.

Sixteen teams competed in the 1999–2000 Cup playoffs, and that same number will be eligible for postseason play after the expansion teams have entered the league. The first-place team in each of the six divisions will qualify, as will the next five best teams in each conference. The three division winners in each conference will be seeded one through three for the playoffs, and the next five best teams, in order of points, will be seeded fourth through eighth. In each conference, team number 1 will play team number 8, number 2 will play number 7, and so on, in the quarterfinals, which will remain best-of-seven series. And the competition for the Cup will continue from there.

Battling for the Stanley Cup

To many, the *Stanley Cup* is the finest trophy in sports, a glittering cup perched atop a silver barrel bearing the names of the greatest teams and players in professional hockey history. It was donated in 1892 by the English governor-general of Canada, Lord Stanley of Preston, who enjoyed the game of ice hockey so much that he bought a silver bowl with an interior gold finish (cost: $48.67 Canadian) and asked that it be given each year to the best team in the Dominion. Initially, it was handed out to the clubs that won the Amateur Hockey Association of Canada championship, and it was their responsibility to defend it against all comers. Challenges came as often as a couple times a season in the early years of the Cup's existence, as teams from other hockey leagues in Canada sought to unseat the reigning champion.

The first winner of the Stanley Cup was the Montreal Amateur Athletic Association team, which seemed appropriate considering that it was one of the oldest hockey clubs in the world. For several years, Cup challenge matches pitted amateur, semi-amateur, and professional teams against each other. But then the pros took over, and in 1910, the forerunner to the NHL, the National Hockey Association, took control of the trophy and began accepting challenges issued by teams from other professional leagues. From 1914 through 1916, the Stanley Cup winner was decided in a playoff between the team that captured the NHA title and the club that finished first in the Pacific Coast Hockey Association. The NHL came into being in 1917, and the following spring its champion, the Toronto Arenas, met the Pacific Coast Hockey Association champion Vancouver Millionaires for the Stanley Cup. Eventually the PCHA folded, and in 1926 the Stanley Cup became the official championship trophy of the NHL. (See Appendix D for a list of Stanley Cup winners — and also-rans — through the years.)

My Cup disappeareth

The Montreal Canadiens won the Stanley Cup in 1924, and not long after their big win, they were honored by the University of Montreal at a dinner. Not surprisingly, the team members who attended the fete brought the trophy with them, and when the gala was over, four of them decided to go to the home of one of the team owners, Leo Dandurand, to drink some more champagne from the Cup. So they all piled into a Model T Ford and drove away. Partway there, the car started to struggle with the load of players as it climbed up a steep hill. The driver stayed put, but the passengers climbed out of the car and began pushing. One of those was Sprague Cleghorn, a tough player who had been holding the Stanley Cup in his arms but decided to put it down on the curb so he could help out. It took some time and sweat, but the men were able to get the car to the top of the hill. And then they hopped back into the Model T and puttered off to Dandurand's home. But shortly after they arrived, the owner looked around the living room and asked, "Where's the Cup?" Suddenly, Cleghorn remembered he had left it by the side of the road. But when they rushed back there in the car, they were relieved to find the trophy sitting just where he had left it.

Battling for the Stanley Cup (after the season)

The Stanley Cup is the only trophy in professional sports that has its own bodyguards. That's right. A team of five men who work for the Hockey Hall of Fame serves as a sort of Secret Service force for the Cup, following it wherever it may go. For example, if a player wants to take the Cup home for a day in the summer, one of those fellows goes with him. It doesn't matter if the player lives overseas; the guardians of the Cup are obliged to follow as they did after the Colorado Avalanche win in 1996: The team's star forward, Peter Forsberg, took the trophy home to Sweden for its first visit to Europe. The same thing happens if a team wants to use the Cup for a fan festival or in a charity event. An escort clad in a Hall-of-Fame blazer is always there to keep track of the trophy for the Hall of Fame — to ensure that nothing happens to it and to answer any questions that people may have about the cup and its rich history.

Many things about the Cup make it unique in professional sports. None of the other major leagues has a trophy as old or as steeped in tradition, for example. And they certainly don't allow players from the winning team to take it home during the off-season. That's a wonderful custom that lets athletes truly savor their hard-fought victory and share their triumph with their family, friends, and fans. It also means that Lord Stanley's Cup has ended up in some very strange places and been put to some odd uses. Players have lugged it into horse stables as well as nursing homes and day care centers. One year it sank to the bottom of Mario Lemieux's swimming pool. The Cup has been used as an ashtray and a planter for geraniums. Dogs have drunk water from it, horses have eaten oats out of it, and fans have sipped fine champagne from the bowl as players toted it from bar to bar. And in the summer of 1997, the Stanley Cup even made a trip to Russia — where 75,000 people were able to cheer it as it was paraded around a soccer stadium in Moscow!

The Players

The NHL has realized so much success over the years for many reasons, but none is as important as the players who fill the rosters of all its teams. We can't think of another league in the world that has so many talented athletes competing against each other on a regular basis — and they are responsible for giving the NHL the speed, power, and finesse that make it the best place to see the game played.

Where do the players come from today?

They come from all over. Consider that at the start of the 1999–2000 season, 17 countries were represented on the 28 team rosters. Fifty-six percent of the players were Canadian, 16 percent were American, and the rest were from countries such as the Czech Republic, Russia, Sweden, and Finland. We do not have any information, however, on how many of the aforementioned players, or their coaches, needed translators or Berlitz lessons.

Where did the players come from in years past?

For decades, Canada has been the home of most of the NHL's players. In fact, it was big news in the 1960s and '70s when an American, or an athlete from another country, made it to the NHL.

Player size

The average NHL player for the 1999–2000 season was 6'1" and 199.3 pounds. In addition, 13 players were 6'6" or taller. "The players now are a lot bigger than they used to be," says Jim Ramsay, who has served as head medical trainer for the Winnipeg Jets (now Phoenix Coyotes) and New York Rangers. "Take a guy like Kevin Lowe, who joined the Edmonton Oilers as a defenseman in 1979 and now is general manager of that same team. At 6'2" and 190 pounds, he was one of the biggest guys on the team. But he wouldn't be any more. Now you have people like Zdeno Chara, who is 6'9" and 246 pounds, and big players are becoming more and more the norm."

Player speed

Amazingly, NHL players have gotten faster even as they have gotten bigger. Although we cannot measure players' speed as precisely as we can their height and weight, we can safely say that the game has never had so much speed.

Player strength

As players have gotten bigger, faster, and more international, they have also gotten stronger, thanks mostly to off-season strength and conditioning regimens and regular weightlifting during the year. "These guys are much more educated about conditioning, and most of them come to training camp at the start of the season in fantastic shape," Ramsay says. "I've been in the league for almost 13 years, and they just keep getting stronger and stronger." (See Chapter 7 for information on conditioning and training.)

Chapter 5

The Minors and Other Hockey Leagues

The National Hockey League may be the biggest fish in the organized hockey pond, but it's certainly not the only one. From Worcester, Massachusetts, to Helsinki, Finland, to Johannesburg, South Africa, to Tokyo, Japan, thousands of amateur and professional hockey teams, composed of both men and women, compete in leagues and tournaments. Some battle for Olympic gold and the World Championship, while others merely strive for a city or district title. And their numbers are growing each year as the game of hockey attracts not only more spectators but also more participants.

The Minor Leagues

Some of the most popular professional hockey teams in the world are in the United States minor leagues. Generally speaking, the people on those clubs are either up-and-comers who are about to break into the NHL or players who aren't quite good enough to land a full-time job there. However you categorize them, they play a hard-nosed brand of hockey that is good fun to watch and gives fans many of the same thrills an NHL game does.

Minor league franchises — the lowdown

It's hard to come up with an exact number of minor league franchises because the teams and leagues change a lot and what's valid this year may not be so 12 months down the road. At the end of the 1999–2000 season, there were seven bona fide professional leagues in the United States:

- ✔ the American Hockey League
- ✔ the International Hockey League
- ✔ the East Coast Hockey League
- ✔ the United Hockey League
- ✔ the Central Hockey League
- ✔ the West Coast Hockey League
- ✔ the Western Professional Hockey League

The **American** and **International** have the highest quality of play and, like Triple A in baseball, are considered just one step below the majors. They boast 19 and 13 teams, respectively.

The **East Coast** league is more like Double A baseball, a couple of notches down from the NHL, and it has 28 teams.

The **United** and **Central** leagues have 14 and 11 franchises, respectively, and are comparable to Single A baseball.

And finally, the **West Coast** and **Western Professional** leagues, which have 8 and 17 teams, feature the youngest and most inexperienced players you can find in professional hockey.

Finding the minor league teams

The minor league teams are all over. The American Hockey League is based in Springfield, Massachusetts, and has clubs from St. John's, New Brunswick, and Portland, Maine, to Syracuse, New York, and Hershey, Pennsylvania, while the International Hockey League, which has its headquarters in Madison Heights, Michigan, includes teams from Cincinnati, Kansas City, Houston, and Orlando.

The franchises in the East Coast Hockey League, which has its home office in Princeton, New Jersey, range from the Toledo Storm to the Jacksonville Lizard Kings. And the United Hockey League, which is based in Lake St. Louis, Missouri, features the Quad City Mallards, the Muskegon Fury, and the Rockford Ice Hogs.

The Central Hockey League runs its operations out of Indianapolis and counts among its franchises the Macon Whoopee and the San Antonio Iguanas. Then, of course, there are the two West Coast organizations, one of which (WCHL) is based in Boise and the other (WPHL) in Phoenix.

NHL affiliations with minor league teams

Minor league affiliations with NHL clubs vary, and they extend all the way down to the lowest levels of the minors. Some teams have straight affiliations similar to what goes on in baseball, in which a team works directly with one NHL club that supplies most of the players. But, unlike baseball, many minor league hockey teams are supplied with players by two NHL franchises. Consider the Lowell Lock Monsters, an American Hockey League club based in Lowell, Massachusetts. Both the Los Angeles Kings and the New York Islanders are responsible for stocking that roster, and both probably put six or seven guys there every year. But they don't fill all the spots. Why? Because NHL clubs have a habit of calling up a minor league team's best players during the season and inserting them in their own lineups. That's fine for the parent franchises, but it deprives the minor league squads of their top players. So no matter what their arrangement with the majors, many minor league teams also go out and get a few players on their own to ensure that they aren't left high and dry if the big league clubs run into a lot of injuries, for example, and have to raid their affiliates.

In addition to the direct and split affiliations, a number of independent clubs have no arrangements with NHL franchises and fill their rosters with whatever players they can find.

Similarities — and differences — between minor leagues and the NHL

Most teams in the minor leagues do not play the same number of games that NHL teams do. Although the teams in the American and International Hockey Leagues have roughly the same amount of games the NHL does (82), the East Coast teams play about 70, the United and Central play about 60, and those in the two Western Leagues play closer to 50. (As a rule, the lower the league level, the shorter the schedule because they all work off each others' players; those who are cut by the American and International leagues often go to play in the East Coast, while those who don't make the East Coast go to the United or Central, and so on.)

And, of course, the minor league players just aren't as good as those in the NHL. The skill level in the NHL is quite a bit higher than what you find in even the upper minor leagues. The general speed of play is probably the biggest difference, and even the top American and International minor leaguers who make it to the NHL have a hard time adjusting to that change.

Popularity of the minor leagues

Minor league hockey is more popular than ever before. Crowds in the International and American Hockey Leagues may average 7,000. Though it brings in fewer fans for its regular-season contests, the East Coast league draws as many as 10,000 for its All-Star Game. Additionally, the number of teams and leagues in the minors has grown dramatically in recent years (only the American and International leagues existed a decade ago). Hockey used to be considered strictly a cold-weather sport, but now franchises exist throughout the Sun Belt. And people there are finding out just what a cool game hockey is.

Canada also has a minor league tradition, mostly in the maritime provinces. Some Canadian minor league franchises have existed for more than half a century.

The Canadian Junior Leagues

Canada has three primary leagues, known as the *juniors*, for 16- to 20-year-old players, and they are considered to be the top feeder system for the NHL. The Ontario Hockey League, the Quebec Major Junior Hockey League, and the Western Hockey League together have more than 50 franchises through-out Canada and the United States. (Yes, Canadian junior league franchises are located in places like Portland, Maine, and Spokane, Washington.) These three leagues make up the Canadian Hockey League. And no organization has produced more NHL stars over the years. Wayne Gretzky came out of the Canadian juniors, and so did Phil Esposito, Bobby Orr, Maurice "Rocket" Richard, Terry Sawchuk, Brett Hull, Bryan Trottier, Mark Messier, Dennis Potvin, Mario Lemieux, Gordie Howe, Eric Lindros, and even our own JD.

Technically, these junior leagues are stocked with amateur players, most of whom have left their homes to compete on the various teams. The players go to school wherever they play and receive lodging and living allowances. One drawback, however, is that any kid who plays in one of the major junior leagues automatically loses his college eligibility in the United States.

Where do these Canadian youngsters come from? Many of them are drafted out of the *midget* leagues as 14- or 15-year-olds by different teams. Or they are selected in open tryouts.

Junior hockey has a rich history in Canada, stretching back to 1890 when the Ontario Hockey Association (OHA) was formed. But it wasn't until 1919 that teams first battled for the Memorial Cup, a sort of Stanley Cup of the junior leagues. Promoted by Capt. James T. Sutherland, a past president of the OHA and also the Canadian Amateur Hockey Association, the Cup was dedicated to the memory of the many Canadian hockey players who gave their lives during World War I. The University of Toronto Schools and the Regina Patricias faced off at the Toronto Arena for the inaugural match more than 80 years ago. Toronto overpowered Regina in a two-game, total-goals-for-the-series match.

A number of classic Memorial Cup matches have taken place since then, and the modern format brings the champions of the three junior leagues together with the host team to compete for the Cup. And for many Canadian hockey players — as well as the communities in which the junior teams are based — there is no greater honor than winning the Cup.

The College Game

College hockey in the United States has undergone a tremendous revival in recent years and is enjoying a fantastic surge in popularity and interest. In 1999–2000, 55 National Collegiate Athletic Association (NCAA) schools were playing Division I (major-college) hockey, 11 were competing in Division II, and another 66 were playing in Division III (smaller colleges). And that's just the men's teams. Women's varsity hockey also gained popularity during the latter part of the decade, and 53 schools fielded women's teams in 1999–2000.

College arenas are generally full, and many of the programs are doing quite well financially. One reason for all this success is that more college players are making it to the NHL than ever before. In fact, more than a quarter of all NHL players today played some hockey at an American college, and the presence of so many former college players in the NHL has made scores of people more aware of the college game and the way it is played. (As you may recall, much the same thing happened with college basketball and the NBA.)

The college game has also benefited from the general increase in enthusiasm for hockey; as more people have gotten interested in the sport, more have been exposed to the college game. In addition, many of the youngsters who are playing in town and school leagues are looking to stay involved with the game as they get older and view college hockey, whether on an intercollegiate or club level, as a viable option. And the very best players can now use college hockey as a much more realistic avenue to the NHL.

Finally, the quality of the college programs has increased, and fans are seeing more good hockey than ever before. Ten years ago, there were maybe 10 really strong programs, but today there are more than 20.

How does Joe College play the game?

The college rinks are roughly the same as those in the NHL, and so are most of the rules. The big difference is that there is no clutching and grabbing, which you see a lot in the pros these days, and no fighting, which leads to an automatic ejection in college. Many fans say those differences make the college game more fluid and open, and therefore more fun to watch. As for the talent on the ice, the NHL teams simply have more quality players. But the gap has narrowed considerably.

The top college teams

Several colleges did very well in the 1990s. Lake Superior State, Maine, and Michigan each won two NCAA Division I titles, while North Dakota, Boston University, Northern Michigan, and Wisconsin all captured titles in the same decade. The rest of the best include St. Lawrence University, New Hampshire, Colorado College, Minnesota, Boston College, Harvard, Michigan State, and Bowling Green.

College grads who have done well in the pros

College players didn't do a thing for years in the NHL, and it wasn't until 1961, when Red Berenson joined the Montreal Canadiens from the University of Michigan, that a U.S. collegiate player made it as a regular in the modern-day NHL. Now, however, the floodgates are open, and the university boys are highly prized. Over the years, some great NHL players have come from the college game. Hall-of-Fame goalie Ken Dryden (Cornell) obviously did very well, and so did another pair of netminders, Mike Liut (Bowling Green) and Mike Richter (Wisconsin).

There hasn't been a shortage of top defensemen, either: Ken Morrow, of Bowling Green, played for 10 years and won four Stanley Cups with the New York Islanders; Chris Chelios of the Detroit Red Wings and the University of Wisconsin has been a perennial All-Star; and Brian Leetch (Boston College) has done a steady job with the New York Rangers. As for forwards, how about these for an all-college five: John LeClair (Vermont), Paul Kariya (Maine), Doug Weight (Lake Superior State), Joe Mullen (Boston College), and Brett Hull (Minnesota-Duluth).

Canadian college teams play some good hockey, but they can't compete with the U.S. colleges. One reason is the great influx of Canadian athletes to U.S. schools; an estimated 45 percent of all collegiate players on American college teams come from Canada. Not surprisingly, that has sapped a lot of Canada's talent pool, and far fewer than 5 percent of all NHL players come from universities up north, which is significantly less than the U.S. schools provide.

International Hockey

Hockey truly is an international game, and according to the world governing body — the International Ice Hockey Federation, or IIHF — the game is now played in more than 50 countries. That includes obvious nations such as Sweden, which has 80,000 registered amateur and professional players and approximately 4,000 teams, and some more surprising countries, such as Mexico, which has 400 players, and Turkey, which has nearly 300.

The IIHF oversees the sport as it is played around the world, puts on the various world and continental championships (for men, women, and juniors), and runs national tournaments for a number of nations. "All told, we put on as many as 30 events a year," says Kimmo Leinonen, the director of marketing and public relations for the federation. Contact the IIHF at the following address and check out its Web site at www.iihf.com (see Figure 5-1).

International Ice Hockey Federation
Parkring 11
8002 Zurich
Switzerland
Phone: 0041 1 289 86 00
Fax General Secretary: 0041 1 289 86 20
Fax PR/Info/EHL/InLine: 0041 1 289 86 22

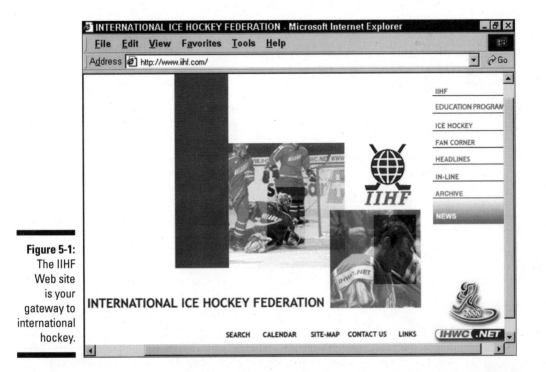

Figure 5-1:
The IIHF
Web site
is your
gateway to
international
hockey.

Not surprisingly, hockey is biggest in Canada, which has 1.5 million registered players, and the United States, which has 350,000. But it is loved in so many other places. The people of India and Hong Kong have ice hockey clubs, for example, and so do people in Thailand and Brazil. And then there is Ecuador, which has only one rink in the entire country and, at last count, four teams.

"Hockey is growing so much overseas," Leinonen says. "And its popularity has spread far beyond the cold-climate countries and cities that used to be the only domain of the sport." Leinonen is especially excited about the potential growth in Asia. "Japan has a very good league, and nations such as Korea are getting more into it," he says. "Then, of course, we had the Winter Olympics in Nagano, Japan, in 1998. In that same year, the Calgary Flames and San Jose Sharks opened their NHL regular-season schedules by playing a pair of games in Tokyo. It's going to be big over there." Correction: It seems like it is going to be big everywhere.

Hockey and the Olympics

The Olympics have produced some of the best hockey ever played. What sports fan can forget the 1980 "Miracle on Ice," when the underdog U.S. squad first beat the faster, stronger, and more experienced Soviet Union team and then went on to whip Finland for a most improbable gold medal? Or the spectacular shoot-out in the 1994 gold medal game between Canada and Sweden? Or the February day in 1998 when the Czech hockey team beat the Russians 1–0 in the final game at the Nagano Olympics? They were stirring moments all, with great goaltending, fierce hitting, magnificent stickhandling, pinpoint passing, and deft playmaking. They were hockey at its finest.

Hockey has been a part of the Olympics since 1920, when an exhibition tournament among seven teams was held during the 1920 Summer Games in Antwerp, Belgium. (That's right, *Summer* Games.) Canada, which was represented by a club team called the Winnipeg Falcons, came out on top, with the United States finishing second and the country then known as Czechoslovakia coming in third.

Four years later, hockey became part of the Winter Games, and once again Canada prevailed. In fact, the Canadians dominated the early years of Olympic hockey, capturing gold medals at the first three Games (1924, 1928, and 1932) and two more times (1948, 1952) in later years. The U.S. team has won the gold twice (1960, 1980), but the real winner in Olympic hockey has been the Soviet Union, which has won eight times, the last one coming as a Unified team in 1992 after the Berlin Wall had fallen and the once-mighty Communist empire was breaking up.

And then there was the surprising British team of 1936, which bested hockey powerhouses Canada, Czechoslovakia, and the United States for first place in that hard-fought tournament. The English were ecstatic after that amazing win, and the entire team was elected to Britain's Hockey Hall of Fame shortly after the Games.

Good as they have been for all these years, the Winter Olympics have gotten even better. And that's because the women now have their own tournament as well, meaning there will be plenty for hockey fans to watch in Salt Lake City in 2002.

Part II
How the Big Boys (And Girls) Do It

The 5th Wave By Rich Tennant

@RICHTENNANT

I would say your stickhandling needs a little work.

In this part . . .

*T*his part is where we tell you all about the world's top professional and amateur players, from the big boys of the National Hockey League to the men and women who make up the strongest college and Olympic teams. Where do they come from? How do they play their games?

We also talk about training and coaching, giving you tips from the best in those fields. And finally, we give you the inside scoop on hitting and intimidating, with JD providing his lists of the greatest fighters, intimidators, and agitators in NHL history.

Chapter 6

Anything You Can Do, I Can Do Better: Women in Hockey

In This Chapter

▶ The roots of the women's game

▶ The differences between men's and women's hockey

▶ The top female players and teams

*H*ockey is not just a sport for men. Women have been taking to the ice since the late 1880s, and while they compete under somewhat different rules and play a slightly slower game, they still put on a terrific show. And more women are lacing up their skates than ever before.

A History of Women's Hockey

Historians say that the first organized all-women's hockey game took place in Barrie, Ontario, in 1892 — more than two decades before the National Hockey League was founded. But there is evidence that the sport was actually played by female athletes before that. For example:

✔ A newspaper account of a game between two unnamed women's teams appeared in the *Ottawa Citizen* on February 11, 1891.

✔ There are also several stories of Lord Stanley of Preston — Canada's sixth governor-general and the man after whom the cherished Stanley Cup is named — having the front lawn of Government House in Ottawa flooded during the winter of 1889 so that he and his wife and children, including his two daughters, could play hockey on the makeshift rink when it froze.

The women's game caught on fairly quickly after that, and in 1894 a female club team formed at Queen's University in Kingston, Ontario. Dubbed the "Love-Me-Littles," the team incurred the wrath of the school's archbishop, who did not want the young women to play. Two years later, women's teams started at McGill University in Montreal and in the Ottawa Valley.

The first women's hockey championship for the province of Ontario was held in 1914, and in 1916 the United States hosted an international hockey tournament in Cleveland, featuring American and Canadian women's squads.

Popularity wanes, then rebounds

Unfortunately, the popularity of women's hockey started to decline in the 1930s and '40s, mostly as a result of the demands of the Depression and World War II. It is important to note, however, that those rather dark years did produce one of the greatest women's hockey teams of all time: the Preston Rivulettes, who lost only twice in 350 Canadian league games during a stretch from 1930 to 1939.

Women didn't start getting back into the game in a big way until the mid-1960s. In 1967, for example, a Dominion Ladies Hockey Tournament was held in Brampton, Ontario, with 22 teams and players ranging in age from 9 to 50 competing. And by the 1970s, things had really picked up. A number of Canadian provinces established associations during that decade to govern female hockey programs. At the same time, several American colleges and high schools began forming varsity and club teams for women players. And overseas, club squads and leagues began taking shape in places like Finland, Japan, Sweden, China, Korea, Norway, Germany, and Switzerland.

In 1982, Canada held its first national championship for women's ice hockey, and eight years later it hosted the first Women's World Ice Hockey Championships, with the home team taking the gold with a 5–2 victory over the Americans. Then in 1992, shortly after the second world championships were completed in Tampere, Finland, the International Olympic Committee voted to include women's hockey in future Winter Games. And the sport made its Olympic debut in Nagano, Japan, in 1998.

The women's game arrives in the 1990s

Women's hockey was never widely played or wildly popular on either a professional or amateur level until the 1990s. But suddenly it became all the rage, and women are taking to the ice in some 30 countries. Women's hockey was a medal sport for the first time at the 1998 Winter Olympics in Nagano, and it gave the sports world quite an introduction as the United States squad beat the Canadian team 3–1 in a beautifully played, hard-fought gold-medal game. A sanctioned world championship for women has been held since 1990 (and dominated by the Canadian team, which beat Team USA for its sixth straight title in the 2000 championship game) and teams from Canada, Sweden, China, Japan, Finland, Russia, Germany, and the United States competed for the 2000 World Championships in Toronto.

Canada and the United States have the most female hockey players, as well as the most talented ones, and their numbers continue to grow. In 1990, for example, the United States had about 5,500 registered women hockey players; by the year 2000, there were more than six times as many.

By the mid-1990s, two woman goalies — Erin Whitten and Manon Rheaume — had played in men's minor league games, and Rheaume actually tended the net in a couple of exhibition contests for the NHL's Tampa Bay Lightning. Some 65 American colleges now have sanctioned women's hockey, either on a club or varsity level, and various women's leagues do exist in Canada and the United States. And there is talk of starting a professional women's league in North America (some already exist in Europe) in the not-too-distant future.

How Women's Hockey Is Different from Men's

"The big difference is that there is no body checking in our game," says Team USA forward (and sometime radio commentator) Cammi Granato. "There is occasionally a discrepancy between referees as to what actually constitutes a body check, and some will let things go a bit more than others. But technically, there are not supposed to be any open-ice hits, though you can, in most cases, make contact along the boards."

According to Sami Jo Small, a goaltender for the Canadian national team, women wear some different equipment to protect their upper body — for obvious reasons. "And we play a somewhat different style game," she explains. "For one thing, you don't see as many shots from the point in women's hockey as you do with the men. One reason for that is that no checking means no taking people out in front of the net, so you see more shots closer in."

"From a purist's standpoint, women's hockey really has a lot to offer," adds Granato. "There is less clutching and grabbing in our game, which often leads to interesting and exciting playmaking. We have more time to make an extra pass, and we rely more on finesse."

Where to Find Teams

Women's hockey teams — and leagues — are everywhere, for 5-year-old kids to 40-year-old hockey moms, and the key to finding the best ones is to check with local ice rinks to see what is available in that area. It also makes sense to check in with hockey associations in your area (see Appendix B). Or you can call the folks at either USA Hockey in Colorado Springs (719-576-8724) or the Canadian Hockey Association in Calgary (403-777-3636) for information.

Top Women's Teams and Players

With the worldwide explosion of women's hockey, you can find terrific young players all across the globe. But right now the best women's games in the world are played in North America, which boasts the top teams and many of the most talented players.

The best teams

The two best women's hockey teams are the national squads from Canada and the United States. The Canadians have won six world championships in a row, and the U.S. team won the gold medal at the Nagano Winter Games. Close behind in talent are the Finns, and both China and Sweden have very strong national teams as well.

Women's college hockey also has more than its share of good players, and there are a number of competitive teams. Among the best U.S. squads are Harvard, Brown, Dartmouth, New Hampshire, and Minnesota-Duluth. And in Canada, the universities of Alberta, Calgary, Toronto, and Concordia (Montreal) are generally the toughest teams to beat.

The top players

Women's hockey has many good players, and several of them compete for the American and Canadian national teams. Following are brief profiles of some of the best athletes both squads have to offer.

Cammi Granato

Granato is probably the best-known player on Team USA, in large part because she served as team captain during the Nagano Games and recorded four goals and four assists during that tournament. A graduate of Providence College, where she played hockey for four years, she has been on the U.S. national squad since 1990 and has scored 86 goals in 104 games in various competitions, which makes her the all-time leading scorer in the history of that team. She grew up in Downers Grove, Illinois, and got interested in the game when she was 5 years old because she had three older brothers who were playing hockey, and Granato (see Figure 6-1) thought it would be fun. (One of her brothers, Tony, went on to enjoy a long and productive career in the NHL, and her father Don is a well-known youth hockey coach in the Chicago area.) In addition to playing, she has worked as a radio color commentator for the NHL's Los Angeles Kings.

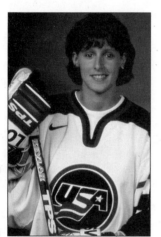

Figure 6-1:
Cammi
Granato.

A.J. Mleczko

A 1999 Harvard graduate, this forward is one of the stalwarts of the U.S. team (see Figure 6-2). She competed in all six games at the Winter Olympics in Nagano, scoring two goals and recording a pair of assists. And the tall (5'11"), left-handed shot was named the 1999 USA Hockey Women's Player of the Year. That honor followed a rather spectacular career at Harvard, where Mleczko served as team captain and broke the women's college scoring record her last year in school, amassing 114 total points in just 34 games. At the same time, she broke Harvard's all-time single-season scoring record for men or women and helped to lead Harvard to a national championship.

Figure 6-2:
A.J.
Mieczko.

Sarah Tueting

This Winnetka, Illinois, native is one of the game's best goaltenders, and she was instrumental in helping the United States capture the gold in Nagano, appearing in four games and compiling a stingy 1.15 goals-against average and a .937 save percentage. Tueting (see Figure 6-3) started the pivotal gold-medal game and held the powerful Canadian team to just one goal, stopping 21 of 22 shots. She attended Dartmouth for two years (1994–96) and was named the Ivy League Rookie of the Year after her first season. But then she decided to take a leave of absence to train with the U.S. Women's Training Program. While in school, Tueting studied neurobiology and was a member of Dartmouth's symphony orchestra.

Figure 6-3:
Sarah
Tueting.

Therese Brisson

Brisson is one of the top defenders in women's hockey and has served as captain of the Canadian squad. She has played with that team since 1993 and over the years has won a number of awards, including Top Defender at the 2000 Esso Nationals and Most Valuable Defense at both the 1995 and 1998 National Championships. She also was named Female Athlete of the Year two times (1988, 1989) at Concordia University in Montreal. Currently, she lives in Fredericton, New Brunswick, and when she isn't playing hockey, she is a professor of kinesiology at the University of New Brunswick.

Hayley Wickenheiser

Wickenheiser was 15 years old when she joined the Canadian national team in 1994, and the hard-skating forward has been an integral member of that team ever since. In 2000 she was named Most Valuable Player at the Esso Nationals and was a member of the All-Star team at the 1999 World Championships. In addition, she has attended the Philadelphia Flyers' rookie camp for the past two years. A native of Shaunavon, Saskatchewan, Wickenheiser is also an accomplished softball player and competes on that national team as well. As is the case with many of her peers on both the U.S. and Canadian squads, Hayley started playing hockey when she was only 5 years old and spent most of her youth competing on teams dominated by boys. In fact, the Canadian national squad was the first all-woman hockey team she ever played on.

Sami Jo Small

This Winnipeg native is a goaltender, and though she did not compete in any of the games in Nagano, she remains a valuable member of the Canadian team. A graduate of Stanford, where she received a degree in mechanical engineering, Small originally went to college on a track scholarship. (She threw the discus and javelin.) And though she played lots of youth hockey back home, she thought she was going to have to give up the game when she moved to California. But then she discovered that Stanford had a men's club team, and she played on that until she left college. Currently, Sami Jo lives in Toronto, playing for the Brampton Thunder in a new national women's hockey league when she is not out on the road with the national team.

Chapter 7

Training

*E*lite hockey players are among the best-conditioned athletes in the world. Whether they compete in the National Hockey League, in the minor leagues, in college, or for one of the international teams, they must be in excellent shape in order to hold their own on the ice. To do that, they work with personal trainers and team personnel throughout the year, following strict fitness regimens so they can perform to the best of their abilities. It wasn't always that way; like athletes in other professional sports, hockey players didn't really begin to understand the value of sophisticated exercise programs until the mid-1970s. But now, extensive training and conditioning routines are part of every player's life.

To give you a sense of what hockey players do to get and stay in shape, we again turned to some experts for help:

✔ Jim Ramsay, who has been a medical trainer in the NHL since the mid-1980s, first for the Winnipeg Jets (now the Phoenix Coyotes) and more recently for the New York Rangers.

✔ Dr. Howie Wenger, a physical education professor at the University of Victoria in British Columbia, Canada, and an exercise physiologist with the Rangers. He has also worked with the Edmonton Oilers, Vancouver Canucks, and Los Angeles Kings. In addition, he has helped develop conditioning programs for several Canadian Olympic teams.

✔ Charles Poliquin, a strength and conditioning coach who counts among his individual clients 120 athletes from the NHL, the National Basketball Association, the National Football League, and a number of Canadian Olympic squads.

No one understands the whole concept of training and conditioning better than they do.

What the Pros Do to Stay in Shape

NHL players work out a lot, as you will see. These guys are constantly working on their conditioning and never seem to let up. "Players will usually take a couple of weeks off at the end of the season," says Jim Ramsay, "but then they get right back into it." And they keep at it until the end of the following season.

Running

Running used to be a part of every athlete's regimen, but not anymore. Very few hockey players ever run during the season, and those who do use it mainly as a warm-up. It's not very popular in the off-season either, and that's because it is high-impact exercise that can lead to knee and back problems. And very few NHL players haven't had knee or back problems during their careers. Still, some do find running an effective training tool, especially for building speed and endurance.

Cycling

Many more players prefer to cycle, especially on exercise bikes, because it has a lower impact on knees, backs, and so on. Some players bike during the season to build or maintain aerobic condition and enhance leg strength. (Power comes from the legs in hockey, and when a player is skating, he is using his legs all the time.) During the season, many NHL teams like their players to get on an exercise bike a couple of times a week for up to half an hour a pop. Also, they have players use it as a cool-down after a game and as a way to rid their bodies of lactic acid and other by-products of strenuous exercise that can delay recovery. As for the off-season, most clubs want their players to ride bikes — both stationary and regular — fairly often, perhaps five or six days a week for about 30 to 45 minutes each time.

Skating

Not surprisingly, skating is a huge part of a hockey player's conditioning program, and your average NHL-er is on the ice most every day during the season, either for practice or for a game. What he does when the season ends is often a different story. Some players get together and rent ice time at a local rink during the summer and meet regularly for informal workouts and scrimmages. Others hardly touch the ice until the following season, but they do a lot of in-line skating or play roller hockey. Those are very sport-specific exercises that use the same muscles a player employs on the ice and give him a chance not only to work on conditioning but also to keep honing his hockey skills (stickhandling, shooting, passing, and so on). The only problem is that it's much harder to stop on those off-ice skates.

Stair climbing

Players use Stairmasters both in and off season the same way they use exercise bikes. Again, they use these machines to build and enhance aerobic fitness. Players generally spend anywhere from 30 to 45 minutes working in one- to three-minute intervals, building up the intensity as they go. "Interval training is important to elite hockey players because they go on and off the ice so frequently," says Ramsay. "We want them to work hard for 45 seconds and then have some time to recover because that's the way they play during the season, with shifts lasting just under a minute, and then they have some time to rest. Recovery is essential so that they can be 100 percent on the next shift."

The types of exercise we have described so far are all considered aerobic, and hockey players need them for a number of reasons. According to Howie Wenger, who has written a splendid book on the subject titled *Fitness for High Performance Hockey* (Trafford Publishing, Victoria, British Columbia, 1-888-232-4444), aerobic fitness is an athlete's ability to take oxygen into his lungs, deliver it to his muscles via the heart and blood, and then use that oxygen in his muscles to generate energy. Athletes who are aerobically fit, Wenger explains, can recover faster between sprints, between shifts and periods, and also between games. They can recover more quickly from soft tissue injuries (bruises, muscle strains) and bone injuries, do more strength and power training, and handle jet lag and heat stress more effectively. In addition, their immune systems are enhanced so they can better withstand minor infections and colds and also build a resistance to lactic acid, which causes fatigue. Given all that, is it any wonder that players today listen to what their trainers and physiologists have to say?

Weightlifting

Strength fitness is another important consideration for hockey players. Dr. Wenger points out that strength means bigger muscles, which translates into better protection against injuries to joints and soft tissue. Strength also makes players more effective around the puck and helps them establish position against opponents. More specifically, abdominal strength allows players to transfer their momentum from the lower body to the upper body and protect the lower back, while leg strength is the first step in improving leg power and explosiveness.

Obviously, the best way to improve strength fitness is through weightlifting, and most NHL players lift weights at least once a week during the season. Trainers tailor individual programs to each player so that the players can maintain their strength throughout the year. The New York Rangers have 12 different weight machines, and a player might do about 15 *mid-range reps* (repetitive lifts of a moderately difficult weight) on each one, working on everything from leg extensions to bicep curls. Some players, such as those nursing knee or shoulder injuries, may spend extra time trying to build those areas up as they try to recover, perhaps lifting weights two or three times a week.

As for the off-season, players increase their time with the weight machines; at a minimum they lift three times a week, and some do it as often as six. Generally, they alternate body parts each time, working on the legs one day, the lower back and chest on another, and so forth, until they have done their whole body in one week.

Keeping Track of Fitness

It's remarkable to see how closely both professional and top amateur teams now monitor the physical fitness of their players. Players take a series of tests at the start of each season and then begin monthly conditioning programs customized for their various needs. "We try to handle everything from workouts to nutrition, taking into account our game days and travel schedule," says Jim Ramsay. "We also look at how much ice time a player gets during a game and what he needs to do to stay in shape with that. An athlete such as Brian Leetch, who plays anywhere from 30 to 40 minutes a game, needs less fitness maintenance than a fourth-liner who may only get onto the ice for five minutes a game." Other considerations are injuries, which would certainly affect the extent to which players can work out, and days off. "Say we have three days between games," Ramsay explains. "The coach might give the players that first day off but work them real hard the second day so nobody has a chance to fall out of condition. And the third day would be a light practice, or recovery day, with some work but not too much."

Players take fitness tests again at the end of the season, and their trainers give them workout programs for the summer. "It used to be that the younger guys came to training camp the following fall in terrific shape, and the veterans were the ones who needed to get in shape," Ramsay says. "But now, it's the other way around. The vets are the ones who are most fit, and the younger kids coming out of college and the Canadian junior leagues aren't conditioned for the NHL." Teams are trying to change this situation by bringing their draft picks in at the start of the summer for fitness tests and then giving them programs to work on so they come to camp in better shape than they otherwise might.

REMEMBER

Something special for the goalies

Ask anyone in hockey and they'll tell you that goalies are an odd bunch who seem to do everything differently. Even their conditioning. They do many of the same aerobic exercises forwards or defensemen perform but are not as likely to hit the weight room. "It's not necessary for a goalie to lift and be strong in his upper body," Ramsay explains. "Obviously, flexibility is very important, so you want them to do a lot of stretching. They also need to work on ways to enhance their speed and balance as well as their hand-eye coordination." Some goalies, JD among them, have used a variety of eye exercises to improve their ability to see the puck through all the traffic in front of the net. Anything for an edge.

A Typical NHL Off-Season Conditioning Regimen

Charles Poliquin helps out a number of NHL athletes in the off-season, and among his most recent clients is Al MacInnis, a hard-shooting defenseman who played his first NHL game in 1981 and has been selected for six All-Star teams. "We train three days out of five," Poliquin says, "and we work out twice each of those days. Some people believe in working out more frequently over a longer period of time, but I think having plenty of rest days and doing more concentrated work brings better results."

- ✔ On **Monday** morning, MacInnis spends about an hour in the weight room working on his chest and back. "We divide the body into three parts for weights," Poliquin says, "and take care of each one on a specific day." After taking a four-hour break, which he does between every workout, MacInnis spends almost an hour Monday afternoon on various abdominal and spinal exercises.

- ✔ **Tuesday** morning, the plan calls for 60 minutes of weightlifting for the legs, and in the afternoon he runs for the same amount of time, either sprints (perhaps 30 yards) or longer distances (up to 600 yards). "I call it energy system work," Poliquin explains, "and what we do depends on what time of the summer it is. I like to do sprint work early on to build speed and then distance as we get closer to the start of the season."

- ✔ **Wednesday** is a day off, but MacInnis is back at it on **Thursday,** spending an hour in the morning on his shoulders and arms in the weight room and then another hour in the afternoon running.

✔ The defenseman takes **Friday** off, and then starts the cycle over again on **Saturday.** "I modify programs every six workouts to maximize adaptation so Al gets stronger faster," Poliquin says. "It also helps to keep boredom from setting in."

"I try to create each program specifically for the athlete involved and his needs," he continues. "A lot also depends on his position. As a defenseman, Al has different needs than a forward. He needs to be stronger in the abs, for example, because he has to clear players out from in front of the net all the time, and that uses those muscles a lot. We also need to look at the style of the player involved. A guy like Doug Gilmour, for example, never stops skating, so he needs to be really fit aerobically — while someone else may stand around more and not be so active."

What You Can Do to Get in Hockey Shape

"The most important thing adults need to know is that most of us can change our physiology quite a bit," says Dr. Howie Wenger. "It's simply a question of how much a person is willing to challenge himself and genetics. But the fact is, we can get most people fit. Making them elite athletes is another thing altogether, but from a fitness point of view, we can make you better."

So there is hope for all us weekend warriors after all. But only if we take care of three primary needs. The first is *stretching*. "Static [stationary] stretches relax the stretched muscles," Dr. Wenger explains. "This allows more blood flow, which enables you to supply more fuel to muscles before and after workouts, remove wastes that cause fatigue after exercise, and cool down the muscles after hard work."

In addition, relaxed muscles offer less resistance to powerful contractions, which should allow athletes to be more explosive. And there is some evidence that relaxed muscles reduce soft tissue injuries.

Secondly, people need some level of *aerobic and cardiovascular fitness*. That's what you get from jogging, cycling, swimming, and rowing, for example. It helps your recovery system so that you can exercise, rest, and then go out and do it again. "It's very important in a sport like hockey because it is not continuous but full of lots of stops and starts," says Dr. Wenger.

And finally, those of us looking to get fit need to work on our *strength*. "There is no question that leg strength is very important to the elite hockey player," says Wenger. "But it's less critical to the recreational athlete, who will likely get what he needs from jogging or cycling. But strength fitness is important to the upper body, especially with regards to the abdominal muscles and the shoulders. If those aren't strong, that leaves you susceptible to lower back strains and groin pulls. To protect yourself from those, you need reasonably good abdominal strength. Shoulders are critical, too, because of all the banging and shooting that takes place in a game."

The Need for Exercise Routines

After Dr. Wenger identified the three primary areas a recreational hockey player needs to work on to get into better shape, he gave us some exercises that can help you get there. The stretches and exercises we are about to discuss are geared toward people from the ages of 15 to 50. But it's important that anyone interested in starting a workout program get clearance from a physician before taking one step on a treadmill or lifting a weight. Also, you should start easy and work your way up to more strenuous circuits; 'tis better to err by doing too little than by doing too much.

Stretching

You should stretch before and after every workout, practice, and game. The most important thing to remember is to stretch until you feel the pull and not to where you feel the pain. Don't worry if you feel limited by a lack of flexibility in the beginning; keep doing these and you should get more limber. Here is a stretching circuit designed by Dr. Wenger, reprinted with permission from his book *Fitness for High Performance Hockey* (illustrated by Kelley Dukeshire). The following stretching circuit is designed to incorporate the major muscles used in hockey. The exercises progress from lying to sitting to kneeling to standing.

1. *Relax* with your knees bent and the soles of your feet together. This comfortable position stretches your groin. You can give added stretch by putting outward pressure on the inside of your knees using your hands.

2. Next, straighten both legs and relax; then pull your left leg toward your chest. Keep the back of your head on the mat. Repeat, pulling your right leg toward your chest.

3. With your opposite hand, pull that bent leg over your other leg toward the floor. Turn your head the opposite way until you get the right stretch feeling in your lower back and hip. Do the other leg.

4. From the bent knees position, cross your left leg over your right and use the left leg to pull your right leg toward the floor until you feel a stretch along the side of your hip and lower back. Turn your head the opposite way. Repeat for the other side.

5. Sit up with your feet a comfortable distance apart. To stretch the inside of your upper legs and hips, slowly lean forward from the hips. Keep your quadriceps relaxed and feet upright. Keep your hands out in front of you for balance and stability. Concentrate on keeping the lower back flat as you do this stretch. Do not strain.

6. To stretch your left hamstring and the right side of your back, slowly bend forward at the hips toward your left foot. Repeat on the other side.

7. From a standing position, move one leg forward *until the knee of the forward leg is directly over the ankle.* Your other knee should be resting on the floor. Now, without changing the position of your knee on the floor or your forward foot, lower the front of your hip downward. This stretch should be felt in front of the hip and possibly in your hamstrings and groin. Do both sides.

8. Hold on to something that is about shoulder height. With your hands shoulder width apart, keep your arms straight, your chest moving downward, and *your feet remaining directly under your hips.* Keep your knees slightly bent.

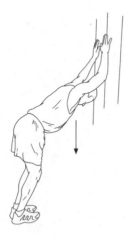

9. With your arms overhead, hold the elbow of one arm with the hand of the other arm. Keeping your knees slightly bent, pull your elbow behind your head as you bend from your hips to the side. Do both sides. Keeping your knees slightly bent gives you better balance and helps protect your back.

10. In a standing or sitting position, interlace your fingers above your head. Now, with your palms facing upward, push your arms slightly back and up. Feel the stretch in your arms, shoulders, and upper back. Do not hold your breath.

11. While standing, bend your left leg so your foot is behind you, then hold the top of your left foot with the right hand and gently pull the heel toward your butt. The knee bends at a natural angle in this position and creates a good stretch in your knees and quads. Do both legs.

12. To stretch your calf, stand a little ways from a solid support and lean on it. Bend one leg and place your foot on the ground in front of you, leaving the other leg straight behind you. Slowly move your hips forward until you feel a stretch in the calf of your straight leg. Be sure to keep the heel of the foot of the straight leg on the ground and *your toes pointed straight ahead.* Do not bounce. Stretch both legs.

Aerobic Fitness

It's good to do aerobic activities — whether it's cross-country skiing, skating, running, or cycling — three or four times a week. Ski machines and stair climbers are fine as well. Ideally, people should get up to 40 or 45 minutes of continuous aerobic workouts on those days. "If you can talk comfortably while you are working out, then you are probably just below the level you need to be at," says Dr. Wenger. In the beginning, it may be better to start with 25 minutes, move up to 30 after a week, and then increase your time by 5-minute intervals each week after that until you get up to 45 minutes. At that point, Howie suggests intensifying the pace, reducing the program to 25 minutes, and then working your way back up again.

Weight Training

The big question here is: How much weight do you lift? Dr. Wenger says it is best to start with a "load" you can do 15 to 20 times without stopping, no more and no less. Keep with that for three or four months before even thinking about moving to a higher weight that you will likely not be able to do as many times in a row.

As for frequency, Dr. Wenger suggests two times a week. You can do one of your upper-body circuits (see sketches) on one of the days you do aerobic fitness (because your aerobic exercises won't usually put a lot of pressure on the upper body) and then do the lower-body and abdominal strength exercises on one of the days you are not running, cycling, or whatever. Again, Dr. Wenger provides some upper- and lower-body exercises for weight training from his book *Fitness for High Performance Hockey*.

Upper body: Circuit 1

Note: You can do these as ***successive sets:*** three to four sets of each before moving to the next. Be sure to take a one- to two-minute rest between each set.

Or . . .

You can do these as ***alternating sets:*** one set of each exercise, then go back through the circuit three or four times. You don't rest between sets or circuits.

1: BENCH PRESS

START   **MIDDLE**   **FINISH**

2: TRICEP EXTENSION

START   **MIDDLE**   **FINISH**

3: LAT PULL-DOWN

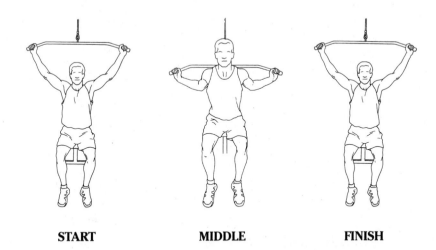

START **MIDDLE** **FINISH**

4: SHOULDER EXTENSION

START **MIDDLE** **FINISH**

5: BICEP CURL

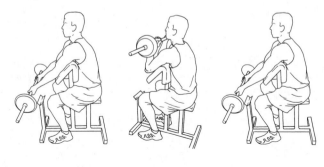

START   **MIDDLE**   **FINISH**

Upper body: Circuit 2

Note: You can do these as ***successive sets:*** three to four sets of each before moving to the next. Be sure to take a one- to two-minute rest between each set.

Or . . .

You can do these as ***alternating sets:*** one set of each exercise, then go back through the circuit three or four times. You don't rest between sets or circuits.

1: BENCH FLY WITH DUMBBELLS

START   **MIDDLE**   **FINISH**

2: SEATED TRICEP EXTENSION WITH BARBELL

Option: seated alternating tricep extensions using two dumbbells.

3: DUMBBELL ROW

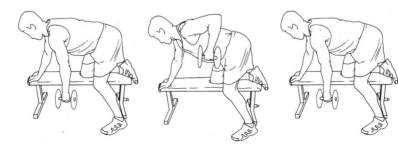

START   **MIDDLE**   **FINISH**

4: ALTERNATING SEATED BICEP CURL WITH DUMBBELLS

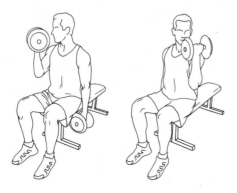

5: STANDING UPRIGHT ROW

START   **MIDDLE**   **FINISH**

Upper-body variations

You can use these exercises as substitutes in the upper-body circuits.

CHEST

You can substitute the *inclined bench press* for the bench press.

FOREARMS

Do *wrist curls* with palms up and down.

UPPER ARMS

This is the *bicep curl*.

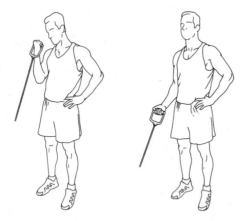

Do the *tricep extension* with the palms down.

✔ Dump it cross-corner deep into the offensive zone (to the boards on either side of the net) for either a winger or centerman to pick up.

✔ Pass to the open man.

However the puck gets into the offensive zone, after it's there, the team needs to set up a play. It has the extra man, and it must use that advantage to score.

Studies in the power play: The Pittsburgh Penguins

The 1996–97 Pittsburgh Penguins possessed one of the most effective power plays in recent years. The key was to get the puck to Mario Lemieux (#1). Once he had it, he tried to suck a defender over to his side, which set up a two-on-one in front, and Mario's passing options were either Ron Francis (#4) or Jaromir Jagr (#5). If he wanted, #5 could circle around behind the net and give Mario another option. Jason Wooley (#3) and Kevin Hatcher (#2) were out near the blue line.

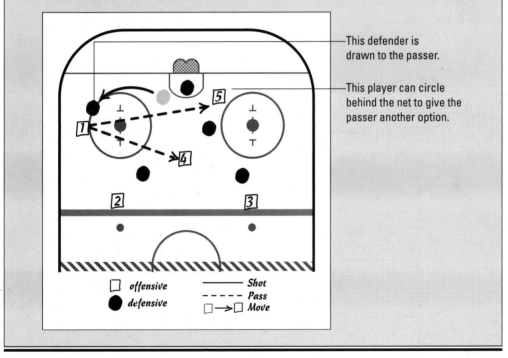

This defender is drawn to the passer.

This player can circle behind the net to give the passer another option.

□ *offensive*   —— *Shot*
● *defensive*   - - - *Pass*
□→□ *Move*

The Key to a Power Play: Control

Control is a key word when it comes to setting up the power play. Control and patience. Most National Hockey League teams use what is known as the *umbrella* (see Figure 9-4). In the middle of the ice, just inside the blue line of the offensive zone, is the *shooter* (#2), the player on the power play team who fires the puck at the net best. To his right, farther down the ice and along the boards, is another forward (#3). And on the opposite side of the zone, perhaps a bit closer to the blue line, is another teammate (#1). Parked in front of the net is another forward (#4), usually a tough guy who can muscle his way around the opposing defensemen, screen the goaltender, punch in rebounds, and deflect in shots. A little bit higher up (closer to the blue line), but still in the middle, is the center (#5).

The basic idea is to move the puck among the five offensive players until one of them has an opening and can shoot. Crisp passes are essential, and so is making use of the man advantage.

- ✔ Get the two-on-one situations.
- ✔ Get the puck to the open man.
- ✔ Get off the shots.

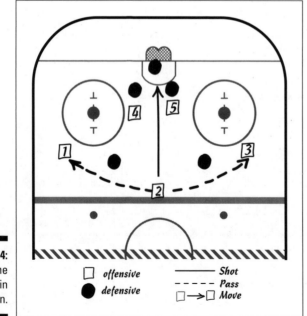

Figure 9-4:
The umbrella in action.

□ offensive   ——— Shot
● defensive   - - - Pass
              □→□ Move

HOCKEY SPEAK

The high triangle

The *high triangle* is essentially the same power play setup as the umbrella. Remember, the key with the power play in the offensive zone is to create two-on-ones with puck or player movement. In this example, the team on the power play has lots of options. If offensive player #2 has the puck, he can shoot it; or if there's a lot of traffic in front of the net, he can pass it to #3, thereby creating a two-on-one with defensive player #4. If that defensive player goes after #3, #3 can then pass the puck into the corner to #5, creating a two-on-one with defensive player #2. This passing can happen all over the offensive zone until the players find an opening to shoot — and, they hope, score.

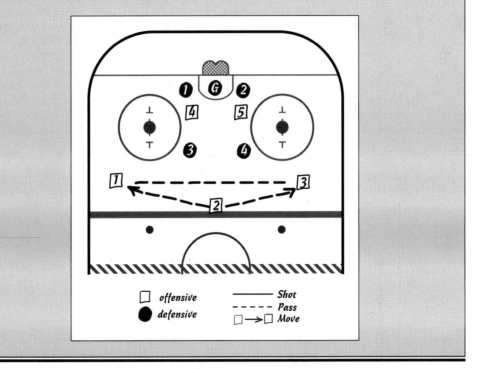

□ offensive
● defensive

——— Shot
------ Pass
□→□ Move

And be sure to take what the other team gives. If a defender comes to you, that means a teammate is open somewhere. Try to find him. And even if you don't have the puck, make something happen.

- ✔ Get in the goalie's way.
- ✔ Look for rebounds.
- ✔ Keep the puck in the zone if a defender tries to shoot it out.

A good professional team can work a power play like magic, but kids don't have to be quite so sophisticated. Forget about slap shots, for example. The big windups look flashy but are far too difficult for younger players to translate into good shots. Kids should concentrate instead on basic wrist shots, which can be even more effective, not only in scoring goals but also in setting up deflections and rebounds.

The Half Board Power Play

When we talk about *half board,* we mean halfway down the boards in the offensive zone, approximately halfway through the face-off circle. In Figure 9-5, if #4 and #5 are right-handed shots, your playmaker, #1, tries to set up on the right side of the offensive zone. If he passes to #4 or #5, they can shoot the puck off the pass because they are facing the passer and don't have to stop the puck to get the shot away. It gives them a quicker, more accurate, and more powerful shot. Also, in the top of Figure 9-5, if #1 has the puck and the defensive players are on #4 and #5, then #3, the pointman, can sneak down low along the back side. In Figure 9-6, if #1 has the puck, he can hit #4 or #5, and hopefully they'll be left-handed shots and able to shoot off the pass. If they're covered, #3 can sneak down as he did in Figure 9-5 — only on the opposite side.

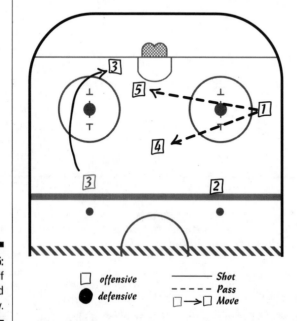

Figure 9-5:
The half
board
power play.

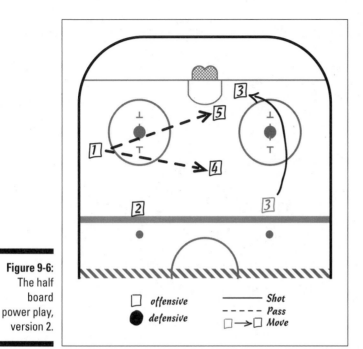

Figure 9-6:
The half
board
power play,
version 2.

The Five-on-Three Advantage

Sometimes when you're on a power play, the opposing team commits a second foul and loses another player to the penalty box — giving your squad a five-on-three advantage! Your chances of scoring go up dramatically in that situation, but you must change your tactics a bit to make sure that happens.

Figure 9-7 shows the basic setup for a five-on-three power play. A lot of teams use four forwards and only one defenseman in a five-on-three situation, hoping to generate as much offense as possible. The defenseman (#2) is in the middle, just inside the blue line. The forwards (#1, #3, #4, and #5) are positioned as indicated, their sticks all facing the middle so that they are better able to shoot quickly. Players #1 and #4 should be right-handed shots; players #3 and #5 should be lefties.

The face-off

First off, you don't want to lose a face-off with a two-man advantage because you want to get control of the puck right away. Two people should always be open, so the centerman should try to get the puck to one of those men when the official drops it.

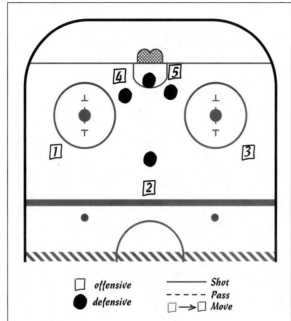

Figure 9-7:
Setting up
for a five-
on-three
power play.

Retain control

After you get the puck, you should not lose control of it. A two-player advantage means that two people should always be open. Try to get the puck as close to the net as possible before you shoot. Be patient in a five-on-three situation, and don't take a lot of shots from the point, or a lot of *one-timers* (shots off the pass) up high in the zone (nearer the blue line). Try to make the perfect play, to get the puck down low, and get it in. Even if the goalie makes a good save on a shot, all is not lost. With its two-man advantage, your team should be able to snatch the rebound before the opposition.

Goalies often go down to the ice when they make the initial save. On the rebound, try to shoot the puck high up and over them.

The best power-play units in hockey today

Plenty of NHL skaters excel on the power play today, but only ten of them are good enough to make the All-JD team. We have put together two units for that squad from current NHL players, and they are so closely matched that we'd be hard-pressed to say one is definitely better than the other. So we'll call them Team I and Team I-A.

Team I has defensemen **Nicklas Lidstrom** of the Detroit Red Wings on the left point, just inside the blue line, and **Al MacInnis** of the St. Louis Blues on the right. Lidstrom is a very slick, underrated player who can carry the puck up ice well and pass with the best of them. MacInnis is famous for having the hardest shot in the NHL, and he is a tremendous weapon because of that. Teams design their power play defenses to stop his shot, and that can open things up for other players.

Up front, the lineup has the Dallas Stars' **Brett Hull** on the left side and the Pittsburgh Penguins' **Jaromir Jagr** on the right. No one shoots off the pass better than Hull, and the puck comes off his stick hard and fast. And Jagr is good at both passing and shooting. He is also strong as a bull and can dig the puck out of the corner well. In addition, he shields the puck with his body and has tremendous reach.

In the slot in the middle is **Peter Forsberg** of the Colorado Avalanche. He wins face-offs, which is what you want your centerman to do during a power play because the more time you have the puck, the more chances you'll have to score. Also, Forsberg is sneaky strong and very hard to knock off his feet. He knows how to score and is very good at finding rebounds.

(continued)

(continued)

Team I-A has **Chris Pronger** of the St. Louis Blues and **Sergei Zubov** of the Dallas Stars on the point. Pronger is a terrific passer, especially out of his own zone, and has a very hard shot. Zubov is great at bringing the puck up ice and also possesses a good shot. In addition, he is a superb passer and especially good at going against the grain with his feeds to teammates, which surprises the penalty killers and often opens things up.

Down low on the left side and near the face-off circle is **Owen Nolan** of the San Jose Sharks. He's a right-handed shot who is extremely strong and shoots the puck well. He is also very hard to knock away from the goal net.

On the right side is **Pavel Bure**, the Florida Panthers' sniper and a pure goal-scorer. Bure loves to score goals, and he is particularly good at speeding up ice and finding an opening. He has a hard, quick shot and would excel on anyone's power play.

And in the center is **Mike Modano** of the Dallas Stars. Modano carries the puck up ice very, very well. He also has good power and strength and knows how to score goals.

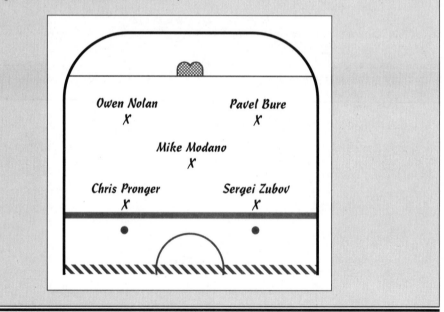

Take your chances close to the net

Create your opportunities closer to the net in a five-on-three, and make the goalie move laterally a lot by passing side-to-side. That strategy creates more openings and more chances to score. Remember that a lot of teams use four forwards and only one defenseman with a two-man advantage in order to get more offense. The defenseman is usually positioned at the center point, while two of the forwards stand just above the face-off circles and the other two position themselves on either side of the goal crease. Teams like to use forwards on their *off* sides, meaning a left-handed shot playing on the right (and vice versa); that puts their sticks toward the middle of the ice and gives them their best chance to get off a quicker shot, firing the puck off the pass for maximum power.

Another thing about the five-on-three: Even the best teams aren't always able to score with a two-man advantage. So don't become discouraged if you don't score every time you have a five-on-three. Keep working hard, and you should be able to create plenty of scoring opportunities, whether or not you're on the power play.

All-time power-play unit

A pair of fast-skating defensemen with quick, accurate shots — **Bobby Orr** and **Paul Coffey** — anchor JD's all-time power-play unit. Orr, who spent most of his career with the Boston Bruins, was one of the best to ever play the game, a brilliant stickhandler and passer who could take over a game. And no defenseman was better at bringing the puck up ice. Coffey, who broke in with the great Edmonton Oilers teams of the 1980s, is a magnificent passer who moves beautifully with the puck.

A pair of familiar names, **Wayne Gretzky** and **Mario Lemieux**, are on the right and left side on this team simply because no one has ever played these positions better. The Great One is the NHL's all-time assists leader, and Mario is among the best scorers and passers the league has ever known. In the slot is **Gordie Howe**, the Detroit Red Wings Hall of Famer who played major-league hockey in five different decades. He was tougher and stronger than most and possessed a wicked shot.

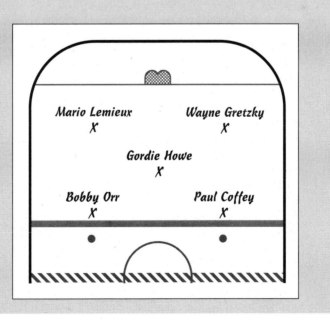

(continued)

(continued)

It wouldn't be right to compile an all-time team without listing a few Honorable Mentions:

- **Doug Harvey**, the Montreal Canadien, was the NHL's first super offensive defenseman.

- **Brad Park** toiled for the Boston Bruins, New York Rangers, and Detroit Red Wings. Though not particularly quick, he was as smart as they come on the power play; Brad knew when to shoot, pass, and skate.

- New York Islanders forward **Mike Bossy** was a pure shooter.

- **Phil Esposito**, of the Rangers, Bruins, and Chicago Blackhawks, was an immovable force in front of the net. His sweeping wrist shot from the slot was deadly.

- Winger **Cam Neely**, a fierce competitor for the Bruins and the Vancouver Canucks, was great at battling the opposing defensemen in front of the net. He had terrific hand-eye coordination and could deflect slap shots from the point into the net with remarkable proficiency. He also had a tough, accurate shot of his own.

Penalty Kills (Or: Killing a Penalty)

Effective penalty killing is as important to a team as a productive power play, and hockey clubs are constantly trying to devise better ways to stave off the opposition when their opponents have the man advantage. (By the way, coaches call their power-play and penalty-killing units "special teams" and put an enormous amount of practice time into making them work properly.)

Clubs that had a man in the penalty box used to take a passive approach and let their opponents skate into their defensive zone before putting up much of a fight. Also, they put their more defensive-oriented players on the ice to kill penalties, often positioning two skaters on either side of the net and up the ice a bit and then two more closer to the blue line in a formation known as the *box* (as shown in Figure 9-8). Or they arranged them in a *diamond,* which puts one man in the slot in front of the goalie, another up top near the blue line, and two teammates in between them latitude-wise and a bit wider on either side (see Figure 9-9).

But a lot of that has changed in recent years. Teams still use the box and diamond, but players for the most part have become much more aggressive when it comes to penalty killing. Many coaches now prefer a pressure game, and they are working harder at stopping the other team before it even has a chance to get into the offensive zone or set up. In addition, they use a lot more skill players on those units, guys with speed and goal-scoring ability who can skate well and anticipate the other team's next move.

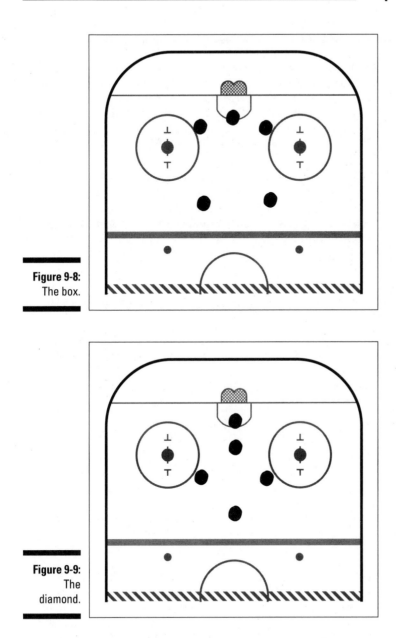

Figure 9-8:
The box.

Figure 9-9:
The diamond.

In the 1990s, many teams started using pairs, or *tandems,* of forwards in their penalty-killing systems. Generally, they use three sets, giving each forward perhaps 40 seconds of ice time. As for their defensemen, they often put their biggest regulars together for a shift to clear out the front of the net and keep the opposing forwards from screening the goalie and having good position for tipping any shots or stuffing in rebounds.

A team needs to be aware of several things as it gets ready to kill a penalty.

✔ First of all, the team that is trying to kill a penalty needs to adapt to the club that's on the power play and how it sets up. If the opponent uses a lot of diagonal passing, for example, with the left defenseman sending the puck to the right wing and vice versa, then the diamond system will most likely work best. But against a team that uses a more traditional power-play format and takes a lot of shots from the point, the box will likely work better.

✔ Whatever system a team uses, the primary objective of the penalty killers remains the same: Get control of the puck as often as possible and "ice" it down to the opposite end of the rink, which the rule book says you can do (see Chapter 3 for the details on icing). Icing eats up precious seconds of time and keeps the puck away from those players on the power play.

✔ In addition, a team should never let more than one of its penalty killers get caught inside the opposition's blue line; that can easily lead to the kinds of odd-man rushes that score goals (two forwards on the attack against one defenseman).

✔ Also, a team must make sure to have a good face-off man on the ice at all times. Taking possession of the puck and keeping it away from the other team is critical to good penalty killing, and winning face-offs is the best way to take possession. Of course, good goaltending also is an obvious key to any club that's down a man.

✔ The team killing a penalty should think about its offense every now and again. If the team works hard and anticipates passes and shots well, it can often create scoring chances for itself, and few things can swing the momentum of a game quicker than a short-handed goal (a score against a team that is on the power play).

The best penalty killers of all time

Two guys deserve special mention for the work they did as penalty killers in the NHL. One is Bob Gainey, who played 16 years with the Montreal Canadiens and won the Frank J. Selke Trophy each of the first four years it was awarded to the NHL forward who "best excels in the defensive aspects of the game." Gainey scored 239 goals in his career and played on five Stanley Cup teams, but he is best remembered as a fierce defender who combined power and speed. Many coaches consider him one of the most complete hockey players to ever lace up a pair of skates. The other is Doug Jarvis, who played in the league for 13 years, some of those as Gainey's teammate in Montreal and the rest for the Washington Capitals and the Hartford Whalers. He scored fewer goals than Gainey (139), won one less Cup than Gainey, and captured the Selke Trophy only once. But he, too, was a tough defender, especially on the penalty kill, and a diligent worker who understood the game and played with a lot of smarts.

Interestingly, Gainey and Jarvis found themselves reunited in the mid-1990s when both of them held jobs with the Dallas Stars; Gainey was the team's general manager, and Jarvis, one of the assistant coaches.

Chapter 10

Intimidation and Hitting

In This Chapter

▶ Talking on the ice

▶ Things that players do to each other besides talking

▶ The best fighters, intimidators, and agitators of all time

Championship hockey isn't only about good skating and shooting. The top clubs must also have people who can throw hard checks, agitate opponents so completely that they get off their games, intimidate the other team with speed and power, and have a physical presence on the ice that keeps the other squad from beating up on their star players. Any professional, international, or collegiate team that both hits and intimidates well can greatly increase its chances of winning.

You want proof of that? Okay, consider the National Hockey League's Philadelphia Flyers of the mid-1970s, the Broad Street Bullies who won two Stanley Cups and so terrified their opponents that players sometimes, and quite suddenly, got "sick" before games against them and insisted on taking a day off. This phantom malady came to be known as the Philly Flu. No one liked facing the 1996 Stanley Cup champion Colorado Avalanche either, and that's partially because they had one of the greatest agitators in the game's history, Claude Lemieux, and a number of other scrappers and hitters who made life miserable for the other team.

What Players Say to Each Other on the Ice

Players don't say much to each other on the ice that we can repeat here, that's for sure. At least not verbatim. But speaking in generalities, we can tell you that NHL players often question one another's lineage and wonder how each other's mother/sister/wife/girlfriend is doing. In most cases, they don't ask about each other's kids or pets, and they're not exchanging stock tips or pasta recipes as they dig for pucks along the boards. In short, the language and the innuendo are as blue as a clear winter sky and as spicy as a bowl of five-alarm chili. Nothing is sacred, and invariably each team, whether it's a high school club or the Boston Bruins, has a couple of guys who are particularly good at one-liners, and they are constantly throwing barbs at the opposition. Why? To get them angry. To get them thinking about something other than the game. To get them to take a bad penalty. To intimidate them. The idea is to get an edge, any edge, and players are always looking to gain some sort of advantage. Sometimes talking does the trick.

Jawing with the opposition is not the only way to achieve that. Many times, players talk to the referees and linesmen, in much gentler ways, about the things a person from the other team might be doing. Say, for example, that one guy is having a good night. He's scored a goal, assisted on another, and is making hits all over the ice. Perhaps he's also working the opponents over with his stick and getting away with a bunch of slashing fouls. A player from the other team might consider going up to the ref during a time-out and complaining. "That guy's had his stick up all night," he'd say. "You've got to start calling that, or someone's going to get hurt." Maybe the player points that out to the official two or three times in the early part of the game. And by doing that, maybe he plants a seed that will blossom later on in the contest when the ref finally does call the guy for slashing.

Teammates talk to each other on the ice all the time. Usually, they're asking for the puck, or telling one another what to do, or warning about where players from the other team are coming from and what they are about to do. The most vocal players on most teams are the goalies, who act as a sort of cruise director when the puck is in their end. They scream at their defensemen to get out of their way; they tell their forwards what to do with the puck as they skate behind the net or into the corners; and they alert their teammates to any opponents who may be bearing down on them for a check. Like catchers in baseball, goalies have the best view of the playing surface, and they are constantly directing traffic.

What Players Do to Each Other on the Ice (Aside from Talking)

Other than talking, players do a number of things to each other on the ice. Hard body checks can work wonders, not only in making a player a little nervous about flying into the corner for a puck or standing in front of the goal looking for a rebound, but also in wearing him out; hitting wears a skater out. Slashing is illegal, but players often do it — especially in the pros — to slow down good players and make them a bit more leery about coming down ice with the puck. Some guys use their elbows a lot when they hit. Whatever the tactics, the aims are the same: to keep the opposing players from being too confident on the ice, to upset their rhythm, to beat them up with a lot of physical contact, and to get them mad so they are more concerned about getting even than they are about scoring goals and winning games.

But hard hitting and agitation are not the only ways one team can intimidate another. Speed is just as useful an approach. It's dangerous, it's scary, and it works. Speed forces opposing players to make mistakes. It gives them less time and space in which to work the puck, and that can often lead to turnovers. A team with a lot of players who can move around the opposition's defensemen with apparent ease, get to the loose puck, and work it back up ice faster than the other team is going to frighten a lot of clubs.

Sheer talent can also have an effect. What rookie wasn't intimidated by Wayne Gretzky, a slightly built man who rarely threw a check and hardly ever got sent to the penalty box? It was his special skill as a hockey player, his unique ability to score and pass so deftly, that terrified the opposition and made him as ominous an opponent as some big gorilla. Same with a great team. Ask players who competed against the top Montreal teams of the 1960s and '70s, or against the Edmonton Oiler and New York Islander squads of the '80s, and they'll tell you about the pit they often felt in their stomachs as they looked across the ice at a Stanley Cup championship club doing its pregame warm-ups. How could they not have the slightest bit of trepidation?

And then, of course, arenas can sometimes be the most intimidating factors of all. The old Montreal Forum — with all its championship banners, its knowledgeable fans, and its great history — was probably worth at least one goal to the Canadiens on some nights. Old Chicago Stadium and Boston Garden had similar feels. They were smaller arenas that had a more intimate atmosphere than their successors, and they made the hometown crowds seem twice as big. "I don't think we're in Kansas anymore," Dorothy said in *The Wizard of Oz*. Some out-of-town rinks can make players feel just as lost.

The Five Best Fighters

Fighting is only an option in the NHL and the North American minor leagues; it is punished by ejection everywhere else, from the Pee-Wees to the Olympics, and therefore is rarely used at those levels. Most NHL teams have at least one player who is good with his fists. In most cases, his presence — on the bench and on the ice — is enough to keep the peace. But if his team needs a lift, or if the opposition has been beating up on one of his teammates, he goes after one of the other squad's tough guys. The scrap usually starts with a check or maybe a slash, and the next thing you know, the two fellows have dropped their gloves and started wrestling with each other while standing on their skates, looking for a chance to land a punch or two before the linesmen come in to break it up.

If the fight is between two tough guys and the officials feel it will help settle the game down, the officials often let them go at it for a spell. But if the fight seems like a mismatch or threatens to get out of control, they try to step in right away.

The NHL has had its share of good fighters over the years, and the following pugilists made our list of the top five:

- **Bob Probert.** At 6'3" and 225 pounds, this right winger is the best heavyweight scrapper ever to play the game. He led the NHL in penalty minutes while with the Detroit Red Wings in 1987–88, spending the equivalent of almost seven full games in the box. Probert has a nasty temperament and a deadly punch, but he can play a little bit as well, scoring 29 goals one season and adding 20 and 19 tallies during two others.

- **John Ferguson.** Mr. Intensity. The longtime Montreal Canadien left wing played 500 games in the NHL during the 1960s, won five Stanley Cups, and amassed more than 1,200 penalty minutes. He also scored 145 goals during his career, showing that he could handle the puck almost as well as he could handle his fists. He was a tough competitor who used to get irate with his teammates if they so much as talked to members of the opposition during warm-ups.

- **Dave Brown.** Another bruiser with size (6'5", 225 pounds) who understood his role as a fighter and represented his team well. While in the minors he led the American Hockey League in penalty minutes with 418 one season, and he racked up more than 270 on two occasions in the NHL, where he played from 1982 to 1996. Brown wasn't much of a scorer, and he never tallied more than 12 goals in a single NHL season. But very few could match him when the gloves came off.

- **Joey Kocur.** Smaller than Probert and Brown but just as ferocious, Kocur led the league in penalty minutes (377) in 1985–86. He had a deadly right and was known as a one-punch guy; if he landed that one punch, he could really do some damage. A native of Calgary, Kocur had a lot of injury trouble with his hands over the years from all the punches he threw, many of which bounced off the helmets of his foes.

- **Marty McSorley.** Another big boy, at 6'1" and 225 pounds, McSorley won the penalty minutes crown in 1992–93 while with the Los Angeles Kings. He is an excellent fighter who served for a time as the Kings' enforcer and made sure no one messed with then-teammate Wayne Gretzky. He can play either forward or defense, and he frequently participates in the power play — something that generally only a club's best offensive players do. McSorley has scored ten or more goals in a season five times during his career.

These guys may not merit being in the top five, but they deserve some kind of honorable mention:

- **Orland Kurtenbach.** The 13-year veteran (1960–73) didn't like to fight, but when he did, there wasn't anybody tougher. He also had great reach, which enabled him to slip in a few good punches while keeping his opponent at bay. Kurtenbach played for four teams over his career, scoring 119 goals and piling up 628 penalty minutes.

✔ **The Hanson Brothers.** They wrapped aluminum foil around their knuckles before each game to give their punches extra zing, and then they took on all comers in the classic 1977 George Roy Hill movie *Slap Shot.* The Hansons pummeled their opponents on the ice, they battled fans in the stands, and they did time in the slammer. "These guys are folk heroes," Paul Newman said to a desk sergeant as a teammate bailed the brothers out of jail. "They're not folk heroes, they're criminals," the cop replied. "Well," Newman countered, "most folk heroes started out as criminals." Real cementheads. But real good. And they knew how to take care of themselves, even if it was only the movies.

The Five Best Intimidators

Intimidation has been a part of organized hockey from the beginning, and the pros who have been best at it over the years make their point without always having to drop their gloves. They use their sticks, their elbows, their speed, or their power to create a sense of fear and foreboding in the athletes they play against and make them a bit more cautious as they skate around the ice. And why is that good? Because it can create scoring chances for their club and give them a better chance of winning.

✔ **Gordie Howe.** Mr. Hockey was best known for his uncanny scoring ability, his durability, his six Most Valuable Player Awards, and his 21 selections to the NHL All-Star squad. But he was also the best intimidator the sport has ever seen, a mean guy who liked to go into the corners with his stick and elbows up. Howe liked getting back at people who did him — or one of his teammates — wrong, but he was a patient man who didn't have to act right away. In fact, he was happy to wait five or six weeks before getting his revenge, and when he did, look out. Most players were peeking constantly over their shoulders when Howe was out on the ice (see Figure 10-1).

✔ **Mark Messier.** Like Howe, Messier is an immensely talented player with a nasty streak who will do whatever it takes to win. His intensity is unsurpassed, and he is famous for "The Look," a glare that emanates toughness, confidence, and abandon. He lifts his teammates with that and uses it to rattle the opposition as well. Messier also intimidates with his speed; he is a fast skater who often puts defensemen back on their heels because they are so worried about his quickness.

✔ **Ted Lindsay.** He is a smallish man, only 5'8" and 160 pounds, but you wouldn't know it from the way he battled during his 17 years with the Detroit Red Wings and the Chicago Blackhawks. Lindsay became known as "Terrible Ted," and that was no reflection on the playing ability of a man who scored 379 NHL goals, helped his teams win four Stanley Cups, played on nine All-Star teams, and won the Art Ross Trophy as the league's leading scorer in 1949–50. He simply competed in a very ill humor. A left winger who played on Detroit's renowned "Production Line" with Gordie Howe and Sid Abel, he also carried the moniker "Scarface" and accumulated more than 700 stitches during his NHL career. In addition, Lindsay piled up more than 1,800 penalty minutes in his time.

- ✔ **Eddie Shore.** The stellar defenseman last played in the NHL in 1940. His reputation survives after all these years as one of the toughest to ever play the game. A four-time MVP, he was the sort of player who had the whole arena standing whenever he had the puck. A prolific scorer, he could also throw a body check as well as anyone, and he never backed down from a fight.

- ✔ **Eric Lindros,** a big brute (6'4", 235 pounds) who uses his stick a lot and is not afraid to run people over, is very talented and very tough. Not many want to mess with him, though a recent spate of concussions has slowed him a bit.

Terrible Ted

Some players can never get the game of hockey out of their system, and Ted Lindsay is still one of those people. Initially, he retired at the end of the 1960 season, when he was 35 years old — ancient by hockey standards back then. Four years later, however, he attempted a comeback with the Red Wings, and to most everybody's surprise he made the team and went on to play one more season. The Terrible One scored 14 goals and ended the year as one of the league leaders in penalties. He dazzled his hometown fans all year with his bone-crunching checks and reckless spirit. In one game, Lindsay received a penalty for spearing a Montreal defenseman who was seven inches taller and 40 pounds heavier. Another Canadien came over to settle matters with Lindsay as his friend was helped off the ice, but the future Hall of Famer gripped his stick with both hands and slashed the Montrealer, who was nearly 20 years younger, across the legs. All that player could do after that was limp away.

As he entered his 70s, Ted Lindsay still had a locker at the Detroit Red Wings practice facility and went out there to work out most every day. He does a variety of activities to keep in shape but rarely plays in NHL old-timer games anymore. It's not that he can't get it done physically; it's just that he gets too intense on the ice and starts knocking people around.

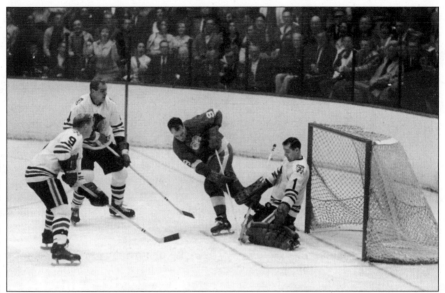

Figure 10-1:
Known for
his scoring,
Howe could
intimidate
with
the best.

The Five Best Agitators

Sometimes the line between agitating and intimidating is very fine, but we think the difference is clear: Intimidators frighten other players, while agitators simply bother them. And the five men we have listed in this section were as bothersome as anyone who ever played the game.

- ✓ **Esa Tikkanen.** A chatterbox who never stopped talking, Tikkanen worked over his opponents in his native Finnish, English, and some bizarre combination of the two that his teammates called "Tikkanese." He had a terrific shot, and his five Stanley Cups show that he was a winner. And remember, he would do anything to win. His coaches always put him out against the other team's top player, and with good reason. Wayne Gretzky said Tikkanen was the best checker he ever faced.

- ✓ **Claude Lemieux.** A big talker who drives opponents crazy with his aggravating tactics, Lemieux rarely fights but does whatever else he can to take players out of their game, using his stick, his elbows, and his mouth. He loves to goad people into taking bad penalties and often does. Another winner, he has played for four Stanley Cup champs.

- ✓ **Ulf Samuelsson.** He agitates so well that most fans think of him as a villain, a hard-hitting player who rarely fights but will gladly take out an opponent. But his teammates love his tough play and the way he battles. And he's been a favorite of his hometown fans wherever he's played. A native of Sweden who entered the NHL in 1984, Ulf has often been among the league leaders in penalty minutes.

✔ **Bobby Clarke.** A career-long Philadelphia Flyer who was a member of those Broad Street Bullies teams in the 1970s, Clarke was as antagonistic as they came. A prolific goal scorer and a great leader, he also racked up more than 1,400 penalty minutes and certainly induced players on opposing teams to take as many themselves. Fiercely competitive, he never stopped looking for an edge. Clarke was elected to the Hockey Hall of Fame in 1987 (see Figure 10-2).

✔ **Dave "Tiger" Williams.** He played on five teams over 14 seasons, and at the end of the 1999–2000 campaign, he still held the NHL record for the most penalty minutes in a career — 3,996 during the regular season and 4,421 including the playoffs. Tiger got many of those from working over the opponents' top players and getting under their skin. A great agitator, he also liked to drop his gloves. But it would be unfair to categorize Williams, who retired in 1988, solely as a fighter; he also tallied 241 goals during his career, an average of 17 a season.

Honorable mention: Tony Leswick, the former New York Ranger, Detroit Red Wing, and Chicago Blackhawk, may not have been one of the five best agitators, but he sure was a hell of a troublemaker. He played for 12 years during the 1940s and 1950s and spent much of his career driving the opposition crazy with his antagonistic play. Hall-of-Fame coach Scotty Bowman says he was "a real pest," which might account for all the time he spent in the penalty box; when Leswick retired in 1958, he had piled up 900 minutes.

Figure 10-2:
Bobby Clarke, agitator par excellence.

Goalies can dish it out, too

You usually don't think of goalies as agitators, but the New York Islanders' Billy Smith (shown here) and Ron Hextall, a longtime Philadelphia Flyer, were two of the best in that regard. Scrappy, competitive, and incredibly possessive of the area in front of the goal, they fought for position outside of the crease and often did things like smack the backs of their opponents' ankles with their sticks to keep them at bay.

Both goalies racked up more than their share of penalty minutes each season and were not averse to dropping their gloves on occasion and mixing it up on the ice. Loved by their teammates, they were loathed by the opposition, who considered them real pains. And you know what? They were.

Part III
It's Easier from the Stands (A Lot Easier)

The 5th Wave   By Rich Tennant

"Of course the drinks taste funny— the ice is from last year's Stanley Cup playoff."

In this part . . .

Hockey is one of the greatest spectator sports around, so in this part we give you advice on how to enjoy it even more as you watch on television or from an arena seat. In addition, we let you know where you can keep up with your favorite game — in newspapers, in magazines, on radio, on television, and (of course) on the World Wide Web.

Chapter 11

How to Watch Hockey on Television

*T*elevision technology has made tremendous advances over the years, and so has the way that networks produce hockey games. It has often been said that the sport doesn't translate well to the home screen, but we think talk like that is so much nonsense. Thanks to great camera work and a rich selection of replays, TV can capture most of the excitement, speed, and hitting of the game and take it inside a fan's living room. It really is the next best thing to being there. Even during intermissions, hockey offers something special that none of the other major sports (baseball, basketball, and football) have: live interviews with players and conversations with coaches on what happened on the ice during the previous period and how things might change for the next one.

Following the Puck (Sometimes)

Perhaps the best way to watch a hockey game is simply to follow the puck. Much of the action centers around that rubber disk, and if you have your eyes on it, you won't miss the big plays.

But plenty happens on other parts of the ice, whether it's a center *back checking* (retreating quickly into his defensive zone to protect the goal), a winger battling for position in front of the net, or a defenseman streaking deep into the offensive zone for a pass (see Chapter 1 for an explanation of the positions). If you want to see more than just what's going on around the puck, we recommend that you let the play-by-play man keep you apprised of where it is and allow your eyes to focus on other aspects of the game, whether it's a play forming down ice or a matchup between one team's big scorer and the other club's top checker.

You can back away from the game for a bit and see what is going on away from the puck, which can be a lot of fun. If Pavel Bure skates onto the ice, who does the opposing coach put out against him? Same with a player like Paul Kariya or Joe Sakic. And don't worry if you miss a great goal; you can watch the instant replay, and the producers will likely show you the play from several different angles. Listen, too, to the color analyst, the person in the television booth who tries to explain to the fans exactly how and why a good play happened and describe the things that caused a mistake. That's JD's job when he takes to the air. A good analyst can make even the least experienced fan understand what's going on.

Watching the Plays Form

One of the best things to watch at a hockey game is how the plays form. They frequently start behind the net with an offense-minded defenseman such as Brian Leetch surveying the setup before him and then beginning to work his way up ice with the puck. Some of his teammates might circle and curl trying to get open, while others crisscross. The team makes passes and takes shots, and when the other team regains possession, the whole thing starts over again, this time from behind the opposite goal.

Video replays give viewers at home a whole range of options when they tune into a hockey game. Watch how the puck got where it did when play has stopped. Who gave it away, and why? Was it the result of sloppy stickhandling? A strong hit? You can learn a lot just by looking carefully at what happened along the way.

Whether the action is live or taped, you'll also enjoy focusing on the one-on-one battles in a hockey game, to see who's winning the face-offs, the scrambles in front of the net, the struggles for the puck along the boards even when they are away from the puck. It's like keying on one player in football; zero in on a particular skater and watch how he moves around the ice, handles the puck, and deals with his opponents and offensive and defensive tactics. You can see a more individual side of the sport and get a better sense of all that goes on during a hockey game.

What to Look For from the Top Teams

Hockey teams, like people, have their own personalities, and many of them play the game quite differently. Understanding a team's character makes it easier to watch them on the tube because you have a sense of what they like to do and know what to look for when they take the ice. Here is a list of some of the top National Hockey League teams and the style of hockey they play.

Old-time television viewing

In the old days, hockey fans at home didn't get to see many plays form because the camera work and coverage was not so advanced. But that isn't a problem today, thanks to vast improvements in production technique and capability. A television network may employ 35 or more workers — ranging from the announcers and statisticians to the cameramen and directors — and use eight or more television cameras for regular-season games. Twenty years ago, the television networks may have used only four cameras. For an important playoff game, the networks may use as many as 14 cameras. In addition, they employ six instant replay tape machines for a regular-season contest and as many as 11 for the playoffs, up from two or three just two decades ago. That enables networks to provide replays to viewers from many more angles than they could in the days when JD played. Viewers can see shots from inside the goal net and in places along the boards that show heart-pounding aspects of checking and scoring in ways that television viewers could have only dreamed about in the 1960s and '70s. And then there is the overhead camera that is suspended from the ceiling of the arena; it provides a picture of the entire rink and finally lets the fans at home watch the important plays form. Television is now almost as good as being there.

Philadelphia Flyers

Toughness is what sells in the City of Brotherly Love, and that's one of the main traits of its hockey club. John LeClair (Figure 11-1) & Co. are big, fast, tough players who have both the talent to score and the ability to deal out punishment in the corners and in front of the net. This is a team that relies a great deal on brute force.

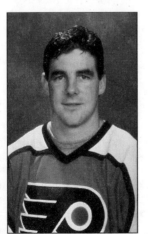

Figure 11-1: John LeClair.

Detroit Red Wings

This is a strong veteran team, and with defensemen like Chris Chelios and Nicklas Lidstrom, it really doesn't need to score many goals to win a game because it doesn't give many up. Defense has been a key part of Detroit's makeup ever since Hall-of-Fame coach Scotty Bowman began running the team in 1993. After all, it is his trademark. The Red Wings are also blessed with the leadership of Steve Yzerman, the scoring of Brendan Shanahan, and the all-around play of Sergei Fedorov. All in all, a very tough squad.

New Jersey Devils

The Devils have played a trap game for years, and that helped them win their first Stanley Cup in 1995 (see Chapter 8 for more on the trapping system). But you could argue that they are even better today because they have more offensive firepower. In fact, New Jersey boasts three lines that can score, which is a big reason why it won the 2000 Stanley Cup. Also, the team has some of the better young talent in the league, with center Scott Gomez and wingers Petr Sykora and Patrik Elias. It has a lot of young players who will provide balance offensively. And, of course, there is goaltender Martin Brodeur. He is very, very strong, and we wouldn't be surprised if he one day sets the record for most wins in the regular season. Plus, he is an exceptional puck handler.

St. Louis Blues

This team has a brilliant young coach in Joel Quenneville and two of the finest passing defensemen in the game, Chris Pronger (Figure 11-2) and Al MacInnis. Plus it features star center Pierre Turgeon and some wonderful players out of Slovakia, led by Pavol Demitra. The Blues never give up many shots, and they generate a lot of offense — all of which makes them very tough.

Dallas Stars

The Stars play a hard-nosed style of hockey, and they have made every player on their roster into a significant checker committed to team defense. As a result, they don't need a lot of offense to win games. Their one-two punch of centers Mike Modano and Joe Nieuwendyk is solid, and then you have the hard-shooting, goal-scoring Brett Hull as well as a terrific defense led by Derian Hatcher and Sergei Zubov. Throw in demanding head coach Ken Hitchcock, and you have the ingredients for an awfully good team — which they were in 1999, when they won the Stanley Cup.

Figure 11-2:
Chris
Pronger.

© 2000 NHL Images/Craig Melvin

Colorado Avalanche

When you talk about Colorado's strengths, you have to start with goalie and team anchor Patrick Roy (Figure 11-3). The Avalanche also has two of the league's greatest forwards in Joe Sakic and Peter Forsberg and two of the best young players in Chris Drury and Milan Hejduk. Basically, the Avalanche is a team that has been rebuilt since it won the Stanley Cup in 1996. It soon started losing a step, but now it is working its way back to the top. The Avalanche is a very creative, offensive-minded team that often plays a wide-open style of hockey (which means the players are willing to take more chances in their offensive end than most to score a goal). And with a great goalie like Roy, it can afford to.

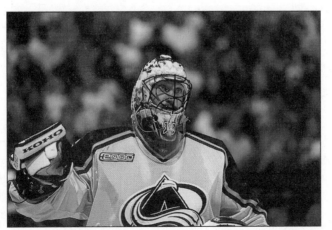

Figure 11-3:
Partick Roy.

© 2000 NHL Images/De Frisco

Toronto Maple Leafs

Of all the top teams today, the Leafs rely on great goaltending more than any-body else. And that's because their style of play is so wide open. Put this group on a pond against any other squad, and they may never lose. The Maple Leafs' centerpiece is Mats Sundin (Figure 11-4) — a big, powerful for-ward from Sweden — and their goalie is veteran Curtis Joseph. The only question is this: Can they be physical enough to compete in the Eastern Conference against tough opponents like Philadelphia and New Jersey?

Figure 11-4:
Mats
Sundin.

© 2000 NHL Images/Dave Sandford

Ottawa Senators

The Senators have a real sense of urgency on defense — that is their priority — and they are tenacious back-checkers who work very hard away from the puck. Yet they can also be very creative on offense, willing to open things up and take some chances to score. They are well coached and play a complete game, excelling on both the offensive and defensive ends of the ice.

What the Camera Doesn't Show You

With all the equipment the television networks have set up around a hockey rink, you don't miss very much of the game, whether it's a coach shouting at the referee from the bench or a pair of forwards from opposing teams hack-ing at each other with their sticks behind the play. And if the producers can't get the shot live, they almost always come up with a replay. They are especially good at isolating cameras on big-time players. A director may trail a scorer like Tony Amonte (shown in Figure 11-5) for a couple of shifts to see how he works the ice and what he is doing. And if he puts the puck in the net, assists on a goal, delivers a big hit, or just misses on a shot, the crew has him on tape and can play it over and over again for the fans.

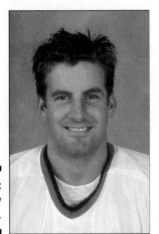

Figure 11-5:
Tony
Amonte.

But still, the cameras don't show you everything; they can miss the action that goes on away from the play. Perhaps two skaters begin battling for the puck at one end of the rink, keep mixing it up even as the play moves toward the opposite net, and then continue going at each other as they finally head up ice themselves. The live camera feed usually won't pick that up, and you can only hope that one of the replay cameras does. Chances are, however, it won't.

Television viewers also don't have the opportunity to hear or see the coaches during a game and don't get much of a sense of what goes on behind the bench as the game progresses, which is too bad because there is so much happening — from the coach sending certain players onto the ice for their shifts to talking strategy with one of his assistants to telling his defensemen how to handle certain players from the other team.

Occasionally, you can hear what's going on while you are watching a game on television, so listen carefully. The ping the puck makes when it hits one of the goalposts but doesn't go in the goal is one of the most distinctive sounds in hockey. (Any puck that hits a goalpost and continues into the net is a goal; any puck that bounces away is not a goal and is still in play.) No matter how loud an arena — or living room — may be, that noise of rubber hitting metal at such a high speed can silence the fans for an instant as they try to figure out exactly what has happened. It's an extreme emotion for both sides; the fans of the squad that has taken the shot are frustrated and can't believe the puck didn't go into the net, and those on the other side are relieved that they survived such a close call and a little nervous about the next shot going in.

The "crunch" against the boards of a player who has just received a solid body check is another sound to listen for. The impact of a great hit can echo throughout an arena, and it is one of the things that gives hockey its special intensity.

Chapter 12

How to Watch Hockey from the Seats

*H*ockey is a great game to watch on television, and an even better one to see in person. In fact, we don't think there's another sport that comes close to matching the speed, excitement, and finesse of a live National Hockey League game or a game played by top international, minor league, or college teams. So do yourself a favor this season: Buy some tickets and get out to see a game. And make sure you remember some of the tips we give in this chapter.

Paying Attention

Hockey is a fast sport, so the key to good watching is paying attention. While you're looking down to squeeze some mustard on your hot dog, your team may score a goal. Or give one up. Eat before or after the game, or between periods when the only action on the rink is the Zamboni resurfacing the ice or some puck-shooting contest for fans from the stands. Thumb through the program during stoppages of play. Chat with your neighbor during the time-outs. But when the official drops the puck and the players start skating, keep your eyes riveted on the ice.

Watching the Whole Rink

There are so many subplots to a hockey game and different things to watch. One of the things we like to do is to follow the matchups on the ice, to see what skaters the coaches put out to play against each other. That's an important consideration in every game — especially during the playoffs, when the stakes are highest. Who's checking Pavel Bure? Or Peter Forsberg? Or your 9-year-old son? Who does coach Scotty Bowman send onto the ice against Paul Kariya and Teemu Selanne? It's a chess game between the two clubs and great fun to watch.

These days, most seats in a hockey arena are good. But we recommend that you get a seat in one of the corners because you can see the entire rink from there (see Figure 12-1). You should get down close to the ice, where you can really get a sense of the hitting, speed, and athleticism of the players. You don't get quite as good a view from that level of the ice (you can see more of the action unfold from a higher position), but you're right there during a game and can see how amazingly talented these people are.

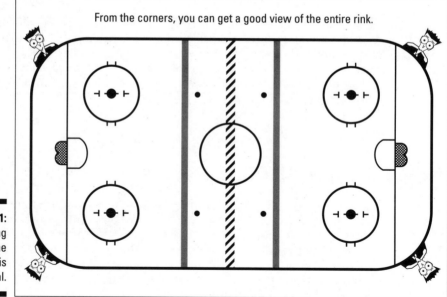

From the corners, you can get a good view of the entire rink.

Figure 12-1: Viewing from the corners is ideal.

What exactly is a Zamboni?

A *Zamboni* is a four-wheel-drive vehicle that scrapes, cleans, and floods the surface of a hockey rink before each period of a game. Invented by a California rink operator named Frank Zamboni, it grew out of an experiment he conducted with a tractor pulling a sled across the ice at his rink. The one-driver Zamboni made its debut in 1949 and soon became a fixture at rinks all over the world. Basically, it scrapes the snow off an ice rink that has had heavy skating activity and lays down a fresh coat of hot water, which creates a new surface of ice in about ten minutes. The procedure improves the quality of the ice and enhances the speed and finesse of the modern game of hockey.

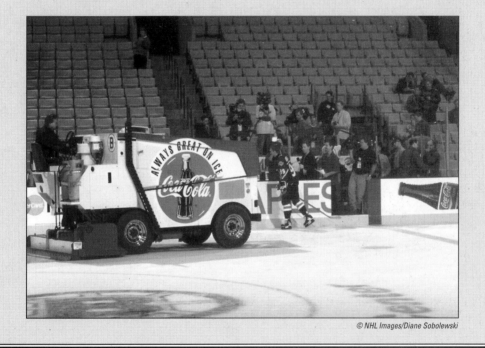

© NHL Images/Diane Sobolewski

Watching an Opposing Player

VIEWER TIP

Focus on the opposing team's star player when he comes to town. Like Eric Lindros or Brett Hull. Or maybe the all-state center on the team your son's high school is playing. Keep your eyes on him for a few shifts, and only him. See what he does without the puck. See what the other team does to him without the puck. See how he gets himself in position to shoot, pass, or check.

If the members of a hockey team don't work together on the ice, they won't win. So as a fan, you should enjoy the effort the players expend each and every night. When you watch players at the NHL level, or even those in a minor-league or collegiate game and international competition, take time to appreciate their ability to perform ballerina-like moves while skating at some 30 miles per hour and carrying a stick. It really is remarkable what these guys can do. The power, strength, and finesse they all possess is truly something to behold.

Enjoying the Culinary Delights

Anyone who goes to more than a few games a year should get to know where the freshest popcorn is made in his or her home arena and where to find the best hot dogs. (Or perhaps you'd prefer gourmet ice cream, freshly made Chinese food, or other fancier eats, which most facilities sell along with more traditional fare.) Each arena has those culinary hot spots, and it pays to discover where they are. Vendors will get to know you and are sure to treat a good fan well, especially if they get a few extra dollars along the way.

Keeping Your Cool

One more thing if you see a game in person: Don't be abusive to the players, officials, security people, ushers, or fans around you. The language at some hockey arenas is as salty as anything you'd find in the locker rooms after the game, and that's not always comfortable when you have your 6-year-old daughter and a couple of her friends in tow. Remember, it's a family game, and a fun game.

- Behave.
- Don't drink too much.
- Don't throw things.
- Don't swear.
- And don't ruin it for everybody else.

JD's Five Favorite Arenas

Our man in the television booth spends more time in hockey rinks during the winter than he does at home, so he knows his way around these buildings pretty well. Here are his top five, in alphabetical order, and two honorable mentions, for purely sentimental value.

Air Canada Centre

This is where the Toronto Maple Leafs now play their home games. The arena was originally designed for the National Basketball Association's Toronto Raptors but has been adapted beautifully for hockey. The camera locations are set up just right, the sight lines are beautiful, and it is a great place to watch a game, either in person or on television. The seating has a fairly steep slope, the skyboxes are plentiful, and the people who work there love it. It's a great new place.

Arrowhead Pond of Anaheim

It's down the street from Disneyland, so you can take your family there before the ref drops the puck. It's also close to where the Angels play baseball. The arena is beautiful, with palm trees on the outside (you don't see those around the Calgary Saddledome in mid-February) and lots of granite and marble inside. An impressive building that feels almost like a palace. The workers are clean, very polite, and pleasant — all of which you would expect from Disney.

Madison Square Garden

History is one of the things that makes "The World's Most Famous Arena" so special, even though the Garden has changed addresses several times over the years. The current edition has been operating on the west side of Manhattan since 1968, and it's one of the loudest buildings in the league. The fans there are among the most passionate and knowledgeable in the game. Oddly located, the rink is actually on the fifth floor of a building that sits atop busy Pennsylvania Station. Great fans who love hockey and know the game well fill the Garden, shown in Figure 12-2. The food is pretty good, too, since the concession stands were renovated a few seasons ago.

Molson Centre

It's tough to replace a legend like the old Montreal Forum, but this building comes close. It opened in 1997, but somehow it manages to carry on much of the tradition and ambiance of the Canadiens and their former arena. All the old championship banners and retired jerseys hang from the rafters, the fans still dress up, and something special remains about going to a game in Montreal. Stop by the concession stands for the best hot dogs in the league — and the buns are toasted, too!

San Jose Arena

The home of the Sharks has had terrific mood and atmosphere from day one. The arena contains excellent facilities for players, broadcasters, and fans alike. The home team comes onto the ice at the start of the game through the mouth of a shark, and the fans all move their arms back and forth like a shark's jaw when their players go on the power play. It's a simple but great place to see a game.

Honorable mention: Lethbridge Arena

JD was a 17-year-old goalie on the Lethbridge Sugar Kings in Alberta, Canada, when they faced off against the Edmonton Maple Leafs in a junior league playoff game back in 1971. The Sugar Kings were losing 2–1, 19 seconds into the third period, when the smallish wooden building suddenly caught fire. The place was packed with some 1,800 fans at the time, and they quickly filed out — as did the players, who didn't have time to take off their skates or get their clothes from the locker room. With most everybody standing across the street on the sidewalk in amazement, the arena burned to the ground in 90 minutes. The game was finished the next night in a nearby arena, with Lethbridge tying the score in the third period and then going on to win 3–2 in overtime. Later that same evening, the Sugar Kings also beat Edmonton in the scheduled game and went on to win the series.

Honorable mention: Maple Leaf Gardens

Known as the "Old Lady of Carlton Street," this building celebrated its 65th anniversary in 1997, and the Toronto Maple Leafs stopped playing their regular season games there in 1999. No other arena in the NHL had been around so long. The seats were too small (at least for us), the concession lines intolerably long, and you needed a road map to get from one part of the building to another. But it was still one of the best venues in the league (see Figure 12-3). It was the site of some of the greatest games in hockey history and had the venerable feel of a church. Old pictures lining the hallway walls added a nice touch.

Figure 12-3:
Maple Leaf
Gardens in
Toronto.

Chapter 13

Online, On the Air, and On the Newsstand

- -

In This Chapter

▶ Surfing the Web for hockey stuff

▶ Flipping through TV and radio stations for the big game

▶ Scouring books, magazines, and newspapers for hockey coverage

- -

*K*eeping up with your favorite sport is, thankfully, not hard to do. Hockey is everywhere, and you can find news about the sport — ranging from player profiles and trades to game summaries and analysis — on your computer or television screen, in the newspapers and magazines, and on the radio. You just need to know where to look.

Hockey Web Sites

There is no shortage of hockey in cyberspace, and a few taps on the mouse can land you on some fascinating and fun-filled sites. Strap on your helmet, and we'll show you some.

nhl.com

The official Web site of the National Hockey League receives more than 40 million hits per month (see Figure 13-1). Want to listen to your favorite team, no matter where you are? nhl.com has live radio broadcasts. The site also offers a wealth of video clips, audio shows, super-detailed statistics from the league's Real-Time Scoring System, player biographies, and team pages. In addition, nhl.com has information on the history of the game and on where to play hockey. No matter where you live or how much you know about hockey, nhl.com is a great place to be.

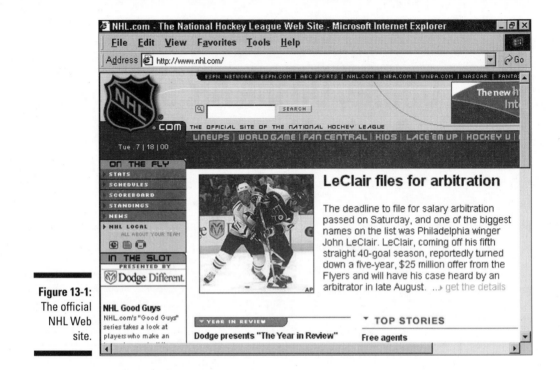

Figure 13-1:
The official
NHL Web
site.

NHL team sites

The league isn't the only hockey organization that has entered the computer age in a big way; all of the NHL's 30 franchises have developed their own Web sites that offer reams of information so fans all over the world can keep up with their favorite clubs like never before (see Table 13-1).

Table 13-1	NHL Team Web Sites
Team	*Site*
Mighty Ducks of Anaheim	www.mightyducks.com
Atlanta Thrashers	www.atlantathrashers.com
Boston Bruins	www.bostonbruins.com
Buffalo Sabres	www.sabres.com
Calgary Flames	www.calgaryflames.com
Carolina Hurricanes	www.caneshockey.com
Chicago Blackhawks	www.chicagoblackhawks.com

Team	Site
Colorado Avalanche	www.coloradoavalanche.com
Columbus Blue Jackets	www.columbusbluejackets.com
Dallas Stars	www.dallasstars.com
Detroit Red Wings	www.detroitredwings.com
Edmonton Oilers	www.edmontonoilers.com
Florida Panthers	www.flpanthers.com
Los Angeles Kings	www.lakings.com
Minnesota Wild	www.wild.com
Montreal Canadiens	www.canadiens.com
Nashville Predators	www.nashvillepredators.com
New Jersey Devils	www.newjerseydevils.com
New York Islanders	www.newyorkislanders.com
New York Rangers	www.newyorkrangers.com
Ottawa Senators	www.ottawasenators.com
Philadelphia Flyers	www.philadelphiaflyers.com
Phoenix Coyotes	www.phoenixcoyotes.com
Pittsburgh Penguins	www.nhlpenguins.com
St. Louis Blues	www.stlouisblues.com
San Jose Sharks	www.sjsharks.com
Tampa Bay Lightning	www.tampabaylightning.com
Toronto Maple Leafs	www.torontomapleleafs.com
Vancouver Canucks	www.vancouvercanucks.com
Washington Capitals	www.washingtoncaps.com

Other hockey sites

How many are there? Let us count them all, or at least the ones we like best. Like espn.com, CBS Sportsline (also known as sportsline.com), and faceoff.com. There are also sites for the Hockey News, the National Hockey League Players Association (nhlpa.com), Fox Sports, CNN/SI, MSNBC, and the

Hockey Forum. One way to find out what's available is to head to Rich Johnson's sportspages.com, which can show you how to access almost any site that has to do with hockey. You can even find daily newspaper coverage of your favorite team by local beat writers, so you can keep up no matter where you are (try www.allsports.com/nhl/media/indexnewspapers.html).

Broadcast TV and Radio

All you need is a TV or radio to take advantage of many hockey resources. The kind of coverage you want is there.

ABC/ESPN

ABC and ESPN have a deal with the NHL to carry league games in the United States through the 2003–04 season. It calls for ABC to air up to seven regular-season games, the All-Star Game, six early-round playoff games, and up to five Stanley Cup Finals games. As for cable coverage in the States, ESPN and ESPN2 will "cablecast" nearly 200 games a year. And ESPN International is working with the NHL to syndicate and distribute a variety of NHL-related programs worldwide, including more than 100 live games per year and also news, magazine, and special event shows. Plus, ESPN and ESPN2 will carry *NHL Cool Shots*, a weekly show created and produced by the league to help fans get to know the players off the ice.

CBC

As you might expect, hockey is very big in the north country, and the Canadian Broadcasting Corporation has the biggest show there, *Hockey Night in Canada*, on which the network airs a doubleheader every Saturday evening during the regular season. It's as much a television happening as *Monday Night Football* in the States. CBC also broadcasts a game every night during the playoffs, if possible — preferably one that includes a Canadian team.

CTV SportsNet

Canada's version of ESPN carries up to 32 NHL regular-season contests a year as well as some first-round playoff action. An up-and-coming cable channel, it is seen throughout Canada.

SRC

The French-language arm of CBC also airs a Game of the Week featuring the Montreal Canadiens throughout the entire season, as well as one series per round for the first two playoff rounds. It also carries the Stanley Cup Finals and the Conference Finals, when it involves two Canadian clubs.

International television and regional cable

There are plenty of other places to find hockey on television, both in and out of North America. More than 170 countries carry NHL games during the regular season and playoffs, for example, and a sizable number air competitions from other professional and amateur leagues throughout the year. And what viewers cannot find on the major broadcast or cable channels they can often locate on one of the many regional cable networks, such as Madison Square Garden in the metropolitan New York area or Fox Sports in Los Angeles, which may cover all a team's games live and provide daily news on the team.

Radio

Sports radio has hit the big time, and there are plenty of stations throughout North America on which you can listen to fans, commentators, players, coaches, and team executives talking hockey. One of our favorite shows is hosted by The Fabulous Sports Babe on ABC Radio. And of course there's JD's own syndicated radio show, *Inside the NHL*, which is carried on Sunday nights for 40 weeks a year on Sports Fan radio. His cohost is Jeff Rimer, who is the Florida Panthers' play-by-play man.

We also like the way ESPN Radio covers the game as well as the attention countless local stations give hockey across the United States and Canada. The NHL has a deal with the Westwood One radio network for the exclusive rights to league games throughout the States.

Hockey in Print

The best place to start with the print media is the NHL, which publishes the *Official Guide and Record Book* before the start of each season. It's a can't-miss for the rabid fan and has everything you'd ever want to know about the league and its players and teams.

Other super NHL publications include the league's official yearbook and its annual All-Star Game program, both of which are wonderful sources of information. (The program, which you can buy even if you don't actually go to the All-Star Game, is one installment in an NHL-licensed publishing effort called FaceOff [416-928-2909, ext. 234].) In addition, the NHL and the Players Association jointly publish *PowerPlay Magazine* (877-687-7529), a youth hockey volume that covers the NHL for youngsters. Finally, the individual franchises each sell official team journals and yearbooks at the arenas that are full of great photos, statistics, and stories about the club and its players.

Magazines

The Sporting News (314-997-7111) provides terrific week-to-week coverage, and *Sports Illustrated* (212-522-1212) does a good job as well, especially around playoff time. And the major newsweeklies, *Time* and *Newsweek,* devote a story to the game every now and again.

But the best publication for the sport is *The Hockey News* (416-340-8000). Based in Toronto, it looks at the game at both a professional and amateur level like no one else. And in addition to its regular weekly edition, *The Hockey News* also publishes some first-rate special issues.

Other magazines of note include:

- *Sports Illustrated for Kids* (212-522-1212)
- *American Hockey Magazine* (719-881-7679) out of Colorado Springs
- *USA Hockey In-Line Magazine* (719-599-5500) out of Colorado Springs
- *Hockey Illustrated* (212-780-3500) based in New York City
- *The Hockey Digest* (847-491-6440) in Evanston, Illinois
- *The Beckett Hockey Monthly* (972-991-6657) out of Dallas — for trading-card enthusiasts
- *Let's Play Hockey* (612-729-0023) from Minneapolis

Newspapers

The local newspapers in each NHL city provide good coverage of their local team, and so do the newspapers in towns that have minor-league or college hockey. On a national basis in the States, *USA Today* does better than most with NHL news, bringing solid information from around the league together in one spot; it contains great box scores and goes to print very late so the morning edition has all the finals. And for Canada, the *Globe and Mail* as well as *The National Post* and the chain of *Sun* newspapers cover the game as well as anyone.

Books

Hockey fans also have a terrific selection of books from which to choose. Perhaps the best one out there is *Total Hockey*, a wonderfully comprehensive publication that has everything from histories of the game and player biographies to statistics and descriptions of how the game is played overseas. Neither of us has ever seen anything like this book, which was edited by Dan Diamond and published by Total Sports (919-573-8020). It is described as the official encyclopedia of the National Hockey League, and it is certainly that — and a lot more.

The NHL also put out a great coffee-table publication to celebrate its 75th anniversary in 1991, appropriately titled *The Official National Hockey League 75th Anniversary Commemorative Book* (McClelland & Stewart, 1991), and it is a classic. So is the *Stanley Cup Centennial* book (Firefly), the NHL-produced book about the Stanley Cup. Read it if you want a colorful and complete history of the league and the greatest trophy in sports.

Another good buy is *A Day in the Life of the National Hockey League* (HarperCollins, 1996), which brilliantly recounts in words and pictures all that went on in the league one March day in 1996.

We recommend you browse your local bookstore or library for any of the countless treatments writers have given the game over the years. You may want to check out the work of veteran broadcaster and journalist Stan Fischler, who has been writing about the sport for more than 40 years and has written some 65 books that discuss everything from the history of the game to its all-time great players.

Two other authors of note are Dick Irvin (son and namesake of the Hall-of-Fame coach and the play-by-play analyst for *Hockey Night in Canada*) and broadcast journalist Brian McFarlane. Both have written several good volumes on the sport.

And then there is our top choice, former Montreal Canadiens goaltender and Hall of Famer Ken Dryden, whose book *The Game* (Times Books in the United States, Macmillan in Canada, 1983) is considered by many, including us, to be the best ever written about hockey (except for this one, of course).

Of course, you can also check out a couple of JD's other literary efforts. One is *For the Love of Hockey,* which features up-close-and-personal stories on some 100 hockey players. Published by Firefly Books, this opus was compiled by Chris McDonell and includes a foreword by JD. And the other is *Wayne Gretzky, My Life in Pictures* (published by Total Sports), which JD wrote with "The Great One" (Gretzky's nickname).

The Hockey Hall of Fame

JD SAYS

Located in Toronto, this is a must-see for anyone interested in the sport. It was established in 1943, and members were first honored two years later. Originally, the Hall was housed in a building on the grounds of the Canadian National Exhibition in Toronto. It moved to its current spot, on the corner of Front and Yonge Streets, in 1993. At the start of the 2000–01 season it boasted 319 members. The Hall is a fascinating shrine to the *coolest game on earth*™, with some wonderful interactive facilities and countless exhibits on the greatest players, games, and coaches the sport has ever known. Nothing captures the history — or excitement — of hockey so well. Visit the Hall's Web site at www.hhof.com (see Figure 13-2).

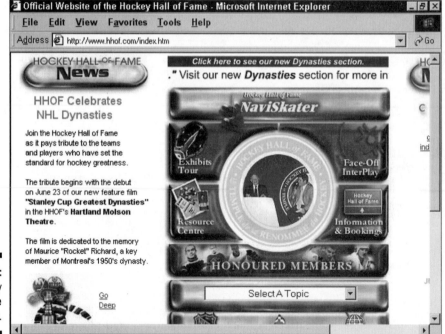

Figure 13-2:
The Hockey
Hall of Fame
on the Web.

Part IV
So You're Ready for Your Shift

The 5th Wave   By Rich Tennant

"Some of the kids have tried street hockey, but most just burn out the brakes on their in-line skates before the season ends."

In this part . . .

This section is for those readers who want to play the game themselves — or those who are looking to get other members of their families involved. We start off with playing tips from current and former pros like Wayne Gretzky and Brett Hull, and then we tell you where to go if you and your children want to play, whether you have any ice or not. Hockey without ice? Read on . . .

Chapter 14

What You Need to Know to Play Hockey and Improve

*T*he best way to pick up any sport, and to get better, is to listen to the professionals and learn what they do. So we got in touch with several of the National Hockey League's best players, past and present, and asked for their advice on different aspects of the game. Now, we'd like you to listen up.

Wayne Gretzky on Passing

"There are two primary kinds of passes," the Great One explains. "One is solid and hard, and the other is known as the feather. If the player you are passing to is standing still, use the *firm pass.* And if he's going at a good rate of speed, use the *feather,* and make sure you get it out ahead of him so he can skate into it" (see Figure 14-1).

"I think it's important to practice the backhand pass as much as the forehand one," Gretzky continues. "And you want to do that as much as possible at a young age so you grow up feeling comfortable with it, especially if you want to be a centerman. Some youngsters ignore the backhand and don't feel relaxed with it as a result."

Number 99 was famous for skating behind the net with the puck in his offensive zone and looking for teammates to get open in front of the net. (He camped out there so often, in fact, that commentators referred to that part of the ice as *Gretzky's office.*) "When I got back there, I preferred to use a backhand pass to get the puck out front," he says. "I liked to use the net as a sort of screen, to buy time from the opposing defensemen who may have been trying to get me, and to buy some time back there. I tried to keep the puck away from them as long as possible so I would hopefully make a play."

Figure 14-1:
Gretzky
prepares
to pass.

© NHL Images/Allsport/Elsa Masch

One final tip: Use plenty of tape on the blade of your stick. "It gives you more control on your passes and shots, and it enables you to pass the puck *flatter* [meaning not lifting it] when you have a decent amount of tape on your blade," Wayne says. "I tried doing it like Bobby Orr, with only a couple of pieces on the blade, but I couldn't do it."

Mark Messier on Face-Offs

"A centerman should always watch the linesman's hands when the puck is about to be dropped [on any face-off]," says the perennial All-Star, shown in Figure 14-2. "Forget about the other player, but keep your eyes on the linesman because he's the one who actually has the puck. In the defensive zone, the best thing to do is try and adjust to what your opponent is doing. Read him. Look at his eyes, where his stick is facing, how his body is turned, how he's holding the stick, and where he's telling his teammates to line up. All that should give you some idea of what he is going to do with the puck, whether he's going to shoot off the draw, pass the puck to one of his defensemen behind him, or over to one of his wingers. And then you should react accordingly.

"Probably the best thing you can do with the puck [in a face-off] in your defensive zone is bring it back behind you so one of your defensemen can pick it up and try to get it outside the zone. To do that, turn the hand you put on the lower part of the stick into a backwards position [palm over the top of the stick], which will give you more power as you bring the stick back when the puck is dropped.

Figure 14-2: Mark Messier.

© NHL Images/Allsport/Glenn Cratty

"We work on set plays off the face-off all the time in practice," Messier says. "And we also practice things that we might do when time is running out and there may be only a minute or so left in the game. It's sort of like the two-minute drill in football, and we have a little bit different way of doing things then. Also, many times in practice, a coach will take a dozen pucks or so and drop them for two centermen so they can work on their face-offs. Your best position for that is having your legs spread for balance and your stick down, so you are set up almost like a tripod.

"Remember, in a power play situation especially, the centerman is the quarterback, and he should know where every player on the ice is," Mark continues. "It is his job to set everybody up and know what he will do with the puck when the linesman drops it. And he should also be aware of the tendencies of the opposing centermen he will face on a particular night and watch them closely from the bench to see what they are doing with the puck after a *draw* [another name for face-off]. That way, he will be better prepared when he steps onto the ice."

Mike Vernon on Defending the Breakaway

"The first thing I try to do is recognize the person that's coming in as soon as he hits the blue line," says the long-time goalie. "Is he a shooter? A *deker* [someone who will first make a move to get the goalie out of position and then shoot]? Or maybe a third- or fourth-line center [who usually won't have the best hands or shot on the team]? Then I adjust my position. I don't want to be too far out of my net, especially if the guy coming down is a Swede or Russian because they generally have a lot of speed and move in very, very quickly. If I go out too far, they'll be on me in a hurry" (see Figure 14-3).

"If I had my choice, I'd rather face a shooter than a deker," explains Vernon. "I believe I have a better chance of stopping him. How do I tell if a guy is going to shoot or deke? Well, the best way is to look at where the puck is on his stick as he's coming down ice. If he's holding it right out in front of him, then I can expect a deke because it's impossible to shoot with your stick that way. If, however, he's carrying it on the side, he can do either, shoot or deke. I believe that if the puck is cocked to one side, I should get ready for the shot first. But at the same time, I need to stay still because if I open up [my legs], the guy coming down on me will stick the puck in the five-hole [the area between a goalie's legs]. I expect most people on a breakaway to fake a shot, try and deke me, and put the puck between my legs. Mario Lemieux did that well. In fact, he did that better than anybody else."

The different holes

Hockey coaches and players have designated seven *holes* in a net guarded by a goalie as a way of communicating where players should aim their shots (and what areas a goalie should be careful to defend). Holes number one and two are above the shoulders of the netminder, and three and four are in the lower corners of the goal, on either side of his ankles. And as mentioned in the preceding text, the five-hole is right between the legs, while six and seven are underneath the armpits. We also think there's an eighth hole — right between the eyes, which is where a person who decides to be a goalie, or a writer, instead of going to law or medical school, deserves to be hit with the puck.

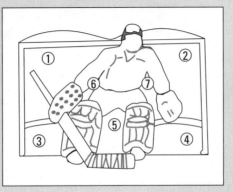

Al MacInnis on Shooting from the Point

This rangy defenseman (shown in Figure 14-4) has won the fastest-shot contest during the NHL All-Star Weekend several times, and his shot from the point was clocked as high as 98 miles per hour. Not surprisingly, goalies don't like to see him wind up. The winner of the Conn Smythe Trophy as the Most Valuable Player in the playoffs for the Calgary Flames when they won the Stanley Cup in 1989, MacInnis grew up on a farm in Nova Scotia and practiced his slap shot whenever he could. He put a sheet of plywood against the barn and shot buckets of pucks against it all summer long. "I would do as many as 300 a day," he recalls. "It helped me build up my strength and work on my timing." When he takes a shot from the point today, MacInnis tries to keep his hands close together, which means that when he takes his windup for a shot, he creates a bigger arc, which in turn gives him more power. At 6'2" and 200 pounds, he is a big player who stands upright when he skates and uses a curved stick with a bit of a wedge to it, giving his shot added lift.

Figure 14-3:
Vernon goes
down for
the save.

© NHL Images/Allsport/Al Bello

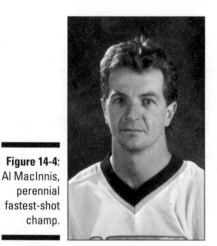

Figure 14-4:
Al MacInnis,
perennial
fastest-shot
champ.

Gary Roberts on Scoring as a Power Forward

Scoring as a power forward requires a set of special talents. A player must not only be big and strong and able to overpower his opponent at either end of the ice, but also have legitimate goal-scoring ability. Gary Roberts is one of

those rare athletes who fills both those bills and is one of the best power forwards in the NHL (see Figure 14-5).

"Body position is really important," Roberts says. "I like to keep my back to
the goalie and be as close to him as I can without being in the crease so the
defenseman can't get in behind me and throw a cross check. One of the key
things that a power forward who wants to score should do is keep his stick
loose so he can knock in rebounds or deflect pucks. Someone on the other
team may be all over you, they may be checking you from behind, whacking
you across the ankles with their sticks, grabbing your jersey. But no matter
what they do, try and keep your stick free so you can somehow get it on the
puck should it come by, even if you're tied up.

"For rebounds, I like to use a stick that's fairly straight with maybe a little toe
curve. The straightness will help you put it on your backhand shots better
than a sharply curved blade, and the toe curve will let you flick the puck
upstairs, 'roofing it' we call it, into the one- or two-hole. I also believe it's best
to have a stick with a stiff shaft because so much of your shooting at that
position comes in close, and you really have to bear down on those two- and
three-footers. You don't have much time with those, only an instant, and a
stiffer shaft will help you get those types of shots off faster and harder."

Figure 14-5:
Power
forward
Gary
Roberts.

Eric Lindros on Shooting off the Pass

"I like to keep both my hands high on the stick when I'm getting ready to shoot off the pass," says the All-Star centerman (see Figure 14-6). "Why? Because it's easier and quicker to move your lower hand down on the stick where it has to be when the pass comes than to try and move it up. Also, it's important to keep my center of gravity low and my legs spread apart just enough so I can adjust to the pass. The idea is to get yourself in the best possible position to shoot because the thing that makes a shot like that work is its quickness and speed. You want to surprise the goaltender, and to do that you need to shoot as quickly as possible. I work on shooting off the pass a lot after practice because it can be so effective. I always have, though it was a problem in junior hockey because I broke so many sticks working on it, and it cost the team money." Clearly the practice paid off because Lindros shoots off the pass as well as anybody. The key for the player feeding the shooter is making a hard, accurate pass. If the pass is both hard and accurate, the shooter can blast a shot so quickly that the goaltender cannot get across the goal fast enough to block it.

Who's the best at setting up a teammate's shot with a pass? "Paul Kariya," Lindros says without hesitation. "We played together during the World Championships in 1993, and he was unbelievable."

Figure 14-6:
Eric Lindros.

© NHL Images/Allsport/Rick Stewart

Brett Hull on Getting Free in Front of the Net

"A lot of it is developing the proper state of mind," says one of the NHL's most prolific scorers of all time. "One thing that's important is learning to take a lot of abuse from the opposition without retaliating or yapping back. And sooner or later, they forget about you.

"When I'm in the slot trying to score, I try to move around a lot," says Hull (see Figure 14-7). "If I get knocked down by a cross check, I stay down for a bit and then get right up, the hope being that the defenseman thinks he has taken you out of the play and forgets about you. Then I try to get up real quick and get open.

"I always try to keep my stick free whenever I am getting tied up in front of the opposition's net," Hull continues, "just in case I can somehow get to the puck, whether for a deflection, a redirection, or a rebound. I've played with some amazing centermen, Wayne Gretzky and Adam Oates to name but two, who had a terrific knack of putting the puck on my stick. Somehow, they would find it. Another guy who was really good at that was Peter Zezel.

"All scorers need good centermen," Hull says, "and it's possible to develop a really strong relationship with one. It's like in football, where a quarterback can throw a pass to a receiver before he even breaks out of his cut. A good centerman knows his wings, and he can move the puck to a spot before you even turn to go there."

Figure 14-7: Brett Hull knows how to slip in and out of the action.

The All-Star right winger goes out of his way not to show up an opponent when he scores a goal. "Usually, I try to go to the bench right away," he says. "I don't pump my arms too much or raise them high because I don't want to embarrass people. I actually think it's better if you can slip in and out without drawing too much attention to yourself. If you make people get emotional about you, then they make it their business to know where you are every second you are on the ice. They are always looking to see where you are. It's much better to be out of sight, out of mind."

Ron Hextall on Handling the Puck as a Goalie

Hextall's grandfather (Bryan Sr.) and father (Bryan Jr.) both played in the NHL, so he's been hanging around hockey rinks as long as he can remember. "I used to watch Eddie Giacomin when my father played in Detroit," Ron says. "He handled the puck as well as anybody, and I watched him all the time when he was with the Wings. And then, when I started playing goalie as a kid, I used to get really bored just standing around. So I started to move with the puck a little bit during games. As I grew up, I began spending lots of time shooting pucks with a forward's stick, maybe two or three hours each day. Also, I played a lot of pond hockey and always tried to work on my shooting and puck handling."

Learning how to handle the puck well is critical for a goalie who wants to get good. "But don't try to do too much with it," says Hextall, shown in Figure 14-8. "Overhandle the puck, and you can get in trouble fast. In addition, be careful when you pass it off to one of your teammates in the defensive zone; move it out from the boards or net and give him the chance to swoop in and take it clean."

Hextall, who in 1989 became the first netminder in NHL history to score a goal in a playoff game, used a blade that he says had "more of a bend to it than a curve. If a blade has a big curve to it, then you could have trouble stopping the puck. I used a stick that looked more like an eight-iron because it was bent backwards a little bit. With it tilted that way, I would shoot the puck harder and higher. And I think it helped me get rid of rebounds more quickly."

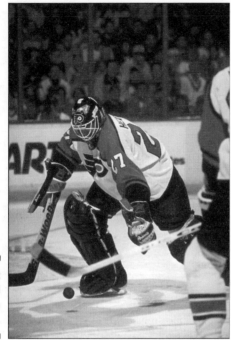

Figure 14-8:
Ron Hextall
pouncing on
the puck.

Mike Gartner on Power Skating

"It was my dad's idea for me to work on my skating at an early age," says the recently retired forward. "He put me in a power skating school when I was 8 or 9 years old, and I remember having to cruise around the ice for an hour and a half at a time without the puck. I hated it, but it made me a much better skater." In fact, it made Gartner one of the strongest in the NHL, and he won the league's fastest man competition during All-Star Weekend each of the three times he entered.

"Technique is very important," Gartner says. "Most players don't bend their knees enough, which means they don't get low enough. That provides the power they need when they finish their stride. It's important to take a full, elongated stride. You also have to remember to use your arms, to pump them like a sprinter does to build up speed. And don't stop moving your legs when you go into a turn; that's the time you want to accelerate" (see Figure 14-9).

Figure 14-9:
Mike
Gartner was
one of the
NHL's
fastest
skaters.

© NHL Images/Allsport/Glenn Cratty

Brian Leetch on Playing Defense

"One of the key things to remember is never look at the puck when an opposing forward is coming down on you," says the perennial All-Star defenseman. "Look at his chest instead, the logo on his sweater, so you won't get mesmerized by the puck." If your opponent is bigger than you, Leetch explains, positioning is critical. "If you're positioned properly, then he will have a harder time trying to outmuscle you," he says. "If your opponent gets even a little position on one side of you, he can use his strength to outmuscle you and get by. If, however, it's a smaller player who relies more on his speed than his strength, you want to give him room to the outside. Let him go to the outside, but be smart with your angle and don't let him beat you to the net."

Leetch, shown in Figure 14-10, has twice won the NHL's Norris Trophy, given each year to the league's top defenseman, and one of the reasons he is so successful is that he prepares. "It helps to know each player that you face," he explains. "Know what their tendencies are, their strengths and weaknesses. That will help you react quicker and figure out the best way to play them. And if there's a new guy on the ice, a player you have never seen before, watch from the bench to see how he does stuff, to understand what his moves are."

Figure 14-10:
Brian
Leetch,
a top
defenseman.

© NHL Images/Allsport/Nat Butler

It's tough trying to clear out a big, strong guy from the front of your net, and if you can't outmuscle him, Leetch suggests that you resort to timing. "Try to get to the player just as the puck is about to arrive," he says. "Don't let him take a clear shot or pass if you can help it."

And if your team gets caught in a *two-on-one* situation (two opposing forwards coming down on your goalie with only one defenseman back), the man defending must let the goalie "play" the shooter (the man with the puck) while forcing him outside and making sure he doesn't pass it across to his teammate. If that happens, the goalie will most likely be out of position, and the other team will have a very good scoring chance.

Mike Richter on Concentration and Focus

"A lot of times, after a stop in play, I will skate to the sideboards from the net," says Mike Richter, the New York Rangers' mainstay goalie (see Figure 14-11). "It has become a routine with me, and when you develop a routine, stick with it. It can help you focus.

Figure 14-11:
As a top goalie, Mike Richter knows the secrets of concentration.

"Different goalies will do different things to help their concentration when there is a stop in play," he continues. "Ron Hextall used to tap his stick. Patrick Roy sometimes talks to the goalpost. Other people I know stare at the dot in the face-off circle.

"When he played for the Chicago Blackhawks, Tony Esposito used to watch the clock and break the game into four- or five-minute segments," adds Richter. "I do the same thing. It can be awfully difficult to concentrate for 60 minutes straight — or at least it might seem that way. So it is better to break it down."

And if things are not going well, the All-Star goalie recommends a quick break. "Go over to your bench when play stops for a bit," he says. "Talk to somebody, loosen up. Then go back out to the net and start to refocus."

Adam Graves on Getting Open in Front

"A lot of times I try to get in behind the defensemen standing in front of the goal," says goal-scoring forward Adam Graves (see Figure 14-12). "Then we have two people screening the goalie, not one. And if you can't deflect the puck, at least you can make it difficult for the goalie to see.

"Also, I try not to be too tight to the goalie," Graves adds. "If you are too close, then it is easier for him to field a deflection. Plus, a shot from one of your teammates will often go flying right by you if you are too close to the goal. Stay back a bit, and you have a better chance of getting not only more shots but also better ones.

"It gets hard sometimes in front, with big defensemen beating on you," he continues. "When someone tries to move me, I think of a tripod, with two skates and a stick, and try to keep my balance that way. Keep your shoulders over your knees in a situation like that, and you'll do okay. Also, keep your stick away from a defenseman who is trying to tie it up. You'll need that to score. But if he is successful at that for some reason, then try to screen the goaltender while you are also trying to get yourself untangled."

Figure 14-12: Adam Graves is a master at getting open in front of the goal.

© 2000 NHL Images/Craig Melvin

Theo Fleury on Scoring without Size

"The key is to try and sneak around," says Theo Fleury, the diminutive (5'6"), high-scoring forward (see Figure 14-13). "Position yourself in such a way that when you get the puck you can shoot it right away, before anyone can hit you or try to knock you down. Personally, I try to get most of my offense off the rush. For someone my size, the chances to score around the net can be tough unless I can knock in a rebound.

"One of the things I try to do all the time is find a seam between the other team's forwards and defensemen in our offensive zone," Fleury says. "Sort of like a wide receiver in football finding the seam in a zone defense. I'll stand near the hash marks toward the face-off dot and then find room to shoot.

"Another thing I try to do is time my rebounds," he explains. "If I see a shot taken from the point, I try to time it so I get to the front of the net about the same time the rebound will. I am not as good as [seven-time NBA rebound leader] Dennis Rodman with rebounds yet, but I am working on it."

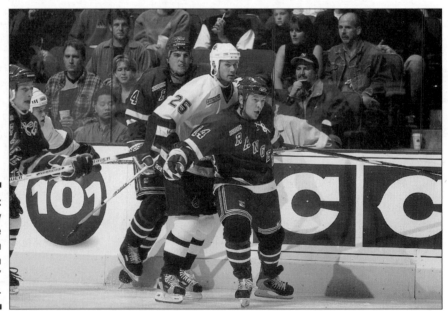

Figure 14-13:
Theo Fleury gets the most from every inch of his 5'6" frame.

© 2000 NHL Images/Jeff Vinnick

Rob Blake on Playing the Body

"The element of surprise is something I like to use," says Rob Blake, the Los Angeles Kings defenseman (see Figure 14-14). "Try to anticipate where the puck is going — and when it will get there — so you can throw a body check that really disrupts the play."

Blake also thinks it is important not to back up too far when the other team is moving down the ice into your defensive zone. "You have to put yourself in the position to be able to throw a check," he explains. "If you keep falling back as the opposing players come in, then you are not giving yourself the chance to do that. Stay up. Don't back up. And put a good hit on the guy who is trying to come down and score."

Figure 14-14:
Rob Blake.

© 2000 NHL Images/Craig Melvin

Chapter 15

Making Hockey a Good Experience for Everyone

*Y*oungsters need to learn and remember many things as they start to play the great game of hockey — and so do their parents and coaches. So we got in touch with our friends at the Canadian Hockey Association, which — like its American counterpart, USA Hockey — has a wealth of important educational materials on the game available for the asking. This chapter presents some of the tips the CHA offers on keeping the game fun and in the proper perspective.

Tips for Young Players

Following is some of the best advice we gleaned on the things a young player should remember as he or she starts playing hockey:

✔ **Enjoy yourself.** Remember, playing hockey is about having fun. Take the game seriously, but not so much so that you do not look forward to your games and practices. And make it fun for those you are playing with.

✔ **Practice, practice, practice.** Both on and off the ice. The only way to get good is to practice, and you don't always need ice to work on your game. Set up a net at home to hone your shot. Try some of the different practice devices that can help with the art of passing. And remember, when you are on the ice, carry a puck with you whenever possible. Get used to stick-handling and let it become second nature; it will, if you do it all the time.

✔ **Be a good sport.** Sportsmanship in any athletic endeavor is essential. And we think all people who play the game should abide by this Fair Play Code found in the Canadian Hockey Association's 3M Coaching Manuals:

1. I will play hockey because I want to, not just because others or coaches want me to.

2. I will play by the rules of hockey and in the spirit of the game.

3. I will respect my opponents.

4. I will control my temper — fighting and mouthing off can spoil the activity for everyone.

5. I will do my best to be a true team player.

6. I will remember that winning isn't everything, that having fun, improving skills, making friends, and doing my best are also important.

7. I will acknowledge all good plays and performances — those of my team and of my opponents.

8. I will remember that coaches and officials are there to help me. I will accept their decisions and show them respect.

Tips for Coaches

The CHA has an Initiation Program that outlines a number of things we think should be of paramount importance for coaches, especially leadership qualities and techniques associated with being a good instructor. And here are some of the most important suggestions:

✔ Be patient.

✔ Communicate well.

✔ Be willing to listen to suggestions.

✔ Motivate players.

✔ Use your influence as a role model effectively.

✔ Know and be yourself — be aware of your own strengths and weaknesses.

✔ Attend to individual differences and needs.

✔ Encourage independence, responsibility, exploration, and growth.

Making hockey fun

The association also offers the following tips on how coaches can stay positive and best handle themselves behind the bench, and how they can make the experience of playing hockey rewarding and fun for everyone involved:

- ✔ Being more positive:

    - Have realistic expectations.

    - Give positive feedback for desirable behavior right away.

    - Praise effort as much as you do results.

- ✔ Reacting to mistakes:

    - Give encouragement immediately after a player makes a mistake.

    - If a player knows how to correct the mistake, encouragement alone is sufficient.

    - When appropriate, give corrective instruction after a mistake, but always do it in an encouraging and positive way.

    - Avoid giving corrective instruction in a hostile or punitive way.

    - Avoid punishing players.

- ✔ Maintaining order and discipline:

    - Make your expectations for behavior very clear.

    - Try to strike a balance between allowing freedom and maintaining structure.

- ✔ Getting positive things to happen:

    - Set a good example of the behavior you want to see in your players.

    - Encourage effort; don't demand results all the time.

    - In giving encouragement, be selective so that it is meaningful.

    - Encourage players to support each other and reward them when they do so.

- ✔ Creating a good learning atmosphere:

    - Set realistic goals for your players.

    - Always give instructions positively, clearly, and concisely.

    - Use proper technique when demonstrating play.

    - Be patient; don't expect or demand more than the maximum effort.

    - Acknowledge and reward effort and progress.

✔ Communicating effectively:

- Ask yourself what your recent actions have communicated to your players.

- Encourage two-way communication between instructors and players.

- Be sensitive to individual needs.

- Communicate when the player is most receptive.

✔ Dealing with disruptive individuals:

- Give them additional responsibilities.

- Appeal to their sense of common courtesy.

- Be positive, not punitive.

- Discuss their behavior with their parent(s).

✔ Gaining respect:

- Establish your role as a competent and willing instructor.

- Be fair and considerate.

- Earn the respect of your players — don't demand it.

Playing fair

As it has done for players, the Canadian Hockey Association has developed a Fair Play Code for Coaches as well:

1. I will be reasonable when scheduling games and practices, remembering that players have other interests and obligations.

2. I will teach my players to play fairly and to respect the rules, officials, and opponents.

3. I will ensure that all players get equal instruction, support, and playing time.

4. I will not ridicule or yell at my players for making mistakes or for performing poorly. I will remember that players play to have fun and must be encouraged to have confidence in themselves.

5. I will make sure that equipment and facilities are safe and match the players' ages and abilities.

6. I will remember that participants need a coach they can respect. I will be generous with praise and set a good example.

7. I will obtain proper training and continue to upgrade my coaching skills.

8. I will work in conjunction with officials for the benefit of the game.

9. I will respect game officials.

Tips for Parents

Parents of hockey players must also uphold a similar code of behavior, especially when they attend games and practices. The Canadian Hockey Association says that setting a good example for kids — being a role model — is important, and it sets forth a series of "do's" that parents and guardians of youth participants should follow:

✔ Make sure that your child gets to all sports activities on time.

✔ Provide and maintain required sports equipment.

✔ Help your child get ready for practices and games.

✔ Let coaches or other team leaders know if your child will be absent or you change your pickup arrangements.

✔ Maintain a positive attitude toward the sport and every athlete's participation in it.

✔ Make sure that the sports organization has effective harassment, sexual abuse, and screening policies for coaches and officials in place.

✔ Let the leaders of your sports organization know of any concerns you may have.

✔ Conduct yourself in a way that promotes fair play.

You're outta here! Undesirable behavior

Be prepared, the CHA says, for officials or organizers of your youth sports organization to ask you to leave a facility if you engage in any of the following inappropriate behavior:

✔ Insulting athletes or officials (for example, name-calling and put-downs)

✔ Arguing or yelling at officials

✔ Suggesting or encouraging aggressive or "dirty" play

✔ Criticizing an athlete too harshly, causing the athlete unnecessary or unhealthy stress

✔ Using physical force or threatening force against another person

✔ Engaging in any type of harassment

Kids just wanna have fun

Finally, how can parents make hockey fun for their children? The CHA suggests the following relatively simple but important guidelines:

- ✔ Be positive and supportive.
- ✔ Be available and show interest in what they are doing; remember, parents are the most important and influential people in kids' lives.
- ✔ Play with them — on the pond, in the driveway.
- ✔ Have fun yourself.

Test your level of respect for the game

The Canadian Hockey Association has developed a "Shared Respect Initiative" that tries to get parents to think about their role in promoting respect for the game of hockey — and for the people who make it the great sport it is. How much do you respect the game of hockey and all its participants? See how you rate by checking off the statements you agree with. (The more you check off, the more respect you have.)

- ❏ The safety of the participants in the game is more important than the final score.

- ❏ I value the contribution of the coach in developing the players' talents, even though I may not always agree with his methods.

- ❏ I understand that officials do not make the hockey rules, they only apply them.

- ❏ I understand that children learn from adults, and my behavior reflects what I want children to learn.

- ❏ I understand that officials are responsible for ensuring that the game is played in a safe and fair manner for all participants.

- ❏ I understand that players, coaches, and officials are learning the game, and that people will make mistakes in the learning process.

- ❏ I may not cheer for the opposition team, but I will also not cheer against them or verbally abuse them.

- ❏ I understand that the biggest reason for players' and officials' quitting the game is abuse.

When players, coaches, parents, and officials recognize the value of each person's contribution to the game, the game is better for everyone. When respect is shared, we all win!

Chapter 16

Where to Go If You — and Your Children — Want to Play

In This Chapter
▶ Making contact with youth and adult leagues
▶ Getting back to basics: pond hockey

*H*ockey isn't only for professionals, and it doesn't matter if you aren't good enough to compete on your country's national team. Men and women of all ages and abilities play and enjoy the sport, and so do boys and girls as young as kindergartners. They participate in various youth and adult leagues around the world, they go to hockey schools and camps during summer vacations, and they organize pickup games on frozen lakes and ponds during winter's icy grip. In fact, plenty of opportunities exist for people who want to play the game, and the number of hockey leagues and associations has been growing steadily in recent years as the sport has become more and more popular.

Youth and Adult Leagues in Canada and the U.S.

You can find hundreds of leagues in North America that offer organized competition for players of all ages. Most leagues run from late fall to early spring, though some leagues operate all year round. Wherever they may be and however they are organized, hockey leagues are fun and a great way for people to enjoy the game.

What to look for

The important thing in finding the right league is determining what caliber of play is best suited for you and/or your children, for there are leagues designed to accommodate a wide range of aspirations and abilities. According to the people at USA Hockey, the sport's national governing body, there are two primary types of leagues:

- Recreational (or house) leagues
- Competitive (or travel) leagues

The recreational leagues usually play all their games in the same arena, hence the nickname "house." They are less serious and not as advanced skill-wise as the travel leagues, in which each team represents a city or region and plays half of its games in out-of-town rinks. Within those two categories, there are several variations. Some leagues don't allow checking of any kind, while others encourage it. Take a look at what's available in your area and see how the leagues fit your wants and needs as a player, or those of your children. Don't get involved in a competitive checking league, for example, if you're just looking for a noncontact recreational game. The idea is to find what works best for you and your level of talent.

How to join

There are a couple of ways to join a good league. One way is simply to contact the local ice rink and see what league, or leagues, operate out of that facility. The other way is to call USA Hockey if you are in the States (719-576-8724), or the Canadian Hockey Association if you are in Canada (403-777-3636). Both those groups are clearinghouses for information on amateur hockey and can not only tell you how to find different leagues all over North America but also advise you on which ones might best meet your needs and those of your children. (See Appendix B for more information on these — and other — organizations.)

Leagues in Other Parts of the World

As we mention in Chapter 5, hockey is played in more than 50 countries, and each one of those has some sort of amateur association that promotes youth and/or adult hockey. The best way to find out what different nations outside North America have to offer is to call the International Ice Hockey Federation, which is based in Zurich, Switzerland, at 41-1-289-8600. The IIHF has a wealth of information on the game as it is played everywhere from Finland and Spain to South Africa and Japan, and it has information on how to contact any of the different international leagues (see Chapter 5 for more info on the IIHF, or visit its Web site at www.iihf.com).

Hockey Camps and Schools in Canada and the U.S.

It has been a time-honored tradition in parts of Canada and the United States for youngsters to head off to hockey camp or school at the start of their summer vacation and work on their games for a few weeks, many times with coaches and players from the National Hockey League. And as the sport has grown in popularity, so has the number of camps and schools that cater to boys and girls. The best way to get information on those camps and schools is to check out the annual Summer Hockey School Guide that *The Hockey News* puts out each spring. It is chock-full of school and camp listings for North America and includes details on each one, such as age groups attending, hours spent on the ice, sleeping accommodations, specialized programs, and entertainment facilities.

Other good sources are USA Hockey and the Canadian Hockey Association, which also have comprehensive directories of hockey schools and camps, and your local ice rink.

For those who want to coach or simply learn more about the game (but not necessarily play), we recommend the Roger Neilson Coaching Clinic held each June in Windsor, Ontario. Roger is a longtime NHL coach who knows the game as well as anyone, and his camp is one of the best around. Check *The Hockey News* for more information.

Camps and Schools in Other Parts of the World

There is no shortage of camps and schools in other parts of the world, especially in northern Europe, and players can find plenty of opportunities abroad. The two best sources for these are *The Hockey News* annual directory and the International Ice Hockey Federation.

Pond Hockey

For those who grew up in ice hockey country — and we both did — nothing is quite like playing the sport on a frozen neighborhood pond or lake. The air is cold and clear, the ice hard and fast, the pickup games spirited and fun. We remember shoveling snow off the ice after evening blizzards, looking for pucks that had been inadvertently shot into the woods around the pond, and building our own goalie nets out of two-by-fours and chicken wire. We loved the sounds our skates made as we cut across the ice and the joy of passing a puck back and forth with a best friend as we scampered around the pond. We recall spending the better part of many winter weekends on the ice, of getting so cold some days that we couldn't feel the freezing wind against our faces anymore and had trouble untying our skates when the sun went down. And who can forget walking back into the warmth of our parents' homes later on and thawing out in front of the fireplace with a mug of hot chocolate?

Knowing when the ice is good — and keeping it that way

Oftentimes, the best ice of the year is the first ice, which comes to Canada and the northern United States in late fall and hasn't been marred by snow. It is clear and smooth, so much so that on most bodies of water you can see right through to the bottom. This is known as *black ice*, and it's as good as anything you'll find in a rink. Actually, it's better.

Black ice lasts only for the early stages of the outdoor hockey season, however, and after a while the skating surface gets whiter, thicker, and in most cases rougher. We never had Zambonis to resurface our ponds and lakes, but many times we tried the next best thing, and that was either hauling buckets of water out to the ponds, which we would pour down on the ice at the end of the day, or running a hose out there. The idea was to use the water to clean off the excess snow from all the skating and put a new layer of water on the surface, which would freeze by morning and make our makeshift rink good as new.

One note of caution about pond hockey: Always make sure that the ice is safe before you skate on it. The best way for youngsters to do that is have a parent come down and take a look at the place where they want to play, or better yet, a local policeman or fireman. If you aren't sure that the ice is thick enough, then wait. You can never be too careful when it comes to ice strength.

Holding your own in pickup games

There is something special about pickup hockey, and it provides the same sort of innocent fun as touch football or sandlot baseball. You go down to the pond, see who shows up, pick sides, and drop the puck. Usually, there are no forwards, no defensemen, and no goalies — just people playing together and having a good time. It doesn't take much to hold your own in games like those; just skate hard and do the best you can. If you get tired, you can slack off a bit and play defense or goalie. And when you get your second wind, you can glide back down ice and battle for the puck in front of your opponents' goal. The beauty of the game as it is played with that attitude is that there is no pressure to perform.

All anyone should care about is having fun. And skating around a pond with a bunch of friends in the middle of winter is good fun.

Pond-hockey etiquette

These are the essential rules for pond hockey:

- ✔ No lifting (sending the puck airborne with either a pass or shot)
- ✔ No checking
- ✔ No slap shots
- ✔ No fighting

Lifting the puck is prohibited strictly as a safety measure because typical pond-hockey attire doesn't include mouth guards, shin guards, thigh pads, shoulder pads, or cups. And since everybody takes a turn at playing goalie whenever the other team skates into the offensive zone, the netminder is without proper protection as well.

Checking is frowned upon for much the same reason, though it is also banned because the ages and sizes of players in a pond hockey game can vary greatly, and no one wants to see a chiseled 18-year-old beat up on a middle-aged skater. Or vice versa.

Slap shots are not allowed because of the danger that their speed presents, and fighting is strictly taboo — though there are still times when we drop our gloves, as players in the NHL often do, and wrestle each other to the ice, trying to pull jerseys over each other's heads and throwing mock punches.

Pond hockey has been around for a long time and will certainly be around for years to come (see Figure 16-1).

Figure 16-1:
An early
game of
pond
hockey at
McGill
University in
Montreal.

Chapter 17

What to Do If You Don't Have Any Ice

In This Chapter

▶ In-line skating
▶ Playing in-line and street hockey

*I*ce is nice, but you can still skate and play hockey without it. Back when we were kids, we shot plastic pucks at nets in the driveway and used tennis balls in the five-on-five games we played on our lawns. But today, we can do so much more off the ice, thanks to the development of "in-line" skates, which allow us to glide across paved surfaces such as driveways and parking lots almost as easily as hockey players streak down a stretch of ice. In fact, in-line skating and hockey have exploded in recent years and are now two of the fastest-growing sports in North America. In-line hockey leagues have sprouted up all over the world, and old-time street hockey, still being played in sneakers, has also never been bigger.

The development of in-line skates has made it possible for people in the Snow Belt to enjoy skating and hockey year round and allowed those who live in more temperate climes to play, watch, and experience different versions of the game that may not be exactly what is found in a National Hockey League arena, but still are pretty close. And it has also helped build hockey's popularity, both as a spectator and participatory sport, even further.

In-line Skating

Originally designed as a form of cross-training for ice hockey players, in-line skating now provides exercise, recreation, and transportation for millions.

The lowdown on in-line skates

In-line skates differ from the old roller skates in that they have four wheels in a straight line while traditional roller skates employ two wheels in front and two in back (see Figure 17-1). Basically, the boot used in the in-line skate is very similar to the one on an ice hockey skate, with thick padding on the ankles, strong support in the front, and a good heel cup to keep the feet in place. Their exterior is made of leather and nylon, and the inside generally consists of a synthetic leather known as *Clarino*. Models that are designed mostly for outdoor use have hard plastic toes for protection.

As for price, good-quality in-line skates for teens and adults start at $150 and run as high as $500. The major variable in price has to do with the type of track, or *chassis,* that is used to hold the wheels. The less-expensive ones are made of plastic or nylon, and those that cost more are made of aluminum. Skates can have different sizes of wheels, with the outside diameter ranging from 56 millimeters to 80 millimeters (2.2 to 3.1 inches). The smaller wheels allow skaters to turn more quickly, while the larger wheels let them go faster. Manufacturers include traditional ice skate makers CCM and Bauer, as well as Nike, which has gotten into both the ice hockey and in-line hockey games in a big way.

Figure 17-1:
A typical
in-line skate.

If you are the parent of a growing youngster, these prices may seem a bit steep for something that your child will outgrow in less than a year. If so, you may want to consider buying a set of pre-owned skates at a used sporting goods store. Remember, though, that the quality and selection of sizes and styles will vary from day to day and week to week at these stores, and if your child needs a certain size at a certain time, you may still have to buy a new pair. And once the kid tries on a shiny new pair of skates, the used ones will be a tougher sell in the future.

In-line skating equipment

Aside from their footgear, in-line skaters generally wear a sort of bicycle helmet, wrist guards, elbow pads, and knee pads. The best place to get all this gear is from the pro shop at your local ice rink or a sporting goods store that specializes in hockey equipment.

In-line Hockey and Street Hockey

In-line hockey is just what you would expect it to be: hockey played on in-line skates. *Street hockey,* on the other hand, is played on foot, using sneakers instead of skates. We often hear of roller hockey, and that's usually just another way of describing in-line skating. (Part of that confusion comes from the fact that the first brand of in-line skates to make any sort of splash was known as "Rollerblades.") But roller hockey can also refer to a sport played with the old quad roller skates, which have two wheels in front and two in back. That sport, however, represents only a small percentage of the off-ice hockey universe, so for the purposes of this section, we cover only the in-line and street hockey versions of the game.

Where and how they are played

Both in-line and street hockey are played all over the world. There are several hundred youth and adult in-line leagues in the United States and Canada alone, and a similar number overseas. There are professional leagues, national amateur events, summer in-line hockey camps, and an annual world championship.

The NHL sponsors an in-line hockey promotion called the NHL Breakout Tour, which rolls into selected NHL cities in the spring, summer, and fall. Players and fans of all ages can be part of weekend-long tournaments at each stop, either as participants or spectators. And the tour concludes each year with a national championship. In addition to the games, the tour includes skill contests that allow players to measure the speed of their slap shots and their sprints down "ice," as well as their shooting accuracy and stickhandling. Tour stops also include merchandise tents where you can purchase NHL Breakout apparel and hockey accessories. (Check out www.nhl.com for more information.)

In-line skating got so big in America that in 1994 USA Hockey started a special organization, USA Hockey InLine, whose mission is to promote the growth of the game and administer the sport as it is played in this country. And three years later it boasted 85,000 members. (Check out the Web site of USA Hockey InLine at www.usahockey.com/inline, as shown in Figure 17-2.) The focus on in-line hockey right now is more recreational than competitive, according to USA Hockey staff. It has been enjoying a tremendous amount of growth, and in many ways helps solve the biggest challenge USA Hockey faces as the sport's national governing body: access to facilities. Hockey has grown so quickly that people sometimes have trouble finding ice time. So in-line hockey is a terrific alternative. There is no dependence on an ice rink to play, or on cold weather.

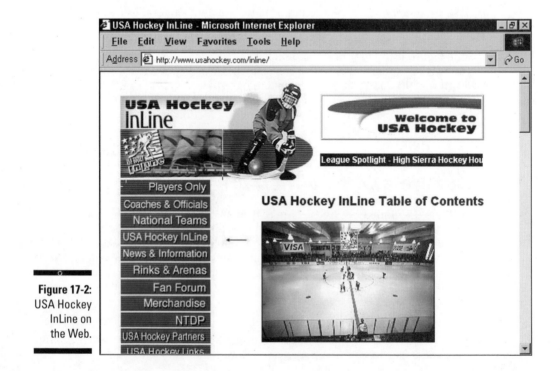

Figure 17-2:
USA Hockey
InLine on
the Web.

Speaking of rinks, in-line and street hockey can be played in any number of locales. Parking lots are popular venues, as are driveways or the concrete floors of ice rinks that haven't been flooded and frozen. That's one of the beauties of those sports: They don't require very fancy or extensive facilities.

What is needed for equipment

Obviously, the key component for in-line hockey is a pair of skates. Helmets are also essential, and if you are playing in a youth league, you will also need a cage to protect your face. Shin guards are worn, and so are elbow pads and gloves. Those items are all similar to the equipment that ice hockey players wear, though they are generally lighter and better ventilated (because in-line hockey is often played in warmer weather, and there's a greater need for the equipment to breathe).

People playing at a higher level of in-line hockey will don additional gear, including a sort of girdle with pads for the thighs, hips, and tailbone, as well as an athletic supporter and cup and shoulder pads. Their hockey pants, which will fit over their shin guards like sweat pants, generally have a special material called *cordura* over the knees to prevent skidding. The sticks feature hard plastic blades, and some of the hard plastic pucks that are used for in-line hockey have nylon pegs on each side to help them slide more easily on rink surfaces.

The gear needed for street hockey is not much different, the two primary exceptions being that sneakers are used instead of skates and hard plastic balls rather than pucks. Additionally, street hockey players don't usually wear shoulder pads and some of the other gear such as girdles.

As for prices, the people at Gerry Cosby's in New York say that helmets for kids run about $55, gloves $45, shin and elbow pads $40, and sticks $15. If you start playing competitively, you will need to spend more money on higher-quality gear and will have to buy things such as girdles ($50–$90), pants ($40–$60), and an athletic supporter and cup ($11).

Competition gloves for adults can run from $130 to $170, and shin and elbow pads can go as high as $60. Total cost to outfit a competitive in-line hockey player (forward or defenseman) is about $400 to $500, while a goalie may go as high as $1,000.

The rules

Well, the rules for in-line hockey and street hockey are more or less the same as ice hockey — with one major exception: There is *no* checking.

Part V
The Part of Tens

The 5th Wave   By Rich Tennant

"Shoot! I thought that thing would finally keep the Red Wings out of the alfalfa!"

Figure 21-4:
Eric Lindros
could hand
out the
punishment.

© 2000 NHL Images/Diane Sobolewski

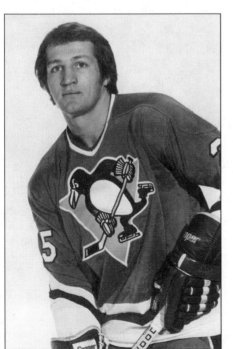

Figure 21-5:
Dennis
Owchar
let his
opponents
know he
was there.

Bob Plager

A onetime member of the St. Louis Blues and New York Rangers, Plager spent 14 seasons in the league and became well known for laying hefty hip checks on his opponents (see Figure 21-6). A tough player, Plager wasn't afraid to drop his gloves, either. Perhaps his most famous fight was with his brother Barclay when the two of them faced off against each other in a Junior Hockey game. It started on the ice with sticks and ended up in the arena hallway with fists.

Figure 21-6: Bob Plager knew how to take out his opponents.

Denis Potvin

Potvin was a longtime New York Islander captain and a brilliant defenseman who helped his team secure four consecutive Stanley Cup titles in the early 1980s. He put up more than 1,000 points and 1,300 penalty minutes in his career. Tough checker. If you played against him and took just a second to admire your shot or pass, WHAM! And then you'd be picking yourself up off the ice. (See Figure 21-7.)

Ulf Samuelsson

Samuelsson (shown in Figure 21-8) is a controversial Swede who has played for the Hartford Whalers, Pittsburgh Penguins, New York Rangers, Detroit Red Wings, and Philadelphia Flyers. He has never scored many goals (only 57 at the end of his 16th year), but he has piled up the penalty minutes (2,453). Like Marchment, Ulfie is a straight-ahead hitter who knows how to catch a player who's not paying attention.

Figure 21-8:
"Ulfie"
Samuelsson
knows how
to hit.

Scott Stevens

This defenseman is a great open-ice hitter, and at the start of the new millennium, he could be the league's best at that. He has a commanding presence and is best known for laying on the big hit just inside his own blue line. Stevens makes people keep their heads up when they come in on him as a result. The winner of the Conn Smythe Trophy for being the most valuable player of the 2000 playoffs, Stevens gets opponents thinking a little bit more about getting hit than they might otherwise.

Chapter 22

The Ten Best Games of All Time

*H*ockey has seen more than its share of classic contests over the years, hard-fought games that filled arenas with tension and energy and displayed superior passing, shooting, hitting, and goaltending.

This chapter contains a list of our top 11 games, arranged chronologically. (Sorry, folks, we couldn't pare the list down to a round 10.) They were all so good that people still feel the excitement when they talk about them.

March 24, 1936

The Montreal Maroons faced off against the Detroit Red Wings in this semifinal playoff game that would become the longest contest in National Hockey League history. The teams battled to a 0–0 tie for an incredible 176 minutes and 30 seconds — nearly three hours — before Detroit's Modere "Mud" Bruneteau took a pass from Hec Kilrea in the sixth overtime period and scored. It was 2:25 a.m. when the red light finally went on — six hours after the opening face-off. The Wings ended up winning the series and then beat Toronto for the Stanley Cup. (Figure 22-1 shows Bruneteau in action.)

Figure 22-1: "Mud" Bruneteau in the mid-1940s.

May 2, 1967

Game Six of the Stanley Cup Finals pitted the Toronto Maple Leafs against the Montreal Canadiens at a time when both teams dominated the NHL. Montreal's Gump Worsley and Toronto's Terry Sawchuk were brilliant in goal, but the Leafs held on to win the game 3–1, sealing the victory — and the championship — with an empty-net goal in the final minute. Toronto hasn't won the Cup since, and this was the last game for the traditional six-team NHL as the league expanded to 12 franchises the next season. Recognizing this, Leafs coach Punch Imlach sent out his older players — Marcel Pronovost, Allan Stanley, George Armstrong, and Bob Pulford — so they could be on the ice as the final seconds of that era ticked away.

April 8, 1971

This was Game Two of the first-round playoff series between the powerhouse Boston Bruins, who had set an NHL record that year by winning 57 games, and the Montreal Canadiens, who had finished 24 points behind in the standings. The Bruins had won the first game in the Boston Garden and were leading 5–1 late in the second period of Game Two when Henri Richard made a nifty move around Bobby Orr and scored to make it 5–2. The Canadiens suddenly caught fire and ended up winning that contest 7–5 and then upsetting the Bruins in a dramatic seventh game. Their ace in the hole was a rookie goaltender named Ken Dryden, who had played in only a handful of regular-season games. Buoyed by that win, the Canadiens went on to take the Cup.

December 31, 1975

The Canadiens battled the Central Red Army team in a tense exhibition contest that ended in a 3–3 tie. Many consider it to be the greatest hockey game ever played. Dryden was spectacular in net, turning away 13 shots; Vladislav Tretiak (shown in Figure 22-2) was even better for the Soviets, making 39 saves. Many people who were there say they had never seen so much emotion in the old Montreal Forum. When Steve Shutt (Figure 22-3) scored a goal, his agent Alan Eagleson got so excited that he hustled down from the stands and hugged Shutt on the bench.

Figure 22-2:
Central Red Army goalie Vladislav Tretiak.

Figure 22-3:
Steve Shutt
of the
Canadiens.

February 22, 1980

The Miracle on Ice, when the U.S. Olympic Team stunned the Soviet Union, and the rest of the sporting world, with its improbable 4–3 upset. Coach Herb Brooks had told his charges before the game, "You were meant to be here. This moment is yours," and they played as if they actually believed him, forcing the Soviet coach to remove Tretiak after one period and going on to win on a Mike Eruzione goal in the third period.

February 27, 1994

The Canadian and Swedish Olympic teams met in the gold medal game at Lillehammer and battled to a tie at the end of regulation in a gritty contest. After a scoreless overtime, then came the shoot-out. Canada's goaltender Corey Hirsch (shown in Figure 22-4) sat on his bench and looked away as his teammates took their penalty shots on Sweden's netminder Tommy Salo. Both men played valiantly, but the Swedes prevailed when Peter Forsberg (Figure 22-5) put the puck past Hirsch. The win meant so much to Sweden that a group of ten Air Force fighters met the team's plane as it entered that country's airspace and escorted it home.

Figure 22-4:
Canadian
Olympic
goalie Corey
Hirsch.

Figure 22-5:
Swedish
Olympic
forward
Peter
Forsberg.

May 25, 1994

The New York Rangers, facing elimination in their Eastern Conference Finals matchup with the New Jersey Devils, skated into the Meadowlands Arena that night down three games to two. Captain Mark Messier had guaranteed victory the day before in practice, but he didn't seem like much of a seer when his Rangers fell behind 2–0 after one period. The Blueshirts closed the gap to 2–1 after the second, and then Messier took over, scoring a hat trick in the final period to deliver a 4–2 win. His final goal was short-handed and came with less than two minutes left. "No one man wins a hockey game," he said in the locker room afterwards. Maybe not. But he had come close.

April 24, 1996

The Pittsburgh Penguins and Washington Capitals met in Game Four of the conference quarterfinals in Landover, Maryland. The score was tied 2–2 after regulation, and the teams headed into overtime. In the second extra frame, Penguins defenseman Chris Tamer knocked his own net off its moorings during a wild scramble in front of the crease, and the officials called a penalty shot — the first time in Stanley Cup history that a penalty shot was awarded in overtime. Joe Juneau took the shot but was stopped by Pittsburgh's Ken Wregget. The Pens went on to win in the fourth overtime on a Peter Nedved goal after almost 140 minutes of hockey. (Nedved is pictured in Figure 22-6.)

Figure 22-6:
Peter
Nedved in a
more
relaxed
setting.

September 7, 1996

Canada and Sweden met in Philadelphia in the semifinal round of the 1996 World Cup. The game had everything: hard hitting, great passing and play-making, fine goaltending. Sweden was the better team, but Canada's grit won it. Up 2–0 after two periods despite being outshot 26–14, Canada let Sweden tie it up in the third. But Theo Fleury (shown in Figure 22-7) put the puck in the net 12 seconds from the end of the second overtime period, and Canada went on to the finals.

Figure 22-7:
Canadian
World Cup
participant
Theo Fleury.

September 12, 1996

Days later, Team USA won the third and final game of its playoff for the World Cup against Canada at the Montreal Forum. This game had hard hitting and great end-to-end action throughout, and it was closer than the 5–2 score might indicate (the United States scored two empty-net goals at the end). Mike Richter played brilliantly, recording 37 saves, while John LeClair had two goals. It was the biggest international win for Team USA since the 1980 Olympic team's gold at Lake Placid. Afterward, veteran referee Kerry Fraser and linesmen Gord Broseker and Ray Scapinello said it was the best game any of them had ever worked.

February 17, 1998

Team USA beat Team Canada in the women's gold medal game of the Nagano Olympics in a brilliant contest that featured spectacular goaltending by America's Sarah Tueting and Canada's Manon Rheaume as well as tight checking and tremendous penalty killing. The U.S. squad took a 1–0 lead in the early part of the second period and made it 2–0 at the start of the third. But the Canadians, who had won four world championships, came storming back, scoring their first goal on a power play with just four minutes to go. The dramatic, end-to-end action continued right to the finish, and Team USA prevailed 3–1 when it scored an empty-net goal with just seconds remaining. Easily the best women's hockey game ever played.

Special Mention: The 1972 Canada-Soviet Series

You cannot overestimate the importance that the people of Canada and the Soviet Union placed on this eight-game series pitting the world's primary hockey powerhouses against each other at the peak of the Cold War. Canadians remember diligently following that series the way some people can still recall watching the Watergate hearings or the perils of Apollo 13. The series was the stuff of folklore in Canada and was recently voted the top sports story of the century there.

The teams played the first four games in Canada (Montreal, Toronto, Winnipeg, Vancouver), and the Soviets surprised the squad of Canadian NHL stars by winning two while tying another and losing only one. Canadian hockey fans seemed shocked at how closely matched the teams were and frustrated at how their team was being handled. A chorus of boos rang down from the stands during Game Four in Vancouver, where the Russians won 5–3, and center Phil Esposito was so irked at that surly response that he grabbed a microphone after the loss and urged the spectators to support — and not berate — the Canadian squad. It didn't help matters any when Canada lost the first game in Russia 5–4 after jumping out to a 3–0 lead. But then the team collected itself enough to win the sixth and seventh games. And in the eighth game, Paul Henderson scored with only 34 seconds remaining to give Canada a 6–5 win and a 4–3–1 record for the series.

An entire nation exalted, and hockey fans all over the world started talking about this exciting matchup. In fact, many of them still talk about it today, and why not? It was one of the best ever.

Chapter 23

The Ten Best Hockey Personalities

*L*ike any sport, hockey has more than its share of personalities. Some do and say outrageously funny things, while others simply play the game with great style and flair. Then, of course, there are combinations of both. After searching far and wide, we came up with this collection of characters, all involved in some way with the game of hockey and all just a little bit out of the ordinary.

Don Cherry

Brash, controversial, and opinionated, the onetime Boston Bruins and Colorado Rockies coach now makes his living in television, offering his opinions in the "Coach's Corner" on the Canadian Broadcasting Corporation's popular *Hockey Night in Canada*. Don Cherry has been a fan favorite since his coaching days, and his blue-collar style and nationalist tilt make him enormously popular in Canada. He loves a good brawl and is known to watch hockey fights on his VCR. He is tough on European players and others not born north of the border, as well as those who decry violence in the sport. His nickname is "Grapes." During his first game back in Boston after leaving the Bruins, he called time-out with his Rockies ahead in the final minute and started signing autographs for the fans around his bench while his former bosses stewed. He is also an eccentric dresser who fancies high-collared, custom-made shirts. (See Figure 23-1.)

Figure 23-1:
Cherry in his
coaching
days.

Phil Esposito

One of the great scorers in National Hockey League history, Esposito played 18 seasons for the Chicago Blackhawks, Boston Bruins, and New York Rangers, recording 717 goals and 873 assists. He was a passionate and super- stitious member of two Stanley Cup championship teams. He donned a black turtleneck underneath his Bruins jersey one night for a game against the Toronto Maple Leafs because he had a cold, and he scored three goals. So he wore it every game after that. He always dressed right to left, putting his right sock on before his left, and so on. Famous for his collection of good luck charms, his locker looked like something from a gypsy's caravan with beads, rabbits' feet, and other trinkets hanging all over the place.

John Ferguson

Ferguson scored 145 goals during his eight years with the Montreal Canadiens (in which he won five Cups), but he was much better known for his fighting, compiling more than 1,200 penalty minutes in his career. He retired in 1971 and then went on to serve as coach and general manager of the New York Rangers and general manager of the Winnipeg Jets. In his autobiography, *Thunder and Lightning,* Ferguson wrote, "When you get right down to it, I made it my business to be an absolutely miserable SOB on the ice, all of the time." He was. At the opening face-off of his first NHL game, he got into a fight with Boston Bruins bad boy Ted Green, who thumped him soundly. He was once scheduled to fight heavyweight boxer — and Canadian champion — George Chuvalo in a three- round bout, but he had to back out when his bosses in Montreal objected.

Nick Fotiu

Nick Fotiu, a Staten Island, New York, native, grew up playing roller hockey and managed to stick in the NHL for 13 seasons. He was a big New York Rangers fan as a kid and wormed his way into Madison Square Garden to see them play whenever he had the chance. (See Figure 23-2.) He never caught a puck in the stands, so he made it a point as a pro to give away as many as he could to fans. It was not unusual for Fotiu to be the last person to leave the ice after pregame warm-ups; he'd skate around the rink and toss pucks up to kids in different parts of the stands. Sometimes, after practice, he'd sit up in the cheap seats in Madison Square Garden with a cup of coffee and think about the good old days when he was a fan in the stands. After leaving the Rangers, Nick went on to play for the Hartford Whalers, Calgary Flames, Philadelphia Flyers, and Edmonton Oilers, retiring in 1989. He scored 60 goals and amassed nearly 1,400 penalty minutes.

Famous for practical jokes, Fotiu once swiped a lobster from a hotel restaurant and put it on his sleeping roommate Bill Goldsworthy's chest. But only after taking the rubber bands off its claws.

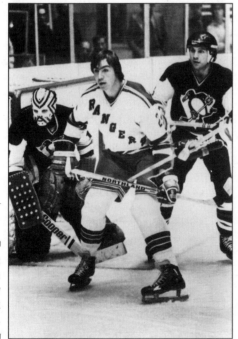

Figure 23-2:
Fotiu with the New York Rangers.

Bernard "Boom Boom" Geoffrion

The longtime Montreal Canadiens star, who also played for a time with the New York Rangers, scored 393 goals and recorded 429 assists over 16 seasons. He won six Stanley Cups as well. He helped to popularize the slap shot, hence his nickname. A Hall of Famer, Geoffrion won the Rookie of the Year award in 1952 and the Most Valuable Player award in 1961, and twice led the league in scoring. During the 1961 season, he hurt his knee and had it set in a cast. But as the Stanley Cup playoffs heated up, he began to get antsy. So he called over teammate Doug Harvey one night as they traveled by train to their next game and said, "Let's get this thing off." The two of them went into the women's room and hacked the plaster off with a borrowed knife. Geoffrion also coached NHL teams in Atlanta, Montreal, and New York, giving memorable pregame speeches, including one in Atlanta that went, "There are three things we must do tonight, and that is shoot and pass."

Bobby Hull

The Golden Jet brought great glamour to hockey in the 1960s and helped popularize the game like no one before him. He became famous for his blonde hair and Greek god–like physique as well as for his slap shot, which other players began imitating, and his all-around abilities. He killed penalties. He anchored the power play. He scored goals. And he signed every autograph. Many believe that Hull's magnetism was one of the main reasons why the league decided to expand from 6 to 12 teams after the 1967 season. He was also a major factor in the creation — and six-year survival — of the World Hockey Association; Hull jumped to the Winnipeg Jets of the upstart league in 1972, signing a deal that paid him the then-enormous sum of $2 million over five years and giving the league instant credibility. If an injury kept him out of a game, attendance figures were down 5,000 fans or so. Hull won three scoring titles and started nine All-Star Games. In 1966 he became the first NHL player to score more than 50 goals in a season. All told, he put the puck in the net 610 times during his 16-year career.

Tom McVie

The longtime minor-league player finally made it to the NHL in 1975–76 when he coached the Washington Capitals. He later coached the Winnipeg Jets and the New Jersey Devils. He played for a spell in the old Western Hockey League for Hal Laycoe, a former NHL defenseman and a stickler for punctuality. One day before a game in Los Angeles, Laycoe called a team meeting by the hotel swimming pool for noon. All players were there by 11:59 a.m., except for

McVie. All of a sudden, however, he stepped out on the balcony of his third-floor room and dove into the pool, clothes and all. "Coach," he shouted when he came out of the water, "you can't fine me for being late."

He would sometimes stuff a regulation-size hockey puck into his mouth to amuse his teammates and skate around practice that way.

Red Storey

Storey was an NHL Hall-of-Fame referee who also worked games in the Canadian Football League, sometimes doing both in the same day. A big man with flame-red hair, he is still revered as an after-dinner speaker in Canada. He is also quick-witted and self-effacing, as evidenced by his encounter with a fan at the old Boston Garden some years ago. A freak snowstorm had held up Storey's arrival, and as a result the game didn't start on time. When Storey finally skated onto the ice, a fan yelled down: "Hey Storey, what time are you going to get going?" Not breaking stride, he said: "If I could tell time, do you think I'd still be a referee?"

Dave "Tiger" Williams

Anyone who racks up just under 4,000 regular-season penalty minutes and spends more than 66 games in the box has to have personality, right? A 14-year veteran who played for five teams, Williams was a fearless player who liked to use his fists — and anything else — to intimidate his opponents. He was an incessant talker who spewed insults and other indelicacies during games. However, he used his hands for more than just fighting, scoring 241 goals. After he'd put a puck in the net, Tiger would skate to center ice with his stick between his legs and ride it like a witch's broom, waving to the fans as he glided by, driving the other team crazy. He also had a fierce temper; he once became so enraged that he threw chairs out of the penalty box and onto the ice. Another time he slammed the door to the box so hard that the glass fell out.

Lorne "Gump" Worsley

Nicknamed after the cartoon character Andy Gump, Worsley was a hefty Hall-of-Fame goaltender who played 861 NHL games, only six of them with a mask (see Figure 23-3). He had a real fear of flying, yet he survived the NHL travel regimen for 21 seasons. He also won four Stanley Cups. When asked by a reporter after a particularly tough game what team was hardest on him, Worsley answered, "The Rangers." And that was the team he played for at the time. He had some difficult moments in New York, thanks in no small part to his coach, Phil Watson. One day after the Rangers had suffered a bad loss, the coach met the press and said, "How can we win when our goalie has a beer belly?" When reporters informed the Gumpster what Watson had said, he replied, "That just shows what a dope we have for a coach. Everybody knows I don't drink beer; just whiskey."

Figure 23-3: "Gump" Worsley during his time with the Montreal Canadiens.

Chapter 24

The Ten Best Minor League Players

*M*any hockey fans have never heard of them, and most of their biggest moments as players occurred before sparse crowds in cities like Hershey, Portland, Muskegon, and Providence. Like thousands of athletes throughout Europe and North America, they hoped to play regularly in the National Hockey League, but in most cases they weren't quite good enough to make much of a mark when they did get the call. But they were dedicated players who loved the game and never gave up on their dreams.

We talked to hockey mavens across the United States and Canada and came up with a list of the top minor league players of all time. One, goalie Johnny Bower, went on to star in the NHL. But the rest didn't have much more than a cup of coffee there, if that. All of them, however, did big things in the minors.

Johnny Bower

Bower was a dominating goalie who played for Providence and Cleveland in the American Hockey League before starting a 15-year NHL career that brought him four Stanley Cup Championships, a Vezina Trophy as the league's outstanding goaltender, and a hallowed spot in the Hockey Hall of Fame. At one point in the minors, Bower had a shutout streak of nearly 250 minutes, which adds up to four-plus games. He won many of the AHL's performance awards, but he still had a hard time breaking into the NHL because the league had only six teams in those days, and not many jobs for netminders, no matter how good they were. He spent eight years in the minors before getting his chance with the New York Rangers in 1953. Bower recorded five shutouts his first season in New York and unseated Gump Worsley as the starter. He went on to play until 1970, spending most of his years with the Toronto Maple Leafs. No one was ever sure about his age, but Bower was said to be 46 years old when he finally retired.

Jock Callander

Callander played center in 800-plus games in the International Hockey League with Toledo, Muskegon, Atlanta, and Cleveland. He also competed in the Central Hockey League in Utah and Montana. His lack of speed kept him in the minors for most of his career, but he was a brilliant playmaker who did a great job on the power play. He spent parts of five years in the NHL with the Pittsburgh Penguins and Tampa Bay Lightning but only played in 109 regular-season games, scoring a total of 22 goals and chalking up 29 assists. He did, however, earn a Stanley Cup Championship ring with the Pittsburgh Penguins in 1992.

Guyle Fielder

Fielder was not very smooth, but he was one of the smartest centermen to ever lace up a pair of skates. He played mostly for Seattle in the Western Hockey League. He got called up to the Detroit Red Wings in the 1950s and skated on a line with Hall of Famers Gordie Howe and Ted Lindsay. But Fielder didn't like it there and eventually asked to be sent back to Seattle. He spent parts of four seasons in the NHL with Detroit, the Chicago Blackhawks, and the Boston Bruins, but he only played in nine regular-season games and never recorded a goal or assist. He is still considered one of the best to ever play in the minor leagues.

Dick Gamble

The left winger scored 468 goals in 898 minor league games during the 1950s and '60s, mostly for teams in Buffalo and Rochester. He had 30 goals or more in 11 seasons. Gamble was a good up-and-down winger who possessed a tremendous shot. He played at various times for the Montreal Canadiens, Chicago, and Toronto in the NHL and competed on two Stanley Cup–winning teams. When he left the game in 1967, he had scored 41 goals in 195 NHL contests.

Fred Glover

Glover scored 20 goals or more in 16 AHL seasons with Indianapolis and Cleveland. He was a tough forward and a never-give-up style of player. His team in Cleveland once won three consecutive championships. He made it to the NHL in 1948 and played 92 games over five seasons for Detroit and Chicago, netting 13 goals and adding 11 assists.

Scott Gruhl

Gruhl was another longtime minor-leaguer who did not skate well but was able to do everything else — be it scoring, checking, or passing — and do it well. In 13 IHL seasons, Gruhl recorded 596 goals, 703 assists, and nearly 2,300 penalty minutes. He played with a lot of energy and passion and was an abrasive sort who was a real pain to play against. But you loved him if he was on your team. He played in only 20 games over three seasons in the NHL for the Los Angeles Kings and Pittsburgh Penguins in the 1980s. His NHL career stats include three goals and three assists.

Willie Marshall

Marshall played 20 seasons in the AHL for teams like the Pittsburgh Hornets, Providence Reds, Baltimore Clippers, Rochester Americans, and Hershey Bears. He was a tough, heady forward who made beautiful passes. He played in 33 NHL games with Toronto in the mid-1950s, scoring one goal. Marshall was another victim of the league's being very small and full of great players in those days. With today's pay scale, he would make $4 million a year. And be worth every penny.

Dave Michayluk

The hardworking forward scored 100 or more points in nine consecutive seasons in the minors, playing in cities such as Kalamazoo, Springfield, and Muskegon. Michayluk made it to the NHL in 1981 and played a total of 14 games over three years for the Philadelphia Flyers and Pittsburgh, scoring just two goals. However, he got his name on the Stanley Cup in 1992 when the Pens won their second consecutive title.

Willie O'Ree

A legend with the San Diego Gulls of the Western League, he became the first player of African descent to compete in the NHL, breaking the so-called color barrier in 1958 when he joined the Boston Bruins. The winger played a total of only 45 games over two seasons in the NHL, scoring just 4 goals and recording 10 assists. But he made a huge contribution just by getting there. He played professional hockey for 11 teams over a 21-year career and is regarded as one of the fastest skaters in the history of the game, even though he lost sight in his right eye after a puck hit him there when he was 18 years old. He twice led the Western League in goals, tallying 38 in both the 1964–65 and 1968–69 seasons. He retired in 1979 but is still an active supporter of the game.

Len Thornson

The high-scoring forward with the IHL's Fort Wayne Komets during the 1960s led the league in scoring three different seasons and posted more than 100 points a year seven times. He wasn't a great skater, but he was a very deceptive puck handler and knew how to shoot.

Chapter 25

Ten Timeless Tips for Better Hockey

*H*owever you look at it, hockey is a great game. But we think that players and fans can enjoy it even more if they just follow some simple advice. You didn't ask for it, but we're going to give it to you anyway. After all, it's our book.

Learn to Skate

You can't run before you walk, and you can't play hockey before you know how to skate. It will make the game more enjoyable, and make you a better player, if you figure out how to scoot around the ice long before you start working on slap shots and no-look passes. Take power-skating lessons if need be, read books of instruction (like ours). But make sure you spend some time learning how to skate well before you do much else with the game.

Wear a Helmet

Ice is slippery stuff, and it's easy to fall down the wrong way during a hockey game, even if you are a pro. So don't take any foolish chances. Wear a helmet, no matter how old you are. Even if you're just gliding quietly around a pond or rink, you never know what could happen. Always be on the safe side.

Don't Skate on Thin Ice

Speaking of ice, make sure the stuff you decide to skate on is thick enough. We know, it's not a problem for the people who use rinks full of refrigeration equipment. But playing on ponds is still big throughout Canada and the northern United States, and people there need to make sure that the surface they're playing on is secure.

Always Keep Your Head Up

There's nothing a hulking defenseman likes to see more than some unsuspecting forward carrying the puck up ice with his head down. OUCH! Get used to handling the puck with your head up. And keep it that way when you go into the boards; this will lessen the chance of a serious neck injury if you fall or get checked into them.

Be a Team Player

Hockey's not like tennis or golf. It's a team sport, and the best teams are the ones that play together. Pass the puck. Get open in front of the net. Cover for your teammates. Work hard for them. And don't let opposing players mess with anyone on your squad. It's important to stick up for each other.

Go and See a Game Live

No sport in the history of the world is more fun to watch in person than hockey. Whether it's your brother's high school game, a big-time college contest, the minor leagues, or the National Hockey League, get some tickets and check it out. A Stanley Cup playoff game is the best, with the forwards whirling around; the defensemen throwing solid body checks; the goalies kicking out hard, low shots from the point; and the crowd building itself into a near frenzy. It's hard to beat a good game.

Make Sure Your Equipment Fits

Few things are worse than a pair of skates that are either too tight or too loose. And a stick that's the wrong length isn't going to produce as many goals. So take the time to get the proper gear and make sure it fits. Also, take care of what you have. Hockey equipment can be expensive, but it will last for quite a while (as long as you aren't growing a couple of inches every year). So wipe down your skate blades and dry out your pads after every game and practice.

Use Your Stick Properly

Shoot with it, pass with it, use it for balance. You can scratch your nose with it, for all we care. Just don't flail it around like some martial arts weapon.

Watch Hockey in All the Right Places

Our favorites are the Madison Square Garden Network; the Canadian Broadcasting Corporation, where *Hockey Night in Canada* is aired; and ABC and Fox SportsNet. Those are the places where JD works when he's not pretending to be William Faulkner. What a surprise, right? Also, check out the 2002 Olympics on NBC. Hey, we're not above making a few shameless plugs.

Be Free

Organized leagues are great fun, but sometimes it's nice to get away from all that structure and just play. We played pond hockey as kids and shot tennis balls off our driveways into nets set up by the garage doors. We played with plastic pucks and sticks in dormitory hallways and scrambled around parking lots in the midst of street hockey games. Street hockey is the sport in one of its purest forms, and it's well worth trying. Just be careful not to break any windows.

Part VI
Appendixes

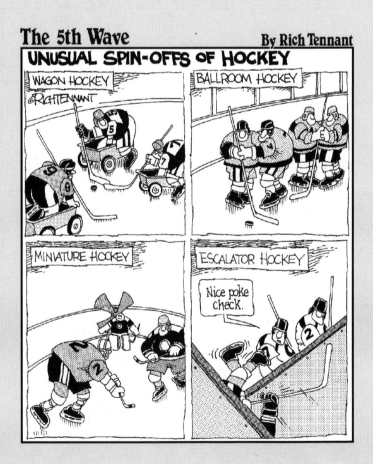

The 5th Wave   By Rich Tennant

UNUSUAL SPIN-OFFS OF HOCKEY

WAGON HOCKEY

BALLROOM HOCKEY

MINIATURE HOCKEY

ESCALATOR HOCKEY

Nice poke check.

In this part . . .

In this part, we show you how to talk hockey like a pro, and after reading this section you should be able to hold your own with even the most knowledgeable players, fans, or coaches. We then provide the names of various hockey organizations around the world, from Pee-Wees to the pros, so that you can track down whatever information you may need to know about watching and playing this wonderful game. We also introduce you to the signals you see the officials make at a hockey game, whether it be ice hockey or roller hockey. We finish with a set of lists that range from Hockey Hall of Fame members to statistics showing you some of hockey's greatest accomplishments.

Appendix A

Hockey Speak

Altercation
Any physical interaction between two or more opposing players that results in a penalty (or penalties) being assessed.

Assist
An assist is credited to a player who helps set up a goal. Assists are awarded to the last players to handle the puck immediately preceding the goal. There is a maximum of two assists per goal.

Attacking zone
When you are on the attack, your attacking zone is between your opponent's blue line and goal line.

Back check
Forwards in their offensive zone skate back quickly to their own defensive zone to protect their goal and keep the opponent from shooting.

Blocker
For the goalie, the glove that goes on the hand that holds the stick.

Blue line
One of two lines running across the width of the rink, one on either side of the red line. The area between the blue lines is called the neutral zone. See Chapter 1 for a diagram of the rink.

Boarding
Violently checking an opponent into the boards from behind. Boarding is illegal and warrants a penalty.

Boards
The wall around a hockey rink (which was at one time really made of wood but which is now usually of fiberglass) measuring about 42 inches high and topped off by synthetic glass to protect the spectators while giving them a good view of the action.

Body check

A body check is when you use your body against an opponent who has possession of the puck. Legal body checking must be done only with the hips or shoulders and must be above the opponent's knees and below the neck. Unnecessarily rough body checking is penalized.

Box

A defensive alignment (similar to the *diamond*) often used by a team defending against a power play. See Chapter 9 for all the details.

Breakaway

A player in control of the puck has a breakaway when the only opponent between him and the opposition's goal is the goalie (and a reasonable scoring opportunity exists).

Breakout

The play used by the attacking team to move the puck out of its own zone and up the ice toward the opponent's goal.

Butt ending

Using the shaft of the stick to jab or attempt to jab an opposing player. Known in Quebec as "donner six pouces" (to give six inches).

Catcher

For the goalie, this is a glove (which looks like a fancy first baseman's mitt) that goes on the non-stick hand.

Center

In a traditional alignment with three forwards, the center plays between the left and right wings. See Chapter 1 for information on the positions.

Changing on the fly

When players from the bench substitute for players on the ice while the clock is running. See Chapter 8 for details on how an NHL coach approaches this task.

Charging

Running, jumping, skating, or charging into another player in an aggressive manner.

Château Bow-Wow

A term for the "doghouse" — where hockey players go when they mess up.

Clearing the puck

When the puck is passed, knocked, or shot away from the front of the goal net or other area.

Crease

The semicircular area in front of each goal is called the crease. (See Chapter 1 for a diagram of the rink.) If an attacking player interferes with the goalkeeper in the crease, a goal may be disallowed and, in certain instances, a penalty may be called. The crease is painted blue. The goal crease is designed to protect the goalies from interference by attacking players. The area marked on the ice in front of the penalty timekeeper's seat is for the use of the referee.

Cross checking

Hitting an opponent with the shaft of the stick while both hands are on the stick and no part of the stick is on the ice.

Defending zone

When the other team is on the attack, the defending zone is the area between your goal line and your blue line.

Defensemen

Two defensemen usually try to stop the opponent's play at their own blue line. The defensemen block shots and also clear the puck from in front of their goal. Offensively, defensemen take the puck up the ice or pass the puck ahead to the forwards; they then follow the play into the attacking zone and help keep it there. See Chapter 1 for the lowdown on positions.

Deke

A deke is a fake by a player in possession of the puck in order to get around an opponent or to make a goalie move out of position. To deke, you move the puck or a part of your body to one side and then in the opposite direction. ("Deke" is taken from "decoy.")

Delay of game

This is called when a player purposely delays the game. Delay of game is commonly called when a goalie shoots the puck into the stands without the puck deflecting off a skater or the glass. Delay of game also occurs when a player intentionally knocks a goalpost out of its stand (usually in an attempt to prevent a goal from being scored).

Delayed offside

In this situation, an attacking player has preceded the puck into the offensive zone (normally a case of offside), but the defending team has gained possession of the puck and can bring it out of their defensive zone without any delay or contact with an opposing player.

Diamond

A defensive alignment (similar to the *box*) often used by a team defending against a power play. See Chapter 9 for all the details.

Dig

An attempt to gain possession of the puck in the corners of the rink.

Directing the puck

Changing the course of the puck in a desired direction by using the body, skate, or stick.

Dive

When a player exaggerates being hooked or tripped in an attempt to draw a penalty.

Elbowing

Using the elbow to impede or disrupt the opponent.

Empty net goal

A goal scored against an opponent that has pulled its goalie from the ice.

Face-off

The action of an official dropping the puck between the sticks of two opposing players to start play.

Fisticuffs

When a player throws a punch (closed fist) and makes contact with an opponent.

Five-hole

The area in the opening between a goalie's leg pads. See the sidebar "The different holes" in Chapter 14 for a description of all the holes.

Flat pass

A pass in which the puck remains on the surface of the ice.

Flex

Hockey sticks come in different degrees of flex — medium, stiff, and extra stiff. A stronger player, who hits more powerful shots usually wants a stiffer stick.

Flip pass

A pass in which the puck is lifted so that it goes over an opponent or his stick.

Forecheck

Forwards forecheck by hurrying into the opponent's defensive zone to either keep the puck there or take it away.

Forward

The center and the wings are traditionally considered to be the forwards. Refer to Chapter 1 for information on these positions.

Freezing the puck

A player freezes the puck by holding it against the boards with the stick or skates. A goalie freezes the puck (when the opposition is threatening to score) by either holding the puck in the glove or trapping it on the ice. *Note:* A delay-of-game penalty can be called if the goalie freezes the puck when the opposition is not threatening.

G

An abbreviation for "goals."

Game suspension

When a player, coach, or manager receives a game suspension, that person can't participate in the next scheduled game.

Goal

A goal is achieved when the entire puck crosses the goal line and enters the net. You can't deliberately kick it in or bat it in with a glove, although a goal is counted when a puck deflects off a player (but not off an official). A goal is worth one point.

Goal judge

A goal judge sits behind each goal (off ice!) and signals when the puck has crossed the red goal line by turning on a red light above his station. The referee can ask the goal judge's advice on disputed goals, but the referee has final authority and can overrule the goal judge.

Goaltender

The goaltender's main job is to keep the puck from entering the goal net. The goaltender is also known as the goalie, the goalkeeper, or the netminder.

GP

An abbreviation for "games played."

Great One

The Great One is none other than Wayne Gretzky.

Habs

A nickname for the Montreal Canadiens. It comes from the French "habitants" (those who live here).

Hat trick

A player who scores three goals in one game achieves a hat trick.

Head butting

Using the head while delivering a body check (headfirst) in the chest, head, neck, or back area; or using the head to strike an opponent.

Heel of the stick

The point where the shaft of the stick and the bottom of the blade meet. See Chapter 2 for a diagram of a stick.

High sticking

Carrying the stick above the shoulder to use against the opponent.

Holding

Using your hands on an opponent or the opponent's equipment to impede your opponent's progress.

Hooking

Applying the blade of the stick to any part of an opponent's body or stick and pulling or tugging with the stick in order to disrupt that opponent.

Icing

An infraction called when a player shoots the puck from his side of the red line across the opponent's goal line (as diagrammed in Chapter 3). Play is stopped when an opponent (other than the goalie) touches the puck. The face-off is held in the offending team's end of the ice. A team that is short-handed can ice the puck without being penalized.

Injury potential penalties

Injury potential penalties include butt ending, checking from behind, head butting, spearing, board checking, charging, cross checking, elbowing, kneeing, high sticking, holding the face mask, slashing, and roughing. A linesman may report these infractions occurring behind the play to the referee (after the next stoppage of play) if the referee did not see them.

In-line hockey

Hockey played on in-line skates. See Chapter 17.

Interference

Making body contact with an opponent who does not have possession of the puck. Interference is also called when a player makes contact with the goaltender.

Kneeing

Using the knee in an effort to impede or foul an opponent.

Left-wing lock

Coach Scotty Bowman often uses this formation, in which his left wing seldom forechecks in the offensive zone but stays back to help out defensively. See Chapter 8.

Linesman

Two linesmen are used to call offside, offside passes, and icing, and to handle all face-offs not occurring at center ice. Although they don't call penalties, they can recommend to the referee that a penalty be called.

Neutral zone

The central ice area between the two blue lines (neither the defending nor the attacking zone). Chapter 1 has a diagram.

Off-ice (minor) officials

These officials include the official scorer, game timekeeper, penalty timekeeper, and the two goal judges. The referee has full control of all game officials and has the final decision.

Offside

A team is offside when a player crosses the attacking blue line before the puck does (as diagrammed in Chapter 3). A face-off then takes place just outside that blue line. The determining factor in most offside situations is the position of the skates: Both skates must be completely over the blue line ahead of the puck for the player to be offside.

Offside pass

An offside pass (also known as a "two-line" pass) occurs when a member of the attacking team passes the puck from behind his own defending blue line to a teammate across the center red line. (See Chapter 3 for a diagram.) If the puck precedes the player across the red line, the pass is legal. Also, an attacking player may pass the puck over the center red line and the attacking blue line to a teammate if the puck precedes that teammate across the blue line. The face-off after an offside pass takes place at the spot where the pass originated.

One-timer

Shooting the puck immediately upon receiving it without stopping it first. A one-timer is an effective way to beat the goalie before he can slide from one side of the crease to another.

Penalty

A penalty is the result of an infraction of the rules by a player or team official. A penalty usually results in the removal of the offending player (or team official) for a specified period of time. See Chapter 3 for more info on the rules of the game, and check out Appendix C for the signals used to indicate penalties. In some cases, the penalty may be the awarding of a penalty shot on goal or the actual awarding of a goal.

Penalty killing

When a team is shorthanded and attempts to prevent the opposition from scoring, this activity is known as "penalty killing." See Chapter 9 for more details on penalty killing.

Penalty shot

A penalty shot is awarded to an offensive player who — on a breakaway — is illegally checked or impeded. The puck is placed at the center face-off spot, and the player may skate in on the opposing goal with no other defenders on the ice besides the goalie.

Penalty-killing unit

The group of players brought in by a shorthanded team in order to defend against a power play.

PIM

An abbreviation for "penalties in minutes" (penalty minutes accumulated).

Pipe

The pipe is the goalpost, and if you hit a puck "between the pipes," you score a goal!

Point

The point is the area just inside the opposition's blue line close to the boards on either side of the rink. A defenseman usually occupies this area when his team is in control of the puck in the opposition's defensive zone.

Poke check

Trying to knock the puck away from an opponent by stabbing at it with the blade of the stick.

Possession of the puck

The last player or goalie to make contact with the puck is the one who has possession. This definition includes a puck that is deflected off a player or any part of his equipment.

Power play

When a team has more players on the ice than the opposition due to one or more penalties against the opposing team. Chapter 9 has all the details about the power play.

Pts.

An abbreviation for "total points."

Pulling the goalie

A team that is losing will sometimes take its own goalie off the ice and use another forward. This situation occurs most frequently near the end of the game when a team is behind and needs some emergency offense.

Red line

The line that divides the rink into two equal parts. This area is center ice. Chapter 1 has a diagram.

Referee

The referee supervises the game, calls the penalties, determines if goals are scored, and handles the face-off at center ice at the start of each game. The NHL uses two referees in each game. The referee has the final decision over all other officials.

Roughing

Engaging in fisticuffs (fighting) or shoving. Chapter 10 is full of information on this type of hitting.

Save

A shot blocked by the goalie — a shot that otherwise would have gone into the net!

Shadow

When a player covers an opponent one-on-one everywhere on the ice in order to limit the effectiveness of this opponent.

Shoot-out

Some minor and international leagues refine the overtime situation by having their teams play a five-minute sudden-death period, and if no one scores, the game is decided by a shoot-out. Each team picks five players, and each one of them takes a penalty shot on the other team's goalie, skating in by themselves with the puck from center ice and trying to score. Whichever team scores more goals wins.

Shorthanded

A shorthanded team is below the numerical strength of its opponents on the ice. When a goal is scored against a shorthanded team, the penalty that caused the team scored against to be shorthanded is terminated, and both teams are again at equal strength.

Slap shot

A slap shot occurs when the player swings the stick back and then quickly forward, slapping the puck ahead with a forehand shot.

Slashing

When a player swings the stick at an opponent. Slashing merits a penalty, whether contact is made or not. Tapping an opponent's stick not slashing.

Slot

The prime scoring area up the middle of the ice, between the face-off circles. When you "clear the slot," you shove an opposing player out of the area in front of your goal.

Smothering the puck

When a goalie or other players fall on the puck. Smothering is legal when done by the goalie or *accidentally* by another player.

Sniper

A player who is a pure goal scorer and who doesn't hit other players or the boards all that much.

Spearing

Poking or attempting to poke an opponent with the tip of the blade of the stick while holding the stick with one or both hands.

Splitting the defense

When a player in possession of the puck goes between two opposing defenders while attacking.

Stanley Cup

The trophy awarded annually to the National Hockey League champion after a best-of-seven Stanley Cup Championship Series.

Stick checking

Using the stick or its blade to poke or strike an opponent's stick or puck in an attempt to get possession of the puck.

Stickhandling

A term for carrying the puck along the ice with the stick.

Street hockey

Hockey played without skates of any kind. See Chapter 17.

Sweater

The term used to designate a hockey jersey.

Sweep check

Using the entire length of the stick with a sweeping motion along the surface of the ice in order to dislodge the puck from an opponent. A team that is shorthanded on a power play often employs a sweep check.

Team official

A person responsible for the operation of a team, such as a coach, manager, or trainer.

Trap

Traps are defensive formations designed to minimize the opposition's scoring opportunities and keep its offense from functioning. The idea is to trap the puck in the neutral zone, halting the opponents and regaining control of the puck. Chapter 8 has some more information on different kinds of traps.

Tripping

Using a stick, arm, or leg to cause an opponent to trip or fall.

Turnover

Just as in basketball or football, you can make a turnover in hockey by losing control of the puck to the opposing team.

Two-line pass

An offside pass (that actually crosses two lines). See Chapter 3.

Umbrella

A formation — resembling an open umbrella — used by a team that is on the power play to take advantage of its numerical superiority. See Chapter 9 for an explanation and a diagram.

Wings

The left wing and the right wing (also known as forwards) move up and down their respective sides of the rink. Offensively, they skate on each side of the center, exchanging passes with him, while trying themselves for a shot on goal or a rebound of a shot from the point. Defensively, they watch the opponent's wings. See Chapter 1 for a description of the positions.

Wrist shot

A wrist shot is used to shoot the puck off the blade of the stick with a flicking motion of the wrist.

Zamboni

The vehicle used to prepare the rink's ice surface before the game and after each period. The Zamboni scrapes a thin layer off the ice, heats the ice, and puts down a fresh layer of heated water that freezes to form a new layer of ice. See Chapter 12 for a picture of this wonderful machine.

Appendix B

Hockey Organizations: From Pee-Wees to the Pros

● ●

*T*wo organizations should be at the head of any list for hockey information: USA Hockey and the Canadian Hockey Association.

USA Hockey is the governing body for the sport of ice hockey in the United States. And for in-line hockey enthusiasts, USA Hockey sponsors USA Hockey InLine. If you want to join USA Hockey, you can reach it at the following address (and its Web site has links to everything you need to know about this organization):

USA Hockey
1775 Bob Johnson Drive
Colorado Springs, CO 80906-4090
719-576-8724
www.usahockey.com

The Canadian Hockey Association links players, coaches, officials, volunteers, and anyone else involved in local hockey associations across Canada to other provincial, national, and international hockey bodies. This organization represents every part of the country and covers hockey levels up to the National Hockey League. Here's how to reach the Canadian Hockey Association:

Canadian Hockey Association
Father David Bauer Arena
2424 University Drive NW
Calgary, AB T2N 3Y9
Canada
403-777-3636
www.canadianhockey.ca

Youth Hockey

Youth hockey is booming in North America, and nowhere is that more evident than in the number of hockey organizations catering to our younger players in recent years! Here is a listing of youth hockey organizations for states and regions in the United States and provinces in Canada. Contact these groups for information about youth hockey leagues, tournaments, schools, and camps in your area; they may be able to refer you to a local organization closer to your home. You can also find a more comprehensive list of U.S. and Canadian youth hockey organizations on the Web at www.dummies.com.

United States

Alaska

Alaska State Hockey Association
Dick Smith, President
615 Highlander Circle
Anchorage, AK 99518
Phone: 907-349-0720

Arizona

Arizona Amateur Hockey Association
Larry Schloss, President
P.O. Box 30674
Tucson, AZ 85751
Phone: 520-298-2511
Fax: 520-733-9520

California

California Amateur Hockey Association
Lynn Beehler, President
1113-C Buckingham Drive
Costa Mesa, CA 92626
Phone: 714-557-1496 (also fax)

Colorado

Colorado Amateur Hockey Association
Tom Fletcher, President
5320 West 67th Avenue
Arvada, CO 80003
Phone: 303-420-2157
Fax: 303-432-0427

Connecticut

Connecticut Hockey Conference
Pat Cavallaro, President
160 Tanglewood Drive
Hamden, CT 06518-2728
Phone: 203-281-3477
Fax: 203-281-3137

Florida

Statewide Amateur Hockey of Florida, Inc.
Frank Scarpaci, President
3205 East Olive Boulevard #96
Pensacola, FL 32514
Phone: 850-478-7784
Fax: 850-478-5256

Idaho

Idaho Amateur Hockey Association
Mike Ten Eyck, President
1271 Londonderry Avenue
Idaho Falls, ID 83404
Phone: 208-529-0221
Fax: 208-533-5057

Illinois

Amateur Hockey Association of Illinois, Inc.
Mike Lebarre, President
8740 Dartmouth
Palos Hills, IL 60465
Phone: 708-599-7791
Fax: 708-430-9811

Maine

Maine Amateur Hockey Association
Howard Feldman, President
33 Western Avenue
Auburn, ME 04210
Phone: 207-784-2197 (also fax)

Massachusetts

Massachusetts Hockey
Allen Wright, President
20 Gregory Lane
West Springfield, MA 01089
Phone: 413-734-3521
Fax: 413-731-5843

Michigan

Michigan Amateur Hockey Association
Jerry Ludden, President
1316 Woodingham Drive
East Lansing, MI 48823
Phone: 517-337-7829
Fax: 517-432-3203

Minnesota

Minnesota Amateur Hockey Association
Elmer Walls, President
566 Memorywood Drive North
Baxter, MN 56425
Phone: 218-829-1841
Fax: 218-828-5118

Missouri

Missouri Hockey, Inc.
Larry Hellwig, President
1366 Kehrs Mill Road
Chesterfield, MO 63017
Phone: 314-537-0639

Montana

Montana Amateur Hockey Association
Wayne Thompson, President
709 32nd Avenue, NE
Great Falls, MT 59404
Phone: 406-727-2251

Nevada

Nevada Amateur Hockey Association
Dennis Degree, President
6900 West Cliff Drive, Suite 500
Las Vegas, NV 89128
Phone: 702-228-0922
Fax: 702-228-1459

New Hampshire

New Hampshire Amateur Hockey Association
Mark Bozek, President
276 Woodcrest Court
Manchester, NH 03109
Phone: 603-623-4427

New Mexico

Land of Enchantment Hockey Association
Bob Nolen, President
790 Camino Encantado
Los Alamos, NM 87544
Phone: 505-662-7227
Fax: 505-665-1226

New York

New York State Amateur Hockey Association
Ralph Scannapieco, President
21 Norma Lane
Kings Park, NY 11754
Phone: 516-269-0866
Fax: 212-647-2493

North Dakota

North Dakota Amateur Hockey Association
Jack Kleven, President
P.O. Box 634
Minot, ND 58701-0634
Phone: 701-838-0714
Fax: 701-839-4045

Oregon

Oregon State Hockey Association
Jim Tarala, President
4840 SW Western Avenue, Suite 7000
Beaverton, OR 97005-3430
Phone: 503-643-3550
Fax: 503-643-5630

Rhode Island

Rhode Island Amateur Hockey Association
Richard Oliver, President
73 Vercant Drive
Cranston, RI 02920
Phone: 401-821-9018
Fax: 401-826-4891

South Dakota

South Dakota Amateur Hockey Association
Tom Honkomp, President
826 17th Avenue South
Brookings, SD 57006
Phone: 605-697-5570 (also fax)

Utah

Utah Amateur Hockey Association
Mike Holmes, President
P.O. Box 563
Bountiful, UT 84011
Phone: 801-292-8910 or 801-918-8910 (cell)
Fax: 801-292-4101

Vermont

Vermont Amateur Hockey Association
Alan Teague, President
1860 Fairfax Road
St. Albans, VT 05478
Phone: 802-524-4183
Fax: 802-524-6511

Washington

Pacific Northwest Amateur Hockey Association
Donna Kaufman, President
3610 Ray Nash Drive, NW
Gig Harbor, WA 98335
Phone: 253-265-6294
Fax: 253-272-1785

Wisconsin

Wisconsin Amateur Hockey Association
Jerry Edwards, President
1118 Eaton Avenue
Beloit, WI 53611
Phone: 608-362-9094
Fax: 608-365-6661

Wyoming

Wyoming Amateur Hockey Association
Bob Collier, President
211 Cactus Circle
Riverton, WY 82501
Phone: 307-857-5111
Fax: 307-857-5125

Regional Organizations

Delaware, Eastern Pennsylvania, New Jersey

Atlantic Amateur Hockey Association
Tom Koester, President
292 Upper Gulph Road
Radnor, PA 19087
Phone: 610-687-1582
Fax: 610-828-2673

Indiana, Kentucky, Ohio, Western Pennsylvania, West Virginia

Mid-American Hockey Association
John Connors, President
909 Cottonwood Street
Morgantown, WV 26505
Phone: 304-599-8111
Fax: 304-293-3850

Alabama, Arkansas, District of Columbia, Georgia, Louisiana, Maryland, Mississippi, North Carolina, South Carolina, Tennessee, Virginia

Southeastern Amateur Hockey Association, Inc.
Knud Aagaard-Svendsen, President
110 Kiveton Park Drive
Roswell, GA 30075
Phone: 770-998-7198
Fax: 770-643-8445

Oklahoma, Texas

Texas Amateur Hockey Association
Charles Callaway, President
P.O. Box 161928
Austin, TX 78716
Phone: 512-328-9282
Fax: 512-328-9283

Iowa, Kansas, Nebraska

Tri-State Amateur Hockey Association
Jim Van Bergen, President
3910 Carey Lane
Ames, IA 50014
Phone: 515-232-7232
Fax: 515-233-5090

Canada

Alberta

Hockey Alberta
Malcolm MacLeod, President
Howard Wurban, Executive Director
#1, 7875 48th Avenue
Red Deer, AB T4P 2K1
Phone: 403-342-6777
Fax: 403-346-4277
Web: www.hockey-alberta.ca/

British Columbia

British Columbia Amateur Hockey Association
Mike Henderson, President
Don Freer, Executive Director
6671 Oldfield Road
Saanichton, BC V8M 2A1
Phone: 250-652-2978
Fax: 250-652-4536
Web: www.bcaha.org/

Manitoba

Hockey Manitoba
George Ulyatt, President
Pat Kirby, Chief Executive Officer
200 Main Street
Winnipeg, MB R3C 4M2
Phone: 204-925-5755
Fax: 204-925-5761
Web: www.hockeymanitoba.mb.ca

New Brunswick

New Brunswick Amateur Hockey Association
Doug Steeves, President
Brian Whitehead, Executive Director
165 Regent Street, Suite 4
P.O. Box 456
Fredericton, NB E3B 4Z9
Phone: 506-453-0862
Fax: 506-453-0868

Newfoundland

Newfoundland and Labrador Hockey Association
George Fardy, President
Craig Tulk, Executive Director
Tamar Walsh, Administrative Assistant
15A High Street
P.O. Box 176
Grand Falls, Windsor, NF A2A 2J4
Phone: 709-489-5512
Fax: 709-489-2273

Northwest Territories

Hockey North
Jim Ramsay, President
Reagan Alexander, Executive Director
Sport North Federation
P.O. Box 223
Yellowknife, NT X1A 2N2
Phone: 867-873-3032
Fax: 867-920-4047

Nova Scotia

Nova Scotia Hockey Association
Denny Deveau, President
Tom Krzyski, Executive Director
6080 Young Street, Suite 910
Halifax, NS B3K 2A2
Phone: 902-454-9400
Fax: 902-454-3883
Web: www.gamesheet.com/nsha

Ontario

Hockey Northwestern Ontario
Joe Tookenay, President
Joseph Ward, Executive Director
600 East Victoria Avenue
P.O. Box 27085
Thunder Bay, ON P7C 5Y7
Phone: 807-622-4792
Fax: 807-623-0037

Ontario Hockey Federation
Allan Morris, President
Scott Farley, General Manager
1185 Eglinton Avenue East, Suite 202
North York, ON M3C 3C6
Phone: 416-426-7249
Fax: 416-426-7347
Web: www.ohf.on.ca

Ottawa District Hockey Association
Ken Corbett, President
Richard Sennott, Executive Director
1900 Merivale Road, Suite 204
Nepean, ON K2G 4N4
Phone: 613-224-7686
Fax: 613-224-6079
Web: www.odha.com

Prince Edward Island

Prince Edward Island Hockey Association
John Brehaut, President
Mike Whelan, Executive Director
P.O. Box 302
Charlottetown, PE C1A 7K7
Phone: 902-368-4334
Fax: 902-368-4337

Quebec

Hockey Quebec
Rene Marcil, President
Guy Blondeau, Executive Director
4545 Pierre de Coubertin Avenue
C.P. 1000, Succ. M
Montreal, QC H1V 3R2
Phone: 514-252-3079
Fax: 514-252-3158
Web: www/hockey.qc.ca/

Saskatchewan

Saskatchewan Hockey Association
Marcel Redekop, President
Kelly McClintock, Executive Director
#2, 575 Park Street
Regina, SK S4N 5B2
Phone: 306-789-5101
Fax: 306-789-6112
Web: www.sha.sk.ca/

Adult Hockey

We don't have a ready-made list of adult hockey organizations, but several are out there. The best way to find out about adult recreational hockey is to contact Hockey North America (800-4-HOCKEY) or visit its Web site at www.hna.com. Hockey North America has more than 20 leagues in the United States and Canada — and you don't need to be a hockey expert, because HNA has plenty of programs for beginners.

NHL Directory of Addresses

This directory gives you contact information for the National Hockey League offices, the NHL Players' Association, and the NHL teams. If you want the Web address for any NHL team, check the listing given in Chapter 13.

NHL offices

National Hockey League, L.P.
1251 Avenue of the Americas
47th Floor
New York, NY 10020
Phone: 212-789-2000
Fax: 212-789-2020

75 International Boulevard, Suite 300
Rexdale, ON M9W 6L9
Phone: 416-798-0809
Fax: 416-798-0819

NHL Players' Association (NHLPA)

777 Bay Street, Suite 2400
Toronto, ON M5G 2C8
Phone: 416-408-4040
Fax: 416-408-3685

NHL teams

Atlanta Thrashers
Philips Arena
One CNN Center
12th Floor South Tower
Atlanta, GA 30303
Phone: 404-827-5300

Boston Bruins
FleetCenter
One FleetCenter, Suite 250
Boston, MA 02114-1303
Phone: 617-624-1900

Buffalo Sabres
Marine Midland Arena
One Seymour H. Knox III Plaza
Buffalo, NY 14203-3096
Phone: 716-855-4100
Fax: 716-855-4110

Calgary Flames
Canadian Airlines Saddledome
P. O. Box 1540 — Station M
Calgary, AB T2P 3B9
Phone: 403-261-0475

Carolina Hurricanes
Raleigh Sports and Entertainment Arena
1400 Edwards Mill Road
Raleigh, NC 27607
Phone: 919-467-7825, ext. 5500

Chicago Blackhawks
United Center
1901 West Madison Street
Chicago, IL 60612
Phone: 312-455-7000

Colorado Avalanche
Pepsi Center
1000 Chopper Circle
Denver, CO 80204
Phone: 303-405-1100

Columbus Blue Jackets
150 East Wilson Bridge Road, Suite 235
Worthington, OH 43085
Phone: 614-540-4625

Dallas Stars
Dr. Pepper StarCenter
211 Cowboys Parkway
Irving, TX 75063
Phone: 972-868-2890

Detroit Red Wings
Joe Louis Arena
600 Civic Center Drive
Detroit, MI 48226
Phone: 313-396-7544

Edmonton Oilers
Skyreach Centre
11230 110th Street
Edmonton, AB T5G 3H7
Phone: 780-414-4000

Florida Panthers
National Car Rental Center
One Panther Parkway
Sunrise, FL 33323
Phone: 954-835-7000

Los Angeles Kings
HealthSouth Training Center
555 North Nash Street
El Segundo, CA 90245
Phone: 310-535-4500

Mighty Ducks of Anaheim
Arrowhead Pond of Anaheim
2695 Katella Avenue
Anaheim, CA 92806
Phone: 714-940-2900

Minnesota Wild
444 Cedar Street, Suite 900
St. Paul, MN 55101
Phone: 651-222-9453

Montreal Canadiens
Molson Centre
1260 Gauchetiere Street West
Montreal, QC H3B 5E8
Phone: 514-932-2582

Nashville Predators
Gaylord Entertainment Center
501 Broadway
Nashville, TN 37203
Phone: 615-770-2300

New Jersey Devils
Continental Airlines Arena
P.O. Box 504
East Rutherford, NJ 07073
Phone: 201-935-6050

New York Islanders
Nassau Coliseum
1255 Hempstead Turnpike
Uniondale, NY 11553
Phone: 516-832-4200

New York Rangers
Madison Square Garden
2 Pennsylvania Plaza, 14th Floor
New York, NY 10121
Phone: 212-465-6486

Ottawa Senators
Corel Centre
1000 Palladium Drive
Kanata, ON K2V 1A5
Phone: 613-599-0250

Philadelphia Flyers
First Union Center
3601 South Broad Street
Philadelphia, PA 19148
Phone: 215-465-4500

Phoenix Coyotes
Cellular One Ice Den
9375 East Bell Road
Scottsdale, AZ 85260
Phone: 480-473-5600

Pittsburgh Penguins
Civic Arena
66 Mario Lemieux Place
Pittsburgh, PA 15219
Phone: 412-873-7604

St. Louis Blues
Kiel Center
1401 Clark Avenue
St. Louis, MO 63103
Phone: 314-622-2500

San Jose Sharks
San Jose Arena
525 West Santa Clara Street
San Jose, CA 95113
Phone: 408-287-7070

Tampa Bay Lightning
Ice Palace
401 Channelside Drive
Tampa Bay, FL 33602
Phone: 813-301-6500

Toronto Maple Leafs
Air Canada Centre
40 Bay Street, Suite 300
Toronto, ON M5J 2X2
Phone: 416-815-5700

Vancouver Canucks
General Motors Place
800 Griffiths Way
Vancouver, BC V6B 6G1
Phone: 604-899-4600

Washington Capitals
MCI Center
601 F Street, NW
Washington, DC 20004
Phone: 202-661-5000

Appendix C
Hockey Signals

This appendix is a collection of the most common signals that the hockey officials make during a game. In fact, these signals are also used in roller (in-line) hockey, too. If you need more details, check out Appendix A, which is a glossary of some common hockey terms. In addition, Part I of this book has more descriptions — and maybe a diagram or two to help you.

Boarding

Boarding is called when you check another player into the boards with more than just your average force. The degree of violence and the manner in which the player is thrown into the boards (tripped, elbowed, body checked, and so on) help determine the penalty.

Gesture: Striking the closed fist once into the open palm of the other hand.

Butt ending

Jab a player with the shaft (butt end) of your stick . . . and you get called for butt ending!

Gesture: Moving the forearm, fist closed, under the forearm of the other hand that is held palm down.

Charging

A charge is called when you run, jump, skate, or charge into another player in an aggressive manner.

Gesture: Rotating clenched fists around one another in front of the chest.

Checking from behind

When you try to get between your opponent and the puck by using your body and/or your stick, you are checking. When you check your opponent from behind, however, you draw the attention of the officials!

Gesture: Placing the arm behind the back, elbow bent, forearm parallel to the surface.

Cross checking

If you pick your stick off the ice and hold it in two hands to check your opponent (using the shaft of the stick), you get whistled for cross checking.

Gesture: Extending both clenched fists forward and back from the chest.

Delayed calling of penalty

If an infraction calls for a minor, major, misconduct, game misconduct, or match penalty on a player of the team *not* in possession of the puck, the referee blows his whistle and imposes the penalty after completion of the play by the team with the puck. (The play is considered completed when the team in possession of the puck loses possession!)

Gesture: Extending the non-whistle hand straight above the head and pointing to the penalized player.

Delayed (slow) whistle

You are onside when either of your skates is on your own side of the blue line (or on the line) at the moment the puck completely crosses the outer edge of that line — no matter where your stick is. However, while an offside call is delayed, if players of the offending team clear the zone, the official drops his arm and the play is no longer offside.

Gesture: Extending the non-whistle hand straight above the head.

Delaying the game

If you shoot, bat, or throw the puck outside the playing area, you are delaying the game. You are also guilty of this infraction if you deliberately move the goal (by displacing a goalpost) to keep the opposition from scoring.

Gesture: Placing the non-whistle hand (palm open) across the chest and then fully extending it in front of the body.

Elbowing

If you use your elbow in any way to contact or foul another player, you are guilty of elbowing.

Gesture: Tapping the elbow with the opposite hand.

Fighting

Fisticuffs are not tolerated!

Gesture: Punching motion to the side with the arm extending from the shoulder.

Goal scored

This is the signal you'll love to see — as long as your team is the one to score the goal!

Gesture: Pointing at the goal (which the puck entered) with the non-whistle hand while blowing the whistle.

Hand pass

This isn't baseball. You can't close your hand on the puck or pick it up from the ice — unless, of course, you're the ref.

Gesture: Placing the non-whistle hand (open hand) and arm alongside the body and swinging forward and up in an underhand motion.

High sticking

You get called for high sticking if you injure an opposing player by carrying any part of your stick above your waist.

Gesture: Holding a clenched fist, with the hands one above the other, at the side of the head.

Holding

Impeding the progress of an opponent by holding is frowned upon!

Gesture: Clasping the wrist of the whistle hand well in front of the chest.

Holding the face mask

If you can't get away with holding your opponent's face mask in football, do you think you can do it in hockey?

Gesture: Holding the closed fist in front of the face, palm in, and pulling down in one straight motion.

Hooking

Imagine that the blade of the hockey stick is a hook. If you use this hook to impede another player (pulling or tugging on the hook), you commit hooking.

Gesture: Tugging with both arms, as if pulling something toward the stomach.

Icing

So you think you can just send that puck from behind your red line down the length of the ice whenever you want? No, you can't. See Chapter 3 for all the details on icing. In roller or in-line hockey, this infraction is known as "clearing."

Gesture: Extending the arm (without whistle) over the head.

Interference

If you impede the progress of another player who does not have the puck, you are interfering. That means you can't check an opponent who does not have the puck. You are also called for interference if you deliberately knock the stick out of your opponent's hands or prevent your opponent from picking up a dropped stick or other piece of equipment.

Gesture: Crossing and keeping the arms in front of the chest with fists closed.

Kneeing

Don't use your knees against your opponent!

Gesture: Tapping the right knee with the right hand once, keeping both skates on the surface.

Match penalty

A match penalty involves the suspension of a player for the remainder of the game. This usually occurs when you try to injure an opponent (such as by kicking). After five minutes playing time, the suspended player can be replaced by another.

Gesture: Patting flat hand on top of the head.

Misconduct

Misconduct includes basic, game, and gross misconduct levels (see Chapter 3 for details).

Gesture: Placing both hands on hips.

Offside

If you precede the puck into the attacking zone (over the blue line), you get called for offside. Offside is explained and illustrated in Chapter 3.

Gesture: Extending the free arm over the head.

Penalty shot

Certain infractions force a referee to award a penalty shot (such as when you take your opponent down from behind if he is on a breakaway). This is a free skate and shot on goal, with only the goalie being allowed to stop the shot.

Gesture: Crossing arms (fists clenched) above head.

Slashing

When you hit another player with your stick, you are guilty of slashing. It doesn't matter if you are holding the stick with one or two hands or even if you miss the player you are aiming for — it's still slashing.

Gesture: Chopping the hand across the straightened forearm of the other hand once.

Spearing

Spearing is sort of the opposite of butt ending. If you poke another player with the blade tip of your stick — or if you only make the attempt — you are guilty of spearing.

Gesture: Making a single jabbing motion with both hands together, thrust forward from in front of the chest then dropping the hands to the side.

Time-out

In the National Hockey League, each team can have one 30-second time-out during a game. This time-out must be taken during a normal stoppage of play.

Gesture: Making a T with both hands.

Tripping

No matter how you trip your opponent — with your stick, knee, foot, arm, or hand — it still adds up to tripping.

Gesture: Striking the side of the leg and following through once, keeping the head up and both skates on the surface.

Wash-out

A referee uses this signal to indicate that no penalty occurred or that no goal was scored — and play can continue. A linesman makes this gesture to show that no icing, offside, or high sticking took place.

Gesture: Swinging both arms laterally across the body at shoulder level with palms down.

Appendix D

Hockey: The Lists

From Hall of Famers to Stanley Cup winners, from career milestones to single-season achievements, this appendix has something for any hockey enthusiast.

The Hockey Hall of Fame

The Hockey Hall of Fame formed in 1943 and opened its doors to the public in 1961 in a building on the grounds of the Canadian National Exhibition in Toronto. The Hall of Fame moved to its new site at BCE Place and welcomed the hockey world on June 18, 1993. Visit its Web site at www.hhof.com.

The Hall of Fame had 319 honored members at the start of the 2000–01 season: 218 were inducted as players, 87 as builders, and 14 as referees/linesmen. The Hall of Fame also recognizes media personnel who have made a significant contribution to hockey. Following is a list of the players in the Hall of Fame, broken down by forwards/defensemen and goalies.

Forwards and defensemen

A forward (F) is usually classified as a center (C), a right wing (RW), or a left wing (LW). A defenseman (D) is, well, a defenseman. Until the 1930s, there was also the position of rover (RO) — a player who roamed the entire rink.

Pos. = position   A = assists   XX = Data unavailable
GP = games played   Pts. = points
G = goals scored   PIM = penalties in minutes

Player	Election Year	Pos.	GP	G	A	Pts.	PIM
Sid Abel	1969	C	613	189	283	472	376
Jack Adams	1959	C	243	134	50	184	307
Syl Apps	1961	C	423	201	231	432	56
George Armstrong	1975	RW	1,187	296	417	713	721
Ace Bailey	1975	RW	313	111	82	193	472
Dan Bain	1945	C	Unavailable				
Hobey Baker	1945	RO	Unavailable				
Bill Barber	1990	LW	903	420	463	883	623
Marty Barry	1965	C	509	195	192	387	231
Andy Bathgate	1978	RW	1,069	349	624	973	624
Bobby Bauer	1996	RW	327	123	137	260	36
Jean Beliveau	1972	C	1,125	507	712	1,219	1,029
Doug Bentley	1964	LW	566	219	324	543	217
Max Bentley	1966	C	646	245	299	544	175
Toe Blake	1966	LW	578	235	292	527	272
Leo Boivin	1986	D	1,150	72	250	322	1,192
Dickie Boon	1952	D	42	10	XX	10	XX
Mike Bossy	1991	LW	752	573	553	1,126	210
Butch Bouchard	1966	D	785	49	144	193	863
Frank Boucher	1958	C	557	161	262	423	119
George Boucher	1960	F/D	457	122	62	184	739
Russell Bowie	1945	C	80	234	XX	234	XX
Punch Broadbent	1962	RW	302	122	45	167	553
John Bucyk	1981	LW	1,540	556	813	1,369	497
Billy Burch	1974	C	390	137	53	190	251
Harry Cameron	1962	D	312	174	27	201	154
King Clancy	1958	D	592	137	143	280	904
Dit Clapper	1947	RW	833	228	246	474	462
Bobby Clarke	1987	C	1,144	358	852	1,210	1,453
Sprague Cleghorn	1958	D	377	163	39	202	489

Player	Election Year	Pos.	GP	G	A	Pts.	PIM
Neil Colville	1967	C/D	464	99	166	265	213
Charlie Conacher	1961	RW	460	225	173	398	523
Lionel Conacher	1994	D	500	80	105	185	882
Roy Conacher	1998	LW	490	226	200	426	90
Bill Cook	1952	RW	586	322	196	518	483
Fred Cook	1995	LW	473	158	144	302	449
Art Coulter	1974	D	465	30	82	112	543
Yvan Cournoyer	1982	RW	968	428	435	863	255
Bill Cowley	1968	C	549	195	353	548	143
Rusty Crawford	1962	LW	245	110	3	113	51
Jack Darragh	1962	RW	250	194	21	215	88
Scotty Davidson	1950	RW	40	42	XX	42	XX
Hap Day	1961	LW	581	86	116	202	602
Alex Delvecchio	1977	C	1,549	456	825	1,281	383
Cy Denneny	1959	LW	368	281	69	350	210
Marcel Dionne	1992	C	1,348	731	1,040	1,771	600
Gord Drillon	1975	LW	311	155	139	294	56
Graham Drinkwater	1950	L/D	37	40	XX	40	XX
Woody Dumart	1992	LW	771	211	218	429	99
Tommy Dunderdale	1974	C	290	225	XX	225	XX
Red Dutton	1958	D	449	29	67	96	871
Babe Dye	1970	RW	270	202	41	243	190
Phil Esposito	1984	C	1,282	717	873	1,590	910
Arthur Farrell	1965	F	26	29	XX	29	XX
Fern Flaman	1990	D	910	34	174	208	1,370
Frank Foyston	1958	C	357	242	7	249	32
Frank Fredrickson	1958	C	327	170	34	204	206
Bill Gadsby	1970	D	1,248	130	437	567	1,539
Bob Gainey	1992	LW	1,160	239	262	501	585
Herb Gardiner	1958	D	233	44	9	53	52
Jimmy Gardner	1962	LW	112	63	XX	63	XX

(continued)

Player	Election Year	Pos.	GP	G	A	Pts.	PIM
Boom Boom Geoffrion	1972	RW	883	393	429	822	689
Eddie Gerard	1945	F/D	201	93	30	123	106
Rod Gilbert	1982	RW	1,065	406	615	1,021	508
Billy Gilmour	1962	RW	32	26	XX	26	XX
Moose Goheen	1952	D	Unavailable				
Ebbie Goodfellow	1963	C	554	134	190	324	511
Michel Goulet	1998	LW	1,089	548	604	1,152	825
Mike Grant	1950	D	55	10	XX	10	XX
Shorty Green	1962	RW	103	33	8	41	151
Wayne Gretzky	1999	C	1,487	894	1,963	2,857	577
Si Griffis	1950	RO/D	117	39	XX	39	XX
Joe Hall	1961	F/D	198	105	1	106	145
Doug Harvey	1973	D	1,113	88	452	540	1,216
George Hay	1958	LW	373	179	60	239	84
Bryan Hextall	1969	RW	447	187	175	362	227
Tom Hooper	1962	F	11	12	XX	12	XX
Red Horner	1965	D	490	42	110	152	1,264
Tim Horton	1977	D	1,446	115	403	518	1,611
Gordie Howe	1972	RW	1,767	801	1,049	1,850	1,685
Syd Howe	1965	F/D	691	237	291	528	214
Harry Howell	1979	D	1,411	94	324	418	1,298
Bobby Hull	1983	LW	1,063	610	560	1,170	640
Harry Hyland	1962	RW	157	199	XX	199	9
Dick Irvin	1958	C	249	152	23	174	76
Busher Jackson	1971	LW	636	241	234	475	437
Ching Johnson	1958	D	435	38	48	86	808
Moose Johnson	1952	LW/D	270	123	XX	123	XX
Tom Johnson	1970	D	978	51	213	264	960
Aurel Joliat	1947	LW	654	270	190	460	752
Duke Keats	1958	C	256	183	19	202	112
Red Kelly	1969	C	1,316	281	542	823	327
Ted Kennedy	1966	C	696	231	329	560	432

Player	Election Year	Pos.	GP	G	A	Pts.	PIM
Dave Keon	1986	C	1,296	396	590	986	117
Elmer Lach	1966	C	664	215	408	623	478
Guy Lafleur	1988	LW	1,126	560	793	1,353	399
Newsy Lalonde	1950	C/RO	315	428	27	455	122
Jacques Laperriere	1987	D	691	40	242	282	674
Guy Lapointe	1993	D	884	171	451	622	893
Edgar Laprade	1993	C	501	108	172	280	42
Jack Laviolette	1962	D/LW	178	58	0	58	0
Jacques Lemaire	1984	C	853	366	469	835	217
Mario Lemieux	1997	C	745	613	881	1,494	737
Herbie Lewis	1989	LW	484	148	161	309	248
Ted Lindsay	1966	LW	1,068	379	472	851	1,808
Mickey MacKay	1952	C/RO	388	246	19	265	79
Frank Mahovlich	1981	LW	1,181	533	570	1,103	1,056
Joe Malone	1950	C/LW	125	146	18	164	35
Sylvio Mantha	1960	D	543	63	72	135	667
Jack Marshall	1965	C/D	132	99	XX	99	XX
Fred Maxwell	1962	RO	Unavailable				
Lanny McDonald	1992	RW	1,111	500	506	1,006	899
Frank McGee	1945	C/RO	23	71	XX	71	XX
Billy McGimsie	1962	F	Unavailable				
George McNamara	1958	D	121	39	XX	39	XX
Stan Mikita	1983	C	1,394	541	926	1,467	1,270
Dickie Moore	1974	RW	719	261	347	608	652
Howie Morenz	1945	C	550	270	197	467	531
Bill Mosienko	1965	RW	711	258	282	540	121
Joe Mullen	2000	RW	1,062	502	561	1,063	241
Frank Nighbor	1947	LW/C	348	136	60	196	266
Reg Noble	1962	LW/C/D	534	180	79	259	770
Buddy O'Connor	1988	C	509	140	257	397	34
Harry Oliver	1967	F	603	216	85	301	147

(continued)

Player	Election Year	Pos.	GP	G	A	Pts.	PIM
Bert Olmstead	1985	LW	848	181	421	602	884
Bobby Orr	1979	D	657	270	645	915	953
Brad Park	1988	D	1,113	213	683	896	1,429
Lester Patrick	1947	D/RO/G	207	130	XX	130	XX
Lynn Patrick	1980	LW	455	145	190	335	270
Gilbert Perreault	1990	C	1,191	512	814	1,326	500
Tommy Phillips	1945	LW	33	57	XX	57	XX
Pierre Pilote	1975	D	890	80	418	498	1,251
Didier Pitre	1962	D/RO/RW	282	238	17	255	59
Denis Potvin	1991	D	1,060	310	742	1,052	1,354
Babe Pratt	1966	D	517	83	209	292	453
Joe Primeau	1963	C	310	66	177	243	105
Marcel Pronovost	1978	D	1,206	88	257	345	851
Bob Pulford	1991	LW	1,079	281	362	643	792
Harvey Pulford	1945	D	96	6	XX	6	XX
Bill Quackenbush	1976	D	774	62	222	284	95
Frank Rankin	1961	RO	Unavailable				
Jean Ratelle	1985	C	1,281	491	776	1,267	276
Ken Reardon	1966	D	341	26	96	122	604
Henri Richard	1979	C	1,256	358	688	1,046	928
Maurice Richard	1961	RW	978	544	421	965	1,285
George Richardson	1950	Unavailable					
Gordon Roberts	1971	LW	166	203	XX	XX	XX
Larry Robinson	1995	D	1,384	208	750	958	793
Art Ross	1945	D	167	85	0	85	0
Blair Russell	1965	RW/C	67	110	XX	110	XX
Ernie Russell	1965	RO/C	98	180	XX	180	XX
Jack Ruttan	1962	Unavailable					
Borje Salming	1996	D	1,148	150	637	787	1,344
Denis Savard	2000	C	1,196	473	865	1,338	1,336
Serge Savard	1986	D	1,040	106	333	439	592
Fred Scanlan	1965	F	31	16	XX	16	XX

Player	Election Year	Pos.	GP	G	A	Pts.	PIM
Milt Schmidt	1961	C	778	229	346	575	466
Sweeney Schriner	1962	LW	484	201	204	405	148
Earl Seibert	1963	D	650	89	187	276	768
Oliver Seibert	1961	D	Unavailable				
Eddie Shore	1947	D	550	105	179	284	1,037
Steve Shutt	1993	LW	930	424	393	817	410
Babe Siebert	1964	LW/D	593	140	156	296	972
Joe Simpson	1962	D	340	76	19	95	176
Darryl Sittler	1989	C	1,096	484	637	1,121	948
Alf Smith	1962	RW.	65	90	XX	90	XX
Clint Smith	1991	C	483	161	236	397	24
Hooley Smith	1972	RW	715	200	215	415	1,013
Tommy Smith	1973	LW/C	XX	240	XX	240	XX
Allan Stanley	1981	D	1,244	100	333	433	792
Barney Stanley	1962	RW/D	216	144	XX	144	XX
Peter Stastny	1998	C	977	450	789	1,239	824
Black Jack Stewart	1964	D	565	31	84	115	765
Nels Stewart	1962	C	651	324	191	515	943
Bruce Stuart	1961	F	45	63	XX	63	XX
Hod Stuart	1945	D	33	16	XX	16	XX
Cyclone Taylor	1947	D/RO/C	186	194	XX	194	XX
Harry Trihey	1950	C	30	46	XX	46	XX
Bryan John Trottier	1997	C	1,279	524	901	1,425	912
Norm Ullman	1982	C	1,410	490	739	1,229	712
Jack Walker	1960	LW/RO	361	135	8	143	18
Marty Walsh	1962	C	59	135	XX	135	XX
Harry E. Watson	1962	C	Unavailable				
Harry P. Watson	1994	LW	Unavailable				
Cooney Weiland	1971	C	509	173	160	333	147
Harry Westwick	1962	RO	87	87	XX	87	XX
Fredrick Whitcroft	1962	RO	9	5	XX	5	XX
Gord Wilson	1962	D	Unavailable				

Goaltenders

GP = games played   GA = goals against   Avg. = average
Min. = minutes   SO = shutouts   XX = data unavailable

Player	Election Year	GP	Min.	GA	SO	Avg.
Clint Benedict	1965	362	22,321	863	57	2.32
Johnny Bower	1976	552	32,077	1,347	37	2.52
Frank Brimsek	1966	514	31,210	1,404	40	2.70
Turk Broda	1967	629	38,167	1,609	62	2.53
Gerry Cheevers	1985	418	24,394	1,175	26	2.89
Alex Connell	1958	417	26,030	830	81	1.91
Ken Dryden	1983	397	23,352	870	46	2.24
Bill Durnan	1964	383	22,945	901	34	2.36
Tony Esposito	1988	886	52,585	2,563	76	2.92
Chuck Gardiner	1945	316	19,687	664	42	2.05
Ed Giacomin	1987	610	35,693	1,675	54	2.82
George Hainsworth	1961	465	29,415	937	94	1.91
Glenn Hall	1975	906	53,464	2,239	84	2.51
Riley Hern	1962	60	XX	281	1	4.68
Hap Holmes	1972	410	6,510	1,191	41	2.90
Hughie Lehman	1958	403	3,047	1,451	23	3.60
Percy LeSueur	1961	156	XX	718	4	4.60
Harry Lumley	1980	804	48,097	2,210	71	2.76
Paddy Moran	1958	201	XX	1,094	2	5.44
Bernie Parent	1984	608	35,136	1,493	55	2.55
Jacques Plante	1978	837	49,533	1,965	82	2.38
Chuck Rayner	1973	425	25,491	1,295	25	3.05
Terry Sawchuk	1971	971	57,114	2,401	103	2.52
Billy Smith	1993	680	38,431	2,031	22	3.17
Tiny Thompson	1959	553	34,174	1,183	81	2.08
Vladislav Tretiak	1989	Unavailable				
Georges Vezina	1945	328	11,564	1,145	15	3.49
Gump Worsley	1980	862	50,232	2,432	43	2.90
Roy Worters	1969	484	30,175	1,143	66	2.27

Stanley Cup Winners

The Stanley Cup is awarded annually to the team that wins the National Hockey League's best-of-seven final playoff round. (The number of times that a team had won the Stanley Cup at that time is in parentheses next to the winning team's name.)

Season	Champion	Finalist	Games	Head Coach
2000	New Jersey Devils (2)	Dallas Stars	6	Larry Robinson
1999	Dallas Stars (1)	Buffalo Sabres	6	Ken Hitchcock
1998	Detroit Red Wings (9)	Washington Capitals	4	Scotty Bowman
1997	Detroit Red Wings (8)	Philadelphia Flyers	4	Scotty Bowman
1996	Colorado Avalanche (1)	Florida Panthers	4	Marc Crawford
1995	New Jersey Devils (1)	Detroit Red Wings	4	Jacques Lemaire
1994	New York Rangers (4)	Vancouver Canucks	7	Mike Keenan
1993	Montreal Canadiens (23)	Los Angeles Kings	5	Jacques Demers
1992	Pittsburgh Penguins (2)	Chicago Blackhawks	5	Scotty Bowman
1991	Pittsburgh Penguins (1)	Minnesota North Stars	6	Bob Johnson
1990	Edmonton Oilers (5)	Boston Bruins	5	John Muckler
1989	Calgary Flames (1)	Montreal Canadiens	6	Terry Crisp
1988	Edmonton Oilers (4)	Boston Bruins	4	Glen Sather
1987	Edmonton Oilers (3)	Philadelphia Flyers	7	Glen Sather
1986	Montreal Canadiens (22)	Calgary Flames	5	Jean Perron
1985	Edmonton Oilers (2)	Philadelphia Flyers	5	Glen Sather

(continued)

Season	Champion	Finalist	Games	Head Coach
1984	Edmonton Oilers (1)	New York Islanders	5	Glen Sather
1983	New York Islanders (4)	Edmonton Oilers	4	Al Arbour
1982	New York Islanders (3)	Vancouver Canucks	4	Al Arbour
1981	New York Islanders (2)	Minnesota North Stars	5	Al Arbour
1980	New York Islanders (1)	Philadelphia Flyers	6	Al Arbour
1979	Montreal Canadiens (21)	New York Rangers	5	Scotty Bowman
1978	Montreal Canadiens (20)	Boston Bruins	6	Scotty Bowman
1977	Montreal Canadiens (19)	Boston Bruins	4	Scotty Bowman
1976	Montreal Canadiens (18)	Philadelphia Flyers	4	Scotty Bowman
1975	Philadelphia Flyers (2)	Buffalo Sabres	6	Fred Shero
1974	Philadelphia Flyers (1)	Boston Bruins	6	Fred Shero
1973	Montreal Canadiens (17)	Chicago Blackhawks	6	Scotty Bowman
1972	Boston Bruins (5)	New York Rangers	6	Tom Johnson
1971	Montreal Canadiens (16)	Chicago Blackhawks	7	Al MacNeil
1970	Boston Bruins (4)	St. Louis Blues	4	Harry Sinden
1969	Montreal Canadiens (15)	St. Louis Blues	4	Claude Ruel
1968	Montreal Canadiens (14)	St. Louis Blues	4	Toe Blake
1967	Toronto Maple Leafs (11)	Montreal Canadiens	6	Punch Imlach
1966	Montreal Canadiens (13)	Detroit Red Wings	6	Toe Blake
1965	Montreal Canadiens (12)	Chicago Blackhawks	7	Toe Blake

Season	Champion	Finalist	Games	Head Coach
1964	Toronto Maple Leafs (10)	Detroit Red Wings	7	Punch Imlach
1963	Toronto Maple Leafs (9)	Detroit Red Wings	5	Punch Imlach
1962	Toronto Maple Leafs (8)	Chicago Blackhawks	6	Punch Imlach
1961	Chicago Blackhawks (3)	Detroit Red Wings	6	Rudy Pilous
1960	Montreal Canadiens (11)	Toronto Maple Leafs	4	Toe Blake
1959	Montreal Canadiens (10)	Toronto Maple Leafs	5	Toe Blake
1958	Montreal Canadiens (9)	Boston Bruins	6	Toe Blake
1957	Montreal Canadiens (8)	Boston Bruins	5	Toe Blake
1956	Montreal Canadiens (7)	Detroit Red Wings	5	Toe Blake
1955	Detroit Red Wings (7)	Montreal Canadiens	7	Jimmy Skinner
1954	Detroit Red Wings (6)	Montreal Canadiens	7	Tommy Ivan
1953	Montreal Canadiens (6)	Boston Bruins	5	Dick Irvin
1952	Detroit Red Wings (5)	Montreal Canadiens	4	Tommy Ivan
1951	Toronto Maple Leafs (7)	Montreal Canadiens	5	Joe Primeau
1950	Detroit Red Wings (4)	New York Rangers	7	Tommy Ivan
1949	Toronto Maple Leafs (6)	Detroit Red Wings	4	Hap Day
1948	Toronto Maple Leafs (5)	Detroit Red Wings	4	Hap Day
1947	Toronto Maple Leafs (4)	Montreal Canadiens	6	Hap Day
1946	Montreal Canadiens (5)	Boston Bruins	5	Dick Irvin

(continued)

Season	Champion	Finalist	Games	Head Coach
1945	Toronto Maple Leafs (3)	Detroit Red Wings	7	Hap Day
1944	Montreal Canadiens (4)	Chicago Blackhawks	4	Dick Irvin
1943	Detroit Red Wings (3)	Boston Bruins	4	Jack Adams
1942	Toronto Maple Leafs (2)	Detroit Red Wings	7	Hap Day
1941	Boston Bruins (3)	Detroit Red Wings	4	Cooney Weiland
1940	New York Rangers (3)	Toronto Maple Leafs	6	Frank Boucher
1939	Boston Bruins (2)	Toronto Maple Leafs	5	Art Ross
1938	Chicago Blackhawks (2)	Toronto Maple Leafs	4	Bill Stewart
1937	Detroit Red Wings (2)	New York Rangers	5	Jack Adams
1936	Detroit Red Wings (1)	Toronto Maple Leafs	4	Jack Adams
1935	Montreal Maroons (2)	Toronto Maple Leafs	3	Tommy Gorman
1934	Chicago Blackhawks (1)	Detroit Red Wings	4	Tommy Gorman
1933	New York Rangers (2)	Toronto Maple Leafs	4	Lester Patrick
1932	Toronto Maple Leafs (1)	New York Rangers	3	Dick Irvin
1931	Montreal Canadiens (3)	Chicago Blackhawks	5	Cecil Hart
1930	Montreal Canadiens (2)	Boston Bruins	2	Cecil Hart
1929	Boston Bruins (1)	New York Rangers	2	Cy Denneny
1928	New York Rangers (1)	Montreal Maroons	5	Lester Patrick
1927	Ottawa Senators (4)	Boston Bruins	2	Dave Gill
1926	Montreal Maroons (1)	Victoria Cougars	4	Eddie Gerard

Season	Champion	Finalist	Games	Head Coach
1925	Victoria Cougars (1)	Montreal Canadiens	4	Lester Patrick
1924	Montreal Canadiens (1)	Vancouver Maroons Calgary Tigers	2 2	Leo Dandurand
1923	Ottawa Senators (3)	Vancouver Maroons Edmonton Eskimos	4 2	Pete Green
1922	Toronto St. Pats (1)	Vancouver Millionaires	5	Eddie Powers
1921	Ottawa Senators (2)	Vancouver Millionaires	5	Pete Green
1920	Ottawa Senators (1)	Seattle Metropolitans	5	Pete Green
1919	No decision*	No decision*	5	
1918	Toronto Arenas (1)	Vancouver Millionaires	5	Dick Carroll

In 1919, the Montreal Canadiens went to the Seattle Metropolitans to play the Seattle metropolitans, Pacific Coast Hockey League champions. After five games (two wins apiece and one tie), the local Department of Health called off the series because of the influenza epidemic and the death of Joe Hall from influenza.

NHL "Mosts"

No sport is without its "most this or that" list, and hockey is no exception. Here are some of the most interesting NHL achievements! (You'll find some of these feats repeated in the next section on NHL career milestones — but with more information on who else ranks in the same category.)

Most Seasons Played: 26, Gordie Howe

Most Games Played: 1,767, Gordie Howe

Most Consecutive Games Played: 964, Doug Jarvis

Most 40-Goal (Or More) Seasons: 12, Wayne Gretzky

Most 50-Goal (Or More) Seasons: 9, Wayne Gretzky, Mike Bossy

Most 60-Goal (Or More) Seasons: 5, Wayne Gretzky, Mike Bossy

Most 100-Point (Or More) Seasons: 15, Wayne Gretzky

Most Three-Goal (Or More) Games in a Career: 49, Wayne Gretzky

Most Career Games for a Goalie: 971, Terry Sawchuk

Most Games in One Season for a Goalie: 79, Grant Fuhr

Most 30-Win (Or More) Seasons for a Goalie: 10, Patrick Roy

Most 40-Win (Or More) Seasons for a Goalie: 3, Jacques Plante

Most Consecutive Complete Games for a Goalie: 502, Glenn Hall

Most Victories in One Season for a Goalie: 47, Bernie Parent

Most Career Shutouts for a Goalie: 103, Terry Sawchuk

Most Shutouts in One Season for a Goalie: 22, George Hainsworth

Longest Winning Streak for a Goalie: 17, Gilles Gilbert

Longest Unbeaten Streak for a Goalie: 32 (24–0–8), Gerry Cheevers

Longest Consecutive Shutout Streak for a Goalie: 461:29, Alex Connell

Most Career Points: 2,857, Wayne Gretzky

Most Career Goals: 894, Wayne Gretzky

Most Career Assists: 1,963, Wayne Gretzky

Most Career Points Scored by a Defenseman: 1,527, Paul Coffey

Most Career Goals Scored by a Defenseman: 403, Ray Bourque

Most Career Assists Scored by a Defenseman: 1,131, Paul Coffey

Most Points Scored in One Season: 255, Wayne Gretzky

Most Goals Scored in One Season: 92, Wayne Gretzky

Most Assists Scored in One Season: 163, Wayne Gretzky

Most Three-Goal (Or More) Games in One Season: 10, Wayne Gretzky

Most Points Scored by a Defenseman in One Season: 139, Bobby Orr

Most Goals Scored by a Defenseman in One Season: 48, Paul Coffey

Most Assists Scored by a Defenseman in One Season: 102, Bobby Orr

Most Points Scored by a Rookie in One Season: 132, Teemu Selanne

Most Goals Scored by a Rookie in One Season: 76, Teemu Selanne

Most Assists Scored by a Rookie in One Season: 70, Peter Stastny, Joe Juneau

Most Points Scored by a Rookie Defenseman in One Season: 76, Larry Murphy

Most Goals Scored by a Rookie Defenseman in One Season: 23, Brian Leetch

Most Assists Scored by a Rookie Defenseman in One Season: 60, Larry Murphy

Most Points Scored by a Goalie in One Season: 14 (0 goals, 14 assists), Grant Fuhr

Most Postseason Games Played in One Postseason by One Team: 26, Philadelphia Flyers (1987)

Most Stanley Cup Wins: 23, Montreal Canadiens

Most Consecutive Stanley Cup Wins: 5, Montreal Canadiens (1956–60)

Most Consecutive Playoff Appearances: 29, Boston Bruins (1968–96)

Longest Playoff Winning Streak: 14, Pittsburgh Penguins (1992–93)

Most Goals in a Playoff Series, One Team: 44, Edmonton Oilers vs. Chicago Blackhawks (1985)

Most Goals in a Playoff Series, Both Teams: 69, Edmonton Oilers vs. Chicago Blackhawks (1985)

Most Goals in a Playoff Game, One Team: 13, Edmonton Oilers vs. Los Angeles Kings (1987)

Most Goals in a Playoff Period, One Team: 7, Montreal Canadiens vs. Toronto Maple Leafs (1944)

Fastest Five Playoff Goals, Both Teams: 3:06, Chicago Blackhawks vs. Minnesota North Stars

Fastest Five Playoff Goals, One Team: 3:36, Montreal Canadiens (1944)

Shortest Playoff Overtime: 0:09, Montreal Canadiens vs. Calgary Flames (1986)

Longest Playoff Overtime: 116:30, Detroit Red Wings vs. Montreal Maroons (1936)

Most Penalties, One Playoff Series, One Team: 119, New Jersey Devils (1988)

Most Penalty Minutes, One Playoff Series, One Team: 351, New Jersey Devils (1988)

Most Penalties, One Playoff Series, Both Teams: 219, New Jersey Devils vs. Washington Capitals (1988)

Most Penalty Minutes, One Playoff Series, Both Teams: 656, New Jersey Devils vs. Washington Capitals (1988)

NHL Career Milestones

This section is a sampling of some great career milestones in the NHL through the 1999–2000 season — and some of these "milestones" are still growing because these lists contain players and coaches who were active that year (these players and coaches are listed in **bold**) and were likely to play or coach beyond 2000. A good place to go for hockey statistics is the World Wide Web. For links to statistics of NHL players past and present, try FOXSports.com/nhl/index. Current season statistics are also readily available at the National Hockey League site, so also give www.nhl.com a visit. And for a listing of all active players' statistics (career and current season), no place is better than the National Hockey League Players Association at www.nhlpa.com.

Forwards and defensemen

Seasons

Gordie Howe (RW)	26
Alex Delvecchio (C)	24
Tim Horton (D)	24
John Bucyk (LW)	23
Stan Mikita (C)	22
Doug Mohns (D)	22
Dean Prentice (LW)	22

Games played

Gordie Howe (RW)	1,767
Larry Murphy (D)	1,558
Alex Delvecchio (C)	1,549
John Bucyk (LW)	1,540

Ray Bourque (D)	1,532
Wayne Gretzky (C)	1,487
Mark Messier (C)	1,479
Tim Horton (D)	1,446
Mike Gartner (RW)	1,432
Harry Howell (D)	1,411
Norm Ullman (C)	1,410
Ron Francis (C)	1,407
Stan Mikita (C)	1,394
Paul Coffey (D)	1,391
Doug Mohns (D)	1,390
Larry Robinson (D)	1,384
Dean Prentice (LW)	1,378
Scott Stevens (D)	1,353
Ron Stewart (RW)	1,353
Marcel Dionne (C)	1,348
Guy Carbonneau (C)	1,318
Red Kelly (C)	1,316
Dave Keon (C)	1,296
Phil Esposito (C)	1,282
Jean Ratelle (C)	1,281
Bryan Trottier (C)	1,279

Goals

Wayne Gretzky (C)	894
Gordie Howe (RW)	801
Marcel Dionne (C)	731
Phil Esposito (C)	717
Mike Gartner (RW)	708
Mark Messier (C)	627
Steve Yzerman (C)	627
Brett Hull (RW)	610
Bobby Hull (LW)	610
Dino Ciccarelli (RW)	608
Jari Kurri (RW)	601
Mike Bossy (RW)	573
Mario Lemieux (C)	563
Guy Lafleur (RW)	560
John Bucyk (LW)	556
Luc Robitaille (LW)	553
Dave Andreychuk (LW)	552
Michel Goulet (LW)	548
Maurice Richard (RW)	544
Stan Mikita (C)	541
Frank Mahovlich (LW)	533
Bryan Trottier (C)	524
Dale Hawerchuk (C)	518
Joe Mullen (RW)	502
Patrick Verbeek (RW)	500

Assists

Wayne Gretzky (C)	1,963
Paul Coffey (D)	1,131
Ray Bourque (D)	1,117
Ron Francis (C)	1,087
Mark Messier (C)	1,087
Gordie Howe (RW)	1,049
Marcel Dionne (C)	1,040
Steve Yzerman (C)	935
Stan Mikita (C)	926
Larry Murphy (D)	910
Bryan Trottier (C)	901
Adam Oates (C)	894
Dale Hawerchuk (C)	891
Doug Gilmour (C)	883
Mario Lemieux (C)	881
Phil Esposito (C)	873
Denis Savard (C)	865
Bobby Clarke (C)	852
Alex Delvecchio (C)	825
Phil Housley (D)	817
Gilbert Perreault (C)	814
John Bucyk (LW)	813
Allan MacInnis (D)	803
Guy Lafleur (RW)	793

Points

Wayne Gretzky (C)	2,857
Gordie Howe (RW)	1,850
Marcel Dionne (C)	1,771
Mark Messier (C)	1,714
Phil Esposito (C)	1,590
Steve Yzerman (C)	1,562
Ron Francis (C)	1,559
Paul Coffey (D)	1,527
Ray Bourque (D)	1,520
Mario Lemieux (C)	1,494
Stan Mikita (C)	1,467
Bryan Trottier (C)	1,425
Dale Hawerchuk (C)	1,409
Jari Kurri (RW)	1,376
John Bucyk (LW)	1,369
Guy Lafleur (RW)	1,353
Denis Savard (C)	1,338
Mike Gartner (RW)	1,335
Gilbert Perreault (C)	1,326
Doug Gilmour (C)	1,305
Alex Delvecchio (C)	1,281

Penalty minutes

Dave Williams (LW)	3,966
Dale Hunter (C)	3,565
Marty McSorley (D)	3,381
Tim Hunter (RW)	3,146
Chris Nilan (RW)	3,043
Bob Probert (LW)	3,021
Rich Tocchet (RW)	2,863
Willie Plett (RW)	2,572
Basil McRae (LW)	2,457
Jay Wells (D)	2,359

Goaltenders

Seasons

Terry Sawchuk	21
Gump Worsley	21
Grant Fuhr	19
Glenn Hall	18
Gilles Meloche	18
Andy Moog	18
Jacques Plante	18
Billy Smith	18
John Vanbiesbrouck	18
Don Beaupre	17
Tony Esposito	16
Eddie Johnston	16
Harry Lumley	16
Rogie Vachon	16
Johnny Bower	15
Reggie Lemelin	15
Cesare Maniago	15

Games played

Terry Sawchuk	971
Glenn Hall	906
Tony Esposito	886
Grant Fuhr	868
Gump Worsley	862
Patrick Roy	841
Jacques Plante	837
John Vanbiesbrouck	829
Harry Lumley	804
Rogie Vachon	795
Gilles Meloche	788

Tom Barrasso	733
Michael Vernon	722
Andy Moog	713
Billy Smith	680
Kelly Hrudey	677
Don Beaupre	667
Mike Liut	663
Dan Bouchard	655
Bill Ranford	647
Turk Broda	629
Ed Belfour	612
Ed Giacomin	610
Bernie Parent	608
Greg Millen	604

Minutes

Terry Sawchuk	57,205
Glenn Hall	53,484
Tony Esposito	52,585
Gump Worsley	50,232
Jacques Plante	49,553
Patrick Roy	49,108
Grant Fuhr	48,946
Harry Lumley	48,107
John Vanbiesbrouck	47,544
Rogie Vachon	46,298
Gilles Meloche	45,401
Tom Barrasso	41,759
Michael Vernon	41,378
Andy Moog	40,151
Billy Smith	38,431
Turk Broda	38,173
Mike Liut	38,155
Kelly Hrudey	38,084
Dan Bouchard	37,919
Don Beaupre	37,396
Ed Giacomin	35,693

Goals-against average

Alex Connell	1.91
George Hainsworth	1.91
Chuck Gardiner	2.02
Lorne Chabot	2.04
Tiny Thompson	2.08
Dave Kerr	2.17
Ken Dryden	2.24
Roy Worters	2.27
Clint Benedict	2.32

Norm Smith	2.32
Bill Durnan	2.36
Gerry McNeil	2.36

Games won

Patrick Roy	444
Terry Sawchuk	435
Jacques Plante	434
Tony Esposito	423
Glenn Hall	407
Grant Fuhr	403
Andy Moog	372
Michael Vernon	371
John Vanbiesbrouck	358
Rogie Vachon	355
Tom Barrasso	353
Gump Worsley	335
Harry Lumley	332
Ed Belfour	308

Shutouts

Terry Sawchuk	103
George Hainsworth	94
Glenn Hall	84
Jacques Plante	82
Alex Connell	81
Tiny Thompson	81
Tony Esposito	76
Lorne Chabot	73
Harry Lumley	71
Roy Worters	66

Coaches

Games coached

Scotty Bowman	1,977
Al Arbour	1,606
Dick Irvin	1,437
Billy Reay	1,102
Jack Adams	982
Sid Abel	963
Bryan Murray	916
Toe Blake	914
Punch Imlach	879
Bob Berry	860

Games won

Scotty Bowman	1,138
Al Arbour	781
Dick Irvin	690
Billy Reay	542
Toe Blake	500
Bryan Murray	467
Glen Sather	464

Most Stanley Cup wins by coach

Toe Blake	8
Scotty Bowman	8
Hap Day	5
Al Arbour	4
Punch Imlach	4
Dick Irvin	4
Glen Sather	4
Jack Adams	3
Pete Green	3
Tommy Ivan	3

NHL Single-Season Milestones

This is a selection of single-season achievements that can give you some idea of how the game has changed from year to year. Players who were active during the 1999–2000 season are in **bold**.

Forwards and defensemen

Goals

1981–82	Wayne Gretzky	92
1983–84	Wayne Gretzky	87
1990–91	**Brett Hull**	86
1988–89	Mario Lemieux	85
1971–72	Phil Esposito	76
1992–93	**Alexander Mogilny**	76
1992–93	**Teemu Selanne**	76
1984–85	Wayne Gretzky	73
1989–90	**Brett Hull**	72
1982–83	Wayne Gretzky	71
1984–85	Jari Kurri	71
1991–92	**Brett Hull**	70
1987–88	Mario Lemieux	70

1988–89	Bernie Nicholls	70
1978–79	Mike Bossy	69
1992–93	Mario Lemieux	69
1995–96	Mario Lemieux	69
1980–81	Mike Bossy	68
1973–74	Phil Esposito	68
1985–86	Jari Kurri	68
1972–73	Phil Esposito	66
1982–83	Lanny McDonald	66
1988–89	**Steve Yzerman**	65
1981–82	Mike Bossy	64
1992–93	Luc Robitaille	63
1986–87	Wayne Gretzky	62
1995–96	**Jaromir Jagr**	62
1989–90	**Steve Yzerman**	62
1985–86	Mike Bossy	61
1974–75	Phil Esposito	61
1975–76	Reggie Leach	61
1982–83	Mike Bossy	60
1992–93	**Pavel Bure**	60
1993–94	**Pavel Bure**	60
1977–78	Guy Lafleur	60
1981–82	Dennis Maruk	60
1976–77	Steve Shutt	60

50-goal seasons

	Seasons	Consecutive
Mike Bossy	9	9
Wayne Gretzky	9	8
Guy Lafleur	6	6
Marcel Dionne	6	5
Mario Lemieux	6	3
Phil Esposito	5	5
Brett Hull	5	5
Steve Yzerman	5	4
Bobby Hull	5	2

Points

1985–86	Wayne Gretzky	215
1981–82	Wayne Gretzky	212
1984–85	Wayne Gretzky	208
1983–84	Wayne Gretzky	205
1988–89	Mario Lemieux	199
1982–83	Wayne Gretzky	196
1986–87	Wayne Gretzky	183
1988–89	Wayne Gretzky	168
1987–88	Mario Lemieux	168

1980–81	Wayne Gretzky	164
1990–91	Wayne Gretzky	163
1995–96	Mario Lemieux	161
1992–93	Mario Lemieux	160
1988–89	**Steve Yzerman**	155
1970–71	Phil Esposito	152
1988–89	Bernie Nicholls	150
1987–88	Wayne Gretzky	149
1995–96	**Jaromir Jagr**	149
1992–93	Pat Lafontaine	148
1981–82	Mike Bossy	147
1973–74	Phil Esposito	145
1989–90	Wayne Gretzky	142

Penalty minutes

1974–75	Dave Schultz	472
1981–82	Paul Baxter	409
1991–92	Mike Peluso	408
1977–78	Dave Schultz	405
1992–93	Marty McSorley	399
1987–88	Bob Probert	398
1985–86	Joey Kocur	377
1988–89	Tim Hunter	375
1997–98	**Donald Brashear**	372
1975–76	Steve Durbano	370

Goaltenders

Shutouts

1928–29	George Hainsworth	22
1925–26	Alex Connell	15
1927–28	Alex Connell	15
1969–70	Tony Esposito	15
1927–28	Hal Winkler	15
1926–27	George Hainsworth	14
1926–27	Clint Benedict	13
1926–27	Alex Connell	13
1927–28	George Hainsworth	13
1997–98	**Dominik Hasek**	13
1953–54	Harry Lumley	13
1928–29	John Roach	13
1928–29	Roy Worters	13

Index

• C •

Notes

Notes

FOR DUMMIES®

A world of resources to help you grow

TRAVEL

0-7645-5453-0

0-7645-5438-7

0-7645-5444-1

Also available:

America's National Parks For Dummies
(0-7645-6204-5)

Caribbean For Dummies
(0-7645-5445-X)

Cruise Vacations For Dummies 2003
(0-7645-5459-X)

Europe For Dummies
(0-7645-5456-5)

Ireland For Dummies
(0-7645-6199-5)

France For Dummies
(0-7645-6292-4)

Las Vegas For Dummies
(0-7645-5448-4)

London For Dummies
(0-7645-5416-6)

Mexico's Beach Resorts For Dummies
(0-7645-6262-2)

Paris For Dummies
(0-7645-5494-8)

RV Vacations For Dummies
(0-7645-5443-3)

EDUCATION & TEST PREPARATION

0-7645-5194-9

0-7645-5325-9

0-7645-5249-X

Also available:

The ACT For Dummies
(0-7645-5210-4)

Chemistry For Dummies
(0-7645-5430-1)

English Grammar For Dummies
(0-7645-5322-4)

French For Dummies
(0-7645-5193-0)

GMAT For Dummies
(0-7645-5251-1)

Inglés Para Dummies
(0-7645-5427-1)

Italian For Dummies
(0-7645-5196-5)

Research Papers For Dummies
(0-7645-5426-3)

SAT I For Dummies
(0-7645-5472-7)

U.S. History For Dummies
(0-7645-5249-X)

World History For Dummies
(0-7645-5242-2)

HEALTH, SELF-HELP & SPIRITUALITY

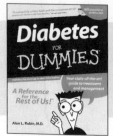

0-7645-5154-X

0-7645-5302-X

0-7645-5418-2

Also available:

The Bible For Dummies
(0-7645-5296-1)

Controlling Cholesterol For Dummies
(0-7645-5440-9)

Dating For Dummies
(0-7645-5072-1)

Dieting For Dummies
(0-7645-5126-4)

High Blood Pressure For Dummies
(0-7645-5424-7)

Judaism For Dummies
(0-7645-5299-6)

Menopause For Dummies
(0-7645-5458-1)

Nutrition For Dummies
(0-7645-5180-9)

Potty Training For Dummies
(0-7645-5417-4)

Pregnancy For Dummies
(0-7645-5074-8)

Rekindling Romance For Dummies
(0-7645-5303-8)

Religion For Dummies
(0-7645-5264-3)

FOR DUMMIES

Plain-English solutions for everyday challenges